# LIFE ON THE MALECÓN

## Children and Youth on the Streets of Santo Domingo

JON WOLSETH

RUTGERS UNIVERSITY PRESS
New Brunswick, New Jersey and London

Library of Congress Cataloging-in-Publication Data
Wolseth, Jon, 1975–
Life on the Malecón : children and youth on the streets of Santo Domingo / Jon
Wolseth.
      pages cm. — (The Rutgers series in childhood studies)
Includes bibliographical references and index.
ISBN 978–0–8135–6288–9 (hardcover : alk. paper) — ISBN 978–0–8135–6287–2
(pbk. : alk. paper) — ISBN 978–0–8135–6289–6 (e-book)
1. Street youth—Dominican Republic—Santo Domingo. 2. Street children—Do-
minican Republic—Santo Domingo. 3. Child welfare—Dominican Republic—Santo
Domingo. 4. Social work with youth—Dominican Republic—Santo Domingo. I.
Title.
HV887.D652S268 2013
362.74—dc23                                                                 2013005959

A British Cataloging-in-Publication record for this book is available from the British
Library.

Visit our website: http://rutgerspress.rutgers.edu

Manufactured in the United States of America

For my nieces, Isabel, Evelyn, and Lindsay

# CONTENTS

# ACKNOWLEDGMENTS

This book is the testament of work in community, and I received untold support from friends, family members, and colleagues throughout all steps in the process of researching and writing. Without this network of assistance and encouragement, this book would not have seen the light of day.

I would like to thank the hundreds of children and youth with whom I worked on the streets in the Dominican Republic over the course of this study, for their willingness to let us build mutual trust and permit me to accompany them on their journeys for a brief period of time. My colleagues at Niños del Camino welcomed me from the beginning. Their passion for their work was infectious from the start. They accepted me for all my quirks. Outreach requires a team you can trust; I found that and more with Ana Sosa, Epifanio de Jesús Castillo, Héctor Ramírez, Eli Barbado, Núria Perelló, Kennedy Estrella, Lidia Miralles, Isabelle Deneyer, Pura González, Liduvina Santos, Ruth Montano, and Agustín Mora. Working alongside them provided some of the best (and most challenging!) times in my life. Special thanks to Ana, Epifanio, Héctor, Eli, and Núria. Knowing them has made me a better person. María Blanco accepted the challenge of having a resident volunteer; Estívaliz Ladrón de Guevara graciously put up with my suggestions and prodding. Dorca Rojas and Martha Alcántara offered a supportive ear and care. Outreach could not have happened without the aid of Wanda Santos, Yolanda Ramírez, Julio César Urbaez, Angela Peña, and Teresa Luciano. Special thanks to Montse Bobés and Dr. Martha Arredondo for their compassion and sense of justice. Miriam Jiménez, Altagracia Concepción, and Víctor Moll always came through in times of need. Dr. Marta Martínez Muñoz offered much-needed perspective.

Peace Corps Dominican Republic supported me at every step. Adele Williams perceptively placed me where I could thrive and trusted in my abilities. I served under two exemplary country directors, Javier Garza and Romeo Massey, both models of service and leadership. Javier's presence in this world is particularly missed. Thank you to all of PCDR's staff and associates, especially Tammy Simo, Liliana Castillo, Nurys Matos, and Jennifer McGowan. I had the pleasure of serving with some of the most enthusiastic and caring volunteers while in PCDR. I drew strength from Laura Ibañez, Emily Hoffman, and Rachelle Olden. Laura, especially, has been a source of constancy and reason. I have also benefited greatly from the friendship of Angela Bennett, Rosa Garza and Chris Moore, Amanda Gilley, Christy Dimos, Joanna Mauer, and Mary Rolle.

A heartfelt thanks to the folks at Rutgers University Press. Even in the face of superstorm Sandy, they were able to shepherd this book to print. Marlie Wasserman is a model editor: no-nonsense and willing to go to bat for her authors. Thank you for sharing my vision, even when I was unable to articulate it fully. I profited from the substantial comments of three anonymous reviewers: thank you for taking the time to provide critical feedback. I especially would like to single out the sociologist who reviewed the manuscript. Your comments gave me confidence at a particularly low moment.

I profited from working with David Lancy, Suzanne Gaskins, Dennis Rodgers, and Gareth Jones on projects associated with this material. Each in their own way pushed me to think about my time in Santo Domingo from a new perspective, shaping many of the concerns that frame this book. Diego Vigil offered a heartening comment after a conference presentation that pushed me forward. Brigittine French and Guadalupe Salazar both, in their own ways, have proved inspirational and encouraging. Florence Babb continues to exert a gentle influence on my intellectual work. Her support of my unconventional path through and around academia has been astonishing. This book also owes an intellectual debt to Margery Wolf, Mac Marshall, Laurie Graham, and Kathy Fine-Dare. Thank you for introducing me to what is possible with ethnography, and an expanded definition of the good of anthropology.

Camaraderie and conversations with Carolyn Hough, Meg McCullough, Anne-Marine Feat, Amanda Hamp, Thomas Blanton, Matt Simpson, Amy Weldon, Harv Klevar, Maryna Bazylevych, Anita Carrasco, Rebecca Bowman, Ginger Meyette, Lori Stanley, Lea Pickard, and Doug White have shaped this book. Anne-Marine, Amy, Matt, Amanda, and Tom made substantive comments on other versions of this material. Harv reminded me to tell the story I wanted to tell.

While teaching at Luther College, I had the pleasure of sharing versions of this material with students, especially in my Street Cultures class. Their feedback and interest were signposts of the direction I needed to go. I especially would like to thank Tyler Foster-Stavneak, James Feinstein, Andrea Kruse, Aaron Rosell, Aparna Ashok, Michaela Hill, Molly Andersen, Alex Lange, Jeni Arbuckle, Dustin Hruby, Courtney Greenley, David Hecht, Alison Sancken, Molly Kline, Anna Morris, Kathleen Durbin, Alex Anderson, Lindsey Bulger, Amanda Kloser, Annie McKay, and Adam Kruse.

My friends have endured my stories and my moodiness. Special thanks to Jacqueline Comito, a model of active engagement in making the world a better place through meaningful work. Mary Holmes and Jackie granted me retreat and provided good counsel. Karin Kohlmeier not only came to see me in Santo Domingo, but also came to the rescue in editing. Jordan Sher, Tim Cravens, and Chris Farley offered perspective and diversion when they visited. Heartfelt thanks go to Rachel Vagts, Corey Shuman, Kyra Bellrichard, and Alexandra Graham for their friendship.

My family has been a constant source of support, even when I had to be a great distance from them. My mother, Sharon Wolseth, and my father, Gary Wolseth, continue to be sympathetic and understanding of my peripatetic life. My sister, Kari Hamilton, and her family aid me in all I do. I would be nowhere without their love.

# LIFE ON THE MALECÓN

# INTRODUCTION

THIS BOOK IS AN ethnographic exploration of life on the streets of Santo Domingo, Dominican Republic, as told through my personal interactions with the children and youth who have chosen to make the street their home. For over two years I served as a Peace Corps volunteer with a Dominican nongovernmental organization (NGO), Niños del Camino (henceforth, Niños), providing outreach services, including educational, medical, and legal assistance, to street children and youth.[1] The overwhelming majority of the children Niños worked with were boys and adolescent males. This was partly because of the relatively few girls and teenage females who make it to the streets. Teenage girls who leave their natal homes lead much less public lives, often being lured to work in brothels or hired as domestics. Although aware that this subpopulation of homeless children existed, Niños defined its boundaries as work with homeless children and youth who lived and slept directly on the streets.

Acting on the decision to make the street their home, however temporarily, kids eke out a living on the avenues, plazas, and abandoned buildings of the city. Their strategies for survival are multiform, as they diversify their approaches to living and working on the margins of society. For some, taking to the streets is but a momentary stopgap as they circulate among natal households, social welfare institutions, and law enforcement agencies. For others, the street is a permanent residence, the final stop on a life trajectory. It is difficult to predict which child will come to the street, which child will remain there. One thing, however, is certain: the longer a child has been sleeping on the streets, the less access he or she has to returning to a natal household or to social services that are willing and able to help.

To better understand the lives of street children and youth, we would do well to examine the external factors that structure and partially determine the conditions in which they live, and the day-to-day workings of children as they confront their physical and social environments. There is a push–pull dynamic, in which economic and social determinants push young people to the streets, while at the same time children and youth may choose the allure of the perceived freedoms and opportunities the street has to offer. Although poverty and lack of economic options are important factors in understanding the phenomenon of working and street children, poverty is not the sole determining cause of their existence. The United Nations Children's Fund (UNICEF) estimates there are over one billion children living in poverty worldwide, yet the number of children who sleep on the streets is but a small fraction of this figure. There is some element of selection on the part of families and communities, and choice on the part of young people involved in being on the streets. These components can be broadly analyzed as the twin threads that weave together any social life: one thread is the structural conditions in which we live, the other thread is the agency we exercise.[2] Each constitutes the other to some degree. Our choices and actions are partially determined by the socioeconomic conditions in which we live, but the choices we make have an impact on those same conditions.

Below, I lay out the structural conditions influencing the life opportunities of children, and then explore the role that agency has in helping children thrive in adverse environments. Both structure and agency have associated research perspectives. In general, researchers more interested in investigating the structural conditions of children's lives take a cultural politics approach, while those who are concerned with agentive decision making are more inclined to focus on children's culture.[3]

## STRUCTURAL FORCES IMPACTING YOUNG LIVES

The structural elements that impact the lives of children and youth are economic, political, and social. There are interlocking forms of exploitation and subjugation that adversely affect the health and welfare of marginalized populations.[4] Macrolevel economic policies and political decisions such as neoliberal reforms and transitioning economies impinge upon the lives of young people, eroding the hope for future advancement. Institutionalized forms of age discrimination, racism, heterosexism, and disability discrimination combine with economic exclusion to create further barriers for the young to reach their fullest potential. This effectively excludes them from many forms of civic and community participation and renders them outside the boundaries of normal, moral citizenship.[5] For example, on the streets of Santo Domingo, lighter-skinned teenage boys who portrayed a more stereotypical masculinity enjoyed more prestige, more opportunities, and more peace of mind than darker-skinned teens, who experienced greater verbal abuse from peers and were under constant threat of being labeled as Haitian by authorities and thus subject to deportation. Teenage girls and effeminate boys were marked out for sexual abuse and exploitation by other street denizens and from police. Finally, mental and physical handicaps, while sometimes made use of as a means of income generation (as in the case of begging), are also forms of difference that can be a source of abuse. In all cases, the young people's perceived identities and class status push them to the edge of social and civic life, even while their existence is central to maintaining the moral order of society.

When forms of exclusion overlap—what anthropologist Diego Vigil calls multiple forms of marginality[6]—the intersections create spaces for social and psychological adaptations to being outside of the centers of power. These adaptations need not be healthy; indeed they often further one's social exclusion by being sources of covert prestige or oppositional identities. On the one hand, marginalized children and youth may try to gain access to privilege and power by attempting to succeed at the forms valued by dominant society—such as increased education—if the pathways to advancement are available and support networks exist. On the other hand, marginalization also creates parallel institutions that foster self-worth, provide a sense of belonging, and have opportunities for advancement not easily gained in dominant society. Institutions such as gangs, street cliques, and drug economies are attractive alternatives for many young people, especially in communities where the institutions valued by dominant society are weak or nonexistent.

One strand of research looking at the structural factors leading to children's marginalization highlights the role public discourse plays in marking out social problems that affect children's lives. Known as the cultural politics of childhood, this approach argues that debates about children's futures are always already debates about other social processes, such as ethnic and race relations, the environment, or economic practices.[7] The cultural politics of childhood seeks to lay bare the governmental and social machinations that affect children's lives, as the economic and political policies nations implement have grave consequences for the well-being of children. Indeed, policies and laws can create, label, and make manifest classes of young people that did not previously exist, social classes that can later evoke national embarrassment, shame, or pity.[8] Street and working children are just such a social class whose existence has been brought into being by the economic and social policies of industrial capitalism.

What we fail to recognize far too often is that working and street children are the logical byproducts of increased income disparities between the lower and ruling classes. In a very real sense, capitalist expansion and exploitation require an underclass of workers, the social cast-offs if you will, who do the dirty work. Single-parent households, usually headed by mothers, are an adaptive norm of the working poor, historically rooted in men's need for mobility to search for seasonal work both in agriculture and in factories. Children's productive labor within the household is needed to make ends meet.[9]

Street and working kids are the cheap labor source that performs the dirty service work of industrialization, akin to their social prototypes at the dawn of the Industrial Revolution. The major difference is that now, as children are legally barred from the formal labor market, instead of doing productive labor, street children are relegated to the service economy.[10] Although it is considered unseemly for children to work in factories, it has somehow become an accepted part of the urban landscape in many cities for children to service the elite. Shining shoes and washing car windows is acceptable informal work for kids. Increasingly, involvement in the sex and drug trades are other options for the enterprising child who realizes that quick gain can be made, even if the risk is higher.

The very presence of street children underscores the inherent contradictions of capitalist growth, a brazen indication that the nation-state cannot take care of its own children. As living metaphors, kids on the street are constant reminders that the promise of progress is only for some. One far too common response to their presence is to eliminate the evidence of their existence. A large body of scholarly literature on Latin America engages with the brutal violence and ire that the presence of homeless children and youth provokes. The reports provide grim glimpses of the social position of street children.[11] As citizens struggle to make their own economic progress in countries experiencing high inflation, low wages, and increased consumer desires, kids living and working on the street are visible markers of economic failure. Once the object of social exclusion, street kids are now increasingly expendable. Vigilante groups of off-duty police and military personnel have taken matters into their own hands, expunging the presence of homeless kids and young adults. The bodies of children appear in trash dumps and in fields on the outskirts of town. They are beaten to death, shot in the back of the head, or even gunned down on the steps of cathedrals where they sleep.[12]

Drawing heavily on distinctions between the private realm of the home and the public venue of the street, researchers have pointed to the idea that street children in much of Latin America are "matter out of place."[13] In other words, children should be neither seen nor heard in public because their rightful place is within the private realm of the home or under the control of institutions like schools or youth detention centers. Increased visibility of unaccompanied children on streets and public plazas questions who controls their lives. Street and homeless kids are outside of the social institutions whose charge it is to teach children the norms and rules of society, educating and civilizing them in the process. Kinship networks, schools, juvenile correctional facilities, churches, orphanages, and child welfare groups all shoulder some of the responsibility in raising and disciplining the modern urban child.[14] But these social institutions lack the resources, stability, or strength to do so. A child begging in the street is anathema to social progress and the self-image of the nation. One response is to remove such children from view by remanding them to correctional or child welfare facilities, thus putting them under proper control.[15] Another far too common response has been to dispose of such "wild" and "uncivilized" children through disappearance and murder.

If these responses sound grim and alarmist, consider that undisciplined children are symptomatic of cultural decline. Debates about what to do with a nation's unruly young indicate the relative worth of certain classes of children. Some crucial aspects of society have broken down, at least in the minds of the global middle and upper class, even as we are unwilling to take financial and ideological responsibility for the way things have become. In much of Latin America, public schools are overcrowded, ineffective, and instruction only offered for half a day: kids spend four hours a day in crumbling classrooms with an underpaid teacher who needs to control forty plus students at a time. Subsidies for social welfare and government programming for children continue to decline as economies constrict, considered to be unnecessary expenditures in the face of internal security issues such as rising rates of urban crime.[16] Governments abdicate responsibility to global NGOs whose limited reach and narrow scope of action necessitate a piecemeal approach. Despite their best efforts, NGOs lack the ability to provide centralized coordination and national vision. Yet it is NGOs that understand the realities and exigencies of the population they work with, the limitations and opportunities that are present.

This is a stark portrait of the social and economic conditions that structure the lives of poor children. Social exclusion, lack of access to education and health care, and diminished economic opportunities continue to prevent many children from advancing. Working and living on the streets of the city is a byproduct of these structural characteristics, a pressure release valve that eases the conditions of poorer households. At the same time, street situations are a dangerous environment because of the high levels of violence, disease, and exploitation that constitute much of day-to-day existence. More than context, this is the patterning of reality through which street children maneuver.

## CHILDREN AS CULTURAL AGENTS

There are limitations on studying children as the products or constructions of economic and political policies and actions. Many researchers attempt to temper this view by listening and representing what children themselves have to say about the uncomfortable social realities they live. Economic and racial exclusion, for example, are lived, visceral experiences. Children have their own opinions about and experiences of what it means to grow up poor or privileged, excluded or at the center of social power.[17] They also find creative ways to manage the stresses of living through interactions with their social environments, including the relationships they foster with others. It is important to realize that children make agentive decisions about their world.

The adaptive role of culture is where children's agency shines. Learning, using, and manipulating knowledge are domains ripe for ethnographic study of children's lives and bear great consequence for our theories about child development and enculturation. Ironically, however, studying children has not been a forte of anthropology. Although there exists an almost hidden literature throughout the history of the discipline, it has only been since the early 1990s that there has been a resurgence of anthropologists focusing explicitly on children as their central research population.[18] This oversight seems peculiar, considering that one of the implied foci of the study of culture is the way in which individuals and groups replicate, transmit, and alter cultural knowledge. The fact that we recognize continuity between generations is testament to the unifying force of socialization. Yet studying children as co-creators in the dialogue of cultural reproduction is a new turn of events in the social sciences, including anthropology.[19]

In this line of inquiry, researchers take children as meaning makers, recognizing that within social groups there is a particular culture of childhood of which most adults have but a distant and incomplete memory. This includes schoolyard games, songs, and folklore.[20] Play is a defining characteristic of children's culture. Indeed, because play is noncrucial, nonserious, and transitory, it is the ideal medium through which children can appropriate, manipulate, and learn about basic categories of social life. Children learn what it means to be gendered through staging games of house and playing with toys.[21] Games of tag or soccer are ideal venues for children to negotiate social hierarchy and power relationships. Through teasing rituals, children reproduce cruel social divisions through their own understandings of the critical differences or distinctions among social classes of people.[22] Children's own culture is not some presocial utopia where everyone gets along, but neither is it only the brutal seriousness of living in social groups. The reality exists somewhere between *Barney* and *Lord of the Flies*.

The literature on children's own worlds and their interpretations of adult realms is growing. One area of particular interest is the lives of children outside the mainstream of social life. Perhaps because of their visibility, or because their lives affront Western middle-class notions of acceptable childhood experiences, marginalized children in the form of child soldiers,[23] juvenile offenders,[24] and street children[25] provide researchers with material for a veritable cottage industry. Within this corpus of studies, researchers have found innovative ways to meld cultural debates on childhood with children's own understandings of the social realities they experience. It is at the extremes of social existence that we are able to witness the rich creative approaches to survival, the agentive approach of children who live outside the protective boundaries of kin and community networks.

Although their lives are often gut-wrenching, marginalized children teach us about resilient living and the very human drive of making meaning to order what, upon first glance, appear like chaotic lives. Research into the lives of street children bears witness to the creative potential of children in adverse social environments. Unlike the study of schoolyard games and play, both social reproduction and survival hinge upon the meaning making that street children and youth engage in. Some of the social structures kids create can be quite complex, as demonstrated in the ethnographic descriptions of the *gallada* system in Colombia or the *arbat* system in Russia.[26] Galladas are complex hierarchical sets of groups whose membership is loosely tied to a street child's age. Members across galladas pool resources, offer protection, and provide network ties to other groups that may facilitate a child's graduation from begging and shoe shining to criminal activities. Gallada networks, thus, offer an introduction to other criminal networks throughout the city and to the possibility of increased earning potential. On the streets of Moscow, the arbat system refers to sets of different subcultures that exist along the main pedestrian mall. Unlike galladas, membership is based on affiliation to different subcultures— hippies, punks, and so on— not age. Each subcultural group has a fictive kinship system of "mothers," "fathers," and "children," within which street children can find a place. Street relationships, including gift exchange expectations, parallel the expectations one would find in naturalized kin systems in Russia. Add to these examples the special sense of self and identity that street children develop, and we begin to see how much street children teach us about the power of culture as a tool for survival.[27]

The streets are a natural laboratory in which to study the transmission of cultural practices because of the swift succession of generations. Instead of waiting twenty or thirty years between elders and children, on the streets the generations of "newbie" and "veteran" are a matter of a few years, if not months. Yet in comparison with other youth subcultures, such as skaters, punks, and skinheads, the stakes on the street are higher still, as not only is subcultural continuity at issue but, more important, individual subsistence is at the heart of survival. In other words, the range of practices learned by kids on the street—from income-generating strategies to conflict management skills to a general street sense—are immediate necessities and require short amounts of time to master. Newer kids on the scene risk continued exploitation by older, more experienced members as long as it takes them to learn the ropes.[28] Short generations thus honor greater knowledge and skill, placing masterful individuals nearer the top of the social hierarchy. These are the kids with greater privileges on the streets, and they earn the right to take advantage of the naïveté of others. This is not always a function of biological age or size, but rather a matter of savvy, reputation for violence, and cunning.

Learning on the streets, however, is not a neutral or nurturing task. The economy of knowledge trades heavily in exploitation. Forms of "apprenticing" require children newer to the streets to trade their physical integrity, health, and personal reputation for knowledge and opportunity. Appropriating money earned by another, sending a kid off to buy drugs, giving a kid the more dangerous or visible role in petty crime, and requiring sexual services form the currency for knowledge transactions. Thus social structure for many street cultures is based on a system of exploitation of newer members. Sexual relationships play a significant role in inducting newer children into street groups as well as maintaining hierarchy within a group. Dyadic friendships are frequent, in which it is understood that a newer street child learns the ropes of the city in exchange for being the sexual companion of the more experienced partner. Gang rape is common punishment for a child who has broken a subcultural norm, such as hording drugs or being perceived as a police informer.[29] Some kids exist for extended periods of time in the position of lackey, maybe never graduating out of the role because of the security of being provided for by members in the group in exchange for these services. Others quickly climb the ranks, jockey for position, and try to diminish the amount they are exploited by others.

Exploitation, however, is not always as brutal and bare as it sounds. It can be wrapped in the velvet of mutual affection, a sense of loyalty, and, perhaps most important, the recognition of need.[30] It is a cultural contradiction of the streets, but one that I saw played out on a daily basis. Group relationships are volatile, but there are enduring bonds made between street youth that can best be described as friendships, no matter how dysfunctional they may appear from the outside. Kids cement their partnerships with each other through engaging in illicit and dangerous activities. Drug consumption is crucial in keeping kids on the street together, as strong bonds are forged through doing drugs together, enabling the habits of every member.[31] Cooperating in adrenaline-producing activities like petty theft, breaking and entering, protecting one's street territory from the incursion of others, or collectively confronting local authorities also cement interpersonal relationships within the group. The maintenance and perpetuation of local street cultures depend upon group cooperation and the active membership and participation of kids in their own exploitation. It's not that kids enjoy being taken advantage of, or even that they enjoy the violent lifestyle found in many street contexts, but rather that they comprehend the benefits involved. Kids take part in their own subjugation on the streets not because they are masochists but because the street offers real connection with others, a connection that many may not have felt before.

## STRUCTURE AND AGENCY ON DOMINICAN STREETS

Like other cultural realities, the street scene in Santo Domingo is partially structured by economic and social constraints. Market reforms over the past thirty years in the Dominican Republic have reworked household economies, kinship patterns, and gender relationships. Transitions from an agro-export economy centered on sugar cane production to export manufacturing have caused great social upheaval and new social class distinctions.[32] The groundbreaking work of Helen Safa is instructive, as she has charted the impact that export manufacturing has had on gender relationships both in the workplace and in the home across the Caribbean. Specifically in the Dominican Republic, her work found that men's status as the household breadwinner has eroded significantly.[33] Although this does lead to women's economic autonomy as they enter the workforce, they still have to contend with entrenched sexism and increased demands on raising families. It is only through calling on extended social networks that women in the workforce are able to sustain themselves emotionally and financially, a process which continues to alter kinship and social relations.

Perhaps the biggest economic shift in the Dominican Republic in recent years has been the concerted effort to increase tourism on the island. Like other shifts in production, the increase in the tourist service economy has sharply increased consumptive desires that cut across all the urban class strata, reaching to the poor. Especially among working-class and working-poor youths, media influence and contact with middle-class foreign tourists brings new music, fashion, and personal consumer goods like electronics and high-end cell phones into closer proximity than ever before. Consumptive desires shift class-consciousness and one's sense of self and identity.

Denise Brennan and Mark Padilla demonstrate the effect of the tourist industry on notions of gender, work, and sense of self among men and women involved in the sex industry, providing ample evidence to demonstrate that the tourist economy has reshaped the identities of Dominican sex workers. Brennan, for instance, demonstrates that the increase in export manufacturing has lead to the feminization of the labor force, reaching its logical conclusion with women who work intermittently in sex tourism.[34] Padilla, perhaps even more convincingly delineates how sex tourism has molded sexuality among young Dominican men, remaking local male gender classifications based on sex roles. For instance, the local classification of *bugarrón*, or men who perform the active role in sex with other men in exchange for money or goods, has taken on particular salience since it is widely known that male foreign tourists specifically seek out young Dominican men for sexual services. The bugarrón has a distinct physical appearance and style that has been formed vis-à-vis the desires of its transnational clients, marking it as a particular and visible form of Dominican masculinity.[35]

These brief examples demonstrate that gender identity in the Dominican Republic is malleable within broader economic and social processes. A similar reworking has occurred for street children in Santo Domingo as a result of increased reliance on the tourist economy. A qualitative shift in the defining characteristics of street kids in the Dominican Republic has occurred since the late 1990s, which has complicated the cultural image of this population. The 2004 popular *bachata* song, "Juancito Nadie," best captures the national myth of the Dominican street child, or *palomo*. Bachata is a genre of music traditionally associated with the rural Dominican countryside, akin to country western music in the United States. The past several decades has seen bachata rise in prominence as a popular genre in the urban areas as well. Sung by Elvis Martínez, the lyrics chronicle the plight of Juancito Nadie—Johnny Nobody—from his days selling flowers in the street to support his mother and her new boyfriend to not knowing where his next meal will come from. In this sense, "Juancito Nadie" identifies the economic conditions that lead children to work on the streets—in this case, a single mother who needs assistance in supporting the household, relying on the twin strategies of sending the eldest boy to work while also hedging her bets by finding a new male partner.

The chorus of the song is revealing both in its sentimental pathos and by highlighting the defining stereotypical behavior of palomos: "They say that glue is bad and I know it harms me, but with it I can escape my suffering." Palomos like Juancito Nadie are glue sniffers—this is what distinguishes them from the other (noble or worthy) kids who work on the street but do not sleep there. The romantic notions found in Martínez's song are, in all actuality, a version of the recent past that no longer holds true when describing Dominican street life in the new millennium. Children and youth do face hardship when living on the streets, but few would give up the freedom and fun they encounter there. More telling, however, is that glue sniffing is no longer the drug of choice for recent arrivals to the street, although it may be the drug that elicits the most pity from observers. In fact, the kids we worked with actively repudiated the identity of palomos as being dirty glue sniffers, something they would not have defined themselves as. Recent children and youth on the streets of Santo Domingo smoked marijuana and crack, did occasional hits of cocaine when money was available, and took great care in maintaining their appearance.

This shift in subcultural characteristics has much to do with the increase in foreign tourism in the Dominican Republic and the reliance on contact with tourists for street children's livelihood, including begging, pickpocketing, and being involved in sex tourism. Much of what constituted their self-conscious cultivation of appearance and behavior was done with an eye toward interacting with tourists and not drawing attention to themselves, if possible, when in tourist areas. They knew that in order to pass in tourist zones and not be harassed by the police they had to take care of their appearance. Glue and solvent sniffing draws undue attention, leaving the user grimy, with a sticky residue around the mouth and nose, as well as lethargic or, conversely, ultraviolent. Recently arrived street children and youth were keen on not being associated with glue sniffers for fear of losing access to their primary means of income.

The structural changes in economic and social practices brought on by the rise in tourism on the island shifts the responses available to children and youth, opening up a number of new desires for material goods not previously considered defining features of their sense of self-worth. Children and youth who are unsatisfied with their socioeconomic position seek out opportunities to fulfill their material and emotional wants without delaying gratification. Although we often conceptualize the streets as a site of lack, for some children and youth the streets are a site of possibility. Having access to entertainment, exciting consumer goods, and new social relationships provides attractive alternatives to their homes. Abusive home environments may also help push children out the door. As kids first become familiar with the streets by working as bootblacks and itinerant salesmen, they may see that some conditions are better than in their homes and that they can better meet their desires and live out greater freedoms on the street.

## ORGANIZATION OF BOOK

In the chapters that follow, I trace out this process, describing the creative ways that children and youth meet the challenges of living on the streets. Each story line chronicles the range of economic and cultural strategies street children and youth utilize to make the urban environment their home. I describe the forms of intimate social relationships and power dynamics that street children face, both among their peers and in relationship to other social institutions such as their families and social welfare organizations. I focus on several narratives, each of which confronts one of three primary themes: outreach work, structural conditions and social connections, and friendship and everyday violence. Each narrative illustrates the predominant theme of the section, even while themes cross-cut the entire narrative and, in most instances, interrelate.

The narrative opens with the theme of outreach work by following the development of the relationship between young José Alberto and myself and the other outreach staff. José Alberto's trajectory—from initial contact on the streets to eventual reinsertion into his home—is an example of what outreach organizations hope will happen with each child they meet. Initial contact with new kids can be a tricky moment filled with wariness. Eventually, outreach staff members are able to build a relationship of mutual trust, a process that takes months. During this time, children and youth slowly open up and reveal aspects of their street situation and the home lives they have left. Because outreach work emphasizes the agentive decision making of clients, street educators do not push children into reuniting with family members, although this is one of the ideal goals of outreach. Instead, through the developed trust, children and youth are made aware of the options out there, assured of support in moving from the streets, and, ideally, given the tools and resources to work out their complicated personal and family issues. Support is key, and outreach workers are often designated as the anchor of stability for children and youth. This can cause problems, as children become more dependent upon outreach educators. Outreach is successful in part because of the emotional connections made between educators and clients. However, as the case of José Alberto illustrates, maintaining a professional relationship in such an emotionally charged context can be difficult, especially when outcomes are different from those one would hope for.

The narrative of José Alberto also serves as an introduction for the reader to the streets of Santo Domingo, especially around the tourist areas of the Colonial Zone and Malecón. Through his story, the reader gains insight into the conditions of street life for younger adolescents, the work lives of outreach educators, and the negotiations and sometimes fraught relationships between educators, the children they work with, and the children's families. In all, Chapter 1 illustrates the work conditions for organizations that emphasize outreach for inducing change in the lives of homeless populations.

Chapter 2 narrates three stories that explore the theme of structural conditions that limit the options and well-being of the homeless, as well as help shape the type of social connections they have with others. The first story line centers on María, a middle-aged mother of two teenage boys, who has lived on the streets with her family for over a decade. The narrative of María's history on the streets highlights the struggle for dignity in the face of institutionalized inequality, especially as she sought adequate care for her failing health. In addition, being a woman on the streets, María was subject to physical and emotional abuse from the men in her life, most notably her partner, Leandro. Although the NGO continued to work with her and provide what outreach services we could, María was outside of the scope of assistance because of her age. Most resources directed toward working with street children are earmarked for children under the age of eighteen; there are no services in Santo Domingo for other homeless populations. Both of María's boys had participated in the early years of the NGO, but were aging out of assistance. Both of her sons were entrenched in their street worlds. Chronic homelessness makes ties to the nonstreet world increasingly tenuous, especially the crucial kinship relationships that prove essential to moving off the streets.

The second and third stories of Chapter 2 are intertwined. Investigating the rumor of a shooting along the Malecón, I discovered that there were, in actuality, two separate events, both of which had severe consequences for a number of the youths we knew. In trying to confirm reports on the street that a young Haitian man had been killed by gunshots, we encountered the teenage Panchito in the hospital with a broken leg and gunshot wounds from another shooting, as the result of being in the wrong place at the wrong time. Panchito's tale presents the ways in which being young, Haitian, homeless, and without family limit access to medical care and social services. His structural position on the margins of Dominican society predisposes him to higher rates of violence, as well as to entering into exploitive relationships, like that with the Colombian Inés. Meanwhile, when we catch up in prison with Blue Eyes, the youth we were looking for in connection with the Malecón shooting, he recounts for us the botched robbery that led to the death of his close friend at the hands of police. Deeply affected by witnessing this event, Blue Eyes is also aware how close to death he had been. Blue Eyes, as well as his friends Alejandro and Nico, all have experienced difficulty in having the justice system treat them with dignity, fairness, and in a timely fashion. A lack of access to legal representation and impartial judges, as well as commonplace police corruption and abuse, limit the likelihood of impartiality and structure the distribution of justice. Because of social and economic inequality inherent within Dominican society, positive outcomes from medical and legal institutions for street children and youth are rare. Structural inequality limits the types of assistance one can expect, as well as distinctly coloring interactions with others outside of one's social class.

Chapter 3 explores the conditions of violent conflict and revenge on the street. The theme of friendship and everyday violence illustrates how gossip and innuendo of violence on the street can point to multiple truths. While violence and mutual exploitation are readily recognizable features of interpersonal relationships between members of the same street cohort, so too these relationships are characterized by affection and friendship. This section focuses primarily on the dyadic relationships formed among street youth and the strength of friendships that develop in a context of violence and exploitation. Eduardo's brutal stabbing raises questions of loyalty and friendship between him and Luisíto, demonstrating the tangled motivations and emotions that underlie such violent action. Remorse and guilt are just as much a part of the emotional landscape as thoughts of revenge. Yet, perhaps paradoxically, the incident serves to draw the two even closer.

Likewise, Juancho and Juan Carlos rely on one another as much as they are dependent upon the crack they use. Even though Juancho sexually exploits his friend by pimping him out, the strength of their bond depends upon how much they share with one another—including drugs, work, and the day-to-day struggle of the streets.

## METHODS: THE ANTHROPOLOGIST
## AS OUTREACH EDUCATOR

Outreach work involves frequenting the public spaces where homeless populations spend their time. One of Niños's primary methods of work was to go where kids spent time, to carry out informal education activities during the day. We eventually expanded our daytime visits to include late-night visits. These weekly visits helped us keep in touch with kids who no longer participated in the daily activities, to make new street contacts in other parts of the city, and be better informed about the life of the kids with whom we worked. The strategy paid off almost immediately, as we were drawn in closer to the kids' world on the street in a way that we had not been before. Over the long course of months we also were able to contact kids we didn't see during the day or who would appear cyclically on the streets. Our collective understanding of the population we were working with also became enriched as we combined our street-based knowledge with periodic visits to juvenile and adult detention centers, and met the families of children and youth through visits to their homes.

The narratives collected within this book constitute a portion of the events of my working life as a street outreach educator. Although I did have the opportunity to collect formal interviews with street kids as part of an evaluation project for the NGO, the bulk of my work life consisted of the day-to-day interactions with kids during outreach activities. This proved a challenge to my previous style of data collection and ethnographic research, in which I was able to build in plenty of time to interview, take notes, and review the data collected. Working as street educator while simultaneously conducting research proved to be a different sort of engaged anthropology. My primary role was that of an employee/volunteer. My first obligation was not to my own research interests, but to provide services and guidance to the kids we worked with and to be a part of the NGO team. Although I often advanced a work agenda that was born from the knowledge I gained on the streets and was sensitive to the needs of individual kids, in actuality, working in an organization with limited monetary and human resources meant prioritizing activities in ways with which I didn't always agree. If the defining methodology of ethnography is participant-observation, in which the ethnographer both observes the action and partakes in daily life of the community of study, I was far more a participant in the daily functioning of the NGO than I would have liked. This presented a number of challenges that have shaped the way this book has taken form.

As part of my work with the NGO and its responsibility to funding agencies, I was required to keep notes on the kids we contacted during our street visits and the nature of the interaction. I kept a notebook with me to jot down names, locations, new contacts, and any sort of identifying information to remind me of the interaction so that I could later write up a brief report for the organization's records. These short reports, and the notes they are based on, would serve to jog my memory later on. I utilized them to reconstruct interactions that are presented in the narrative that follows. The quoted speech contained within this narrative reflects a deep familiarity with the speakers. While the dialogues are reconstructed from notes taken shortly after the events took place, the way of speaking and information conveyed has been modeled as closely as possible after actual speakers and situations. The narrative is accurate and faithful to the social reality it depicts. The aggregated personalities and situations presented allow for the maintenance of the anonymity and privacy of individual children and youth.

I had hoped to be able to work out a way to utilize a child-driven data collection method, in which children are able to record their lives through use of documentary technologies like cameras, voice recorders, and video recorders.[36] There were a number of limitations that prevented me from implementing such a methodology. As a volunteer, my research goals were subsumed by the practical considerations of working as part of a team and the demands of the delivery of services. Being an employee/volunteer limited my ability to take time out and introduce a tape recorder and microphone to our activities. Instead of focusing on the ways in which kids presented themselves to the outside world, through the democratic introduction of recording devices, I paid attention to the types of stories that circulated within the different groups of kids with whom we worked. Kids would spontaneously have discussions or relive experiences from the night before or pass on street gossip to one another during our work activities and visits. One of the key means for street educators to understand the local environment is to pay attention to the circulation of narratives and gossip. Indeed, educators are part of the gossip circle, as kids pass on relevant information about themselves and others. This could take the form of who has been recently picked up by the police, local disputes with other street denizens, who controls territory where kids congregate, or how kids are fueling their drug habits. Although there is a certain amount of guile involved in this information, as kids would leave out important incriminating details, I was routinely surprised at the trust and openness they had in sharing information with us, whether or not we asked them.

I feel I gained as much of a child-centered perspective as I had initially hoped. Both methodologies highlight children's cultural creativity and spontaneity. The difference lies in the performance. Instead of presenting themselves to some unknown larger potential audience, the children and youth I worked with on the streets of Santo Domingo put forth narratives mainly to constitute and regulate their relationships with their peers. Kids place outreach educators in the roles of soundboard, confidant, and, in the words of Dominican Spanish, someone to whom they can *desahogarse*, or unburden themselves. Desahogarse is not so much confessional as it is a releasing of inner feelings and conflicts, a sort of verbal letting off steam to someone who will not judge.

The narratives collected in this book center around the lives of several different types of street scenes. Although based on real events, the narratives have been altered in significant ways to protect the identity of the people discussed and to aid in the flow of the story. Characters are sometimes composites of a number of kids I met, and narrative time has been compressed, but the tangibility and plausibility of street life has remained. Each character represents a possible trajectory or career on the street. The narrative follows along with the character, paralleling the types of intervention (or inability to intervene) created by the outreach team. Our ability to respond to the needs of the children we worked with was conditioned by the available resources, the cooperation we received from children and their families, and exigent details of life on the street. Our interventions were not always successful. Indeed, success is best defined in small victories, momentary changes in attitude and behavior or self-reflection, and not whether children ultimately made it off the streets and back to a dysfunctional home. It is this operating definition of success that proves outreach work to be undervalued by funding agencies and even within organizations that have some outreach component.

Outreach is most concerned with building relationships from which other work can develop and keeping attuned to changes within the local street environment. It is emotional work. I found myself jerked in multiple directions as I gained respect and admiration for the kids with whom I worked. In a few cases, like that of José Alberto, I found the line between work and private life blurred as the level of investment and friendship increased. In the course of the more than two years I spent working as a street educator, the kids ceased to be cases. They were, for me, children with pluck and verve and a great deal of cunning. I admire them greatly, even while there were a few with whom I dreaded working or who pushed me to the edge of compassionate understanding. It is my hope that the narratives told within the course of this book do justice to their rich cultural and emotional lives, drawing out the contradictions of everyday life on the streets. I ask that you withhold judgment of the lives contained within these pages. Instead, attempt to understand how kids who live on the margins of society and are excluded from mainstream structures of social and economic power create for themselves a life of meaning, utilizing culture in order to thrive.

The insights into street life that I gained during my time working in the arena of child social services in the Dominican Republic were possible only because of my position as a street outreach educator and anthropologist. I gained access to information, areas of the city, and rapport with numerous kids and adults on the street because of my position as advocate and street educator, not because I was an ethnographer. I utilized my skills as an ethnographer, however, to better understand my own working conditions and the lives of those with whom I came into contact. In a very real sense, this is an ethnography of the experience of being a street educator, a personality that also populates street life along with drug dealers, prostitutes, cops, con men, and homeless children.

# 1 · OUTREACH WORK

## LIVING AND SLEEPING ON THE MALECÓN

The jukebox in the corner of the *colmado* (corner shop) blasted out the greatest hits of the 1980s—Air Supply, REO Speedwagon, Journey. In their best campy English, Eli and Núria sang along, the words coming out of their mouths in twisted variations. They didn't speak English, but they knew all the mangled words to "All Out of Love." Just seeing them hold the green bottle up to their lips like a microphone—doing a mock duet—was enough to make me almost spit my beer out through my nose. "Bravo! Bravo!" I proclaimed. "Just like I remember it from elementary school." Eli and Núria laughed. We sat on the high metal bar stools with the green jumbo bottle of Presidente beer between the three of us. The jukebox began playing a Poison song unfamiliar to the two Spaniards. Núria turned conversation to her literacy classes at the drop-in center. Facing the two young women, I could look out across the street to where a bright orange hamburger cart sat. Four blue plastic chairs were arranged on the sidewalk for customers. My thoughts about dinner were interrupted when I saw passing by the food cart a kid, no more than thirteen years old, carrying a large burlap sack swung over the shoulder. He was barefoot and skinny. Not overly skinny—not crack-addict-show-your-ribs-and-long-bones skinny—but skinny like he's going to be a lanky guy when he grows up. Skinny like he had potential. In his mouth he had this ridiculous corn-cob pipe that glowed red embers in the evening, punctuating the night. He reached down to the curb and around the plastic chairs of the hamburger stand to pick up the loose bottles by the neck. Like an expert, he gathered four at a time in one hand. In a practiced move, the sack came off his shoulder and opened to receive the added glass to his collection, returning quickly to position. He was crossing the street, coming toward the colmado.

I laid my hand on Eli's knee. "I think we have a new contact," I said, jutting out my pursed lips to indicate the figure of the boy coming toward the opened walls of the shop. The kid was going to do a sweep of the shop for empty bottles as well. Some of the patrons indicated to him the green and brown glass accumulated around their chairs.

The kid was fast, almost done with the whole room in less than five minutes. He approached the bar and did a final once-over, having to ask customers to reach the bottles, the bar being blocked by the metal stools. As he moved to pick up our empty bottle, I leaned forward and asked, "What's your name, kid?"

He eyed me with distance. "José Alberto."

"What are you doing out so late on a Tuesday, José Alberto?"

"Working hard, can't you see?" he replied, eyes drifting behind the counter where the Presidente ad displayed a digital clock, "Besides, it's not that late. It's 9:30."

"Well, so it is. And what time were you thinking of heading home tonight?"

"What's it matter to you? I'm already on my way."

At my obvious faux pas, Eli took over. "So where's home, little one?" She had a way of smoothing over every situation with the well-learned Dominican sugary way of addressing people—little one, honey, sweetness, my love, dear one.

"San Cristóbal."

I offered him some chips, which he accepted, still kind of cagey.

"Listen," I said as he took a chip with a grimy hand, dirt pushed deep under his fingernails. "I don't think you're heading to San Cristóbal tonight. Not with those bottles and—" I glanced down "—not without something on your feet."

"Which is OK," Núria interjected. "We understand there are times when you may not want to go home. You ever heard of Niños del Camino?"

And so, between the three of us, we kept José Alberto's attention, describing what it was we did, how we operated.

"I want to show you a game. Put out your hand, like this," I placed my left hand out as if I were going to shake to greet him. He extended his hand. I grabbed hold, sliding my curled fingers into his so that our thumbs were up and in a ready position. "It's a thumb battle. You have to try to hold my thumb down and I try to get yours."

"Oh! I know this one!" José Alberto smiled for the first time, a shy grin but wide. Our thumbs began dancing around, trying to catch the other one off guard.

He still hadn't committed to saying he slept on the streets. Kids rarely did unless they were with a child we already knew. So I had to keep it hypothetical, in the realm of what could be possible. "If by chance you were not to return to San Cristóbal tonight, where could we go to visit you tomorrow morning?" He remained concentrated on the thumbs and didn't answer. I'm not going to push it, I thought, just let it go. It sometimes took three chance encounters before a kid would talk to you about where they slept.

We were tied, one win apiece. The competition was stiff—he was serious in his play. Our hands moved forward and back in the air as we jockeyed for position. In a triumphal move, he slipped his thumb on the nail of mine and pushed down. "Champion!" he cried out, relishing the win. I laughed at the grand look on his face.

It was almost 10 P.M. Núria and Eli made signals as if to go. "José Alberto, it's getting late. We're going to get on our way. What's my name?"

He looked at each of us in turn. "Eli. And she's Núria. And he's Jon."

"Oh, but you are a smart kid. You've got our names down."

"If you decide to participate," Núria said, leaving the final instructions, "the bus passes along the Malecón at around 9 in the morning. I'll be on board and so will Eli."

"If I go," he returned to being his cagey self, "I'll be around the obelisk. If I go."

"Maybe we'll see you tomorrow."

I ruffled his spongy, dense hair, a thick weave of tight black curls, with my hand to say goodbye. The three of us made for the opposite direction from José Alberto who, with his bag full of bottles, headed toward the sea.

The morning was bright and clear as I walked along the Malecón, admiring the rocky shore and the palm-tree-lined walk. The Malecón does not lie right on the water, but rather sits about ten or fifteen feet above. Down below are the periodic coves with their fine sand covered in the refuse of the city. The Malecón, beautiful as it is, overlooks one giant trash dump. All the garbage from the streets of Santo Domingo gets washed down the Ozama River into the sea and ends up piling onto the shore.

There are two monuments along George Washington Avenue—the official street name for the Malecón—that are referred to as obelisks. Natives of the city distinguish them by giving them genders—the feminine obelisk and the masculine obelisk. As can be imagined, the masculine obelisk is not unlike a shorter version of the Washington Monument; a tall, phallic missile pointing to the sky. The feminine version is yoni-shaped, a rectangular base rising up with a "U" dip in the top.

The road curved around the feminine obelisk, passing in front. At the backside, a good twenty feet above the shoreline at this point, I could look down onto the inlet. The beach was invisible because of the green and white plastic soda bottles that had been washed up. From a distance, it gave the illusion of being covered by a foam mattress.

I saw no evidence around this obelisk that José Alberto would have been there. I knew that Francisco slept under the oversized Jacaranda trees in the small park across the street. Maybe he would know where I could find José Alberto.

The park was a small space with a wide open area where there sat a bust of either Shakespeare or Cervantes—I could never tell which, but assumed it must be some classical European writer from the full tutu-like bronze collar that billowed out from the neck. In a ring around the statue were a series of stone benches, equally spaced. It was there I found Francisco, lying with his arm over his eyes, flat on his back.

Santo Domingo is a tropical city. The sun reflects off the asphalt and, combined with the humidity, makes the temperature suffocating at times. This didn't matter to Francisco. He believed in layers, lots of layers. His fourteen-year-old body was always wrapped in multiple articles of clothing. Beneath jeans, he had on a pair of shorts over another pair of exercise shorts. On top, two t-shirts, a long-sleeve button-down followed by a zip-up hooded sweatshirt. None of the other kids we worked with went through as much trouble to layer themselves.

Once, we visited Francisco's home, located an hour and a half out from the capital along a dirt track so pitted the pick-up truck inched down the road. We mistook Francisco's mother for his grandmother because she was so beaten down, haggard, with one stray tooth and sunken cheeks. She should have been in her sixties by the way she looked, but Francisco, at fourteen, was the oldest of eleven children. His brothers and sisters ran around the dirt patio, the youngest five naked and shoeless, their bellies protruding in evidence of parasites dancing inside. The house itself was a collection of sticks, cardboard, and metal cans flattened out, all held together with mud. It was a nearly empty square 10 × 10 box placed on the dirt. I saw no bed. The way Francisco layered his clothes could have been from fear of losing what little he had. It is not true that when you have nothing it is easier to let go. Sometimes you hold on all the more tightly.[1]

It was still early at eight in the morning, and the traffic along the Malecón was just starting to pick up. The great rumbling of a passing semi made Francisco squirm a bit on the bench, although he did not open his eyes. I decided to finish what the truck started and sat myself on the edge of the bench, down by his feet. I reached my hand up to his arm and shook slightly. He simply shrugged my hand off. I tried again, a bit firmer. His arm lying across his eyes flew off and reached for my hand. I was too fast. What he managed to grab was his own bicep. Laughing, I said, "Not so quick in the morning, are you?"

By this time Francisco was awake, eyes opened, if still unfocussed. He lifted his head to see me smiling brightly at him, "Christ, Jon. What the hell are you doing here?"

"Just a wake-up call so you don't miss the Niños del Camino bus today."

"What time is it?"

"About 8:45." I lied. I didn't want him to think he got up too early. The bus usually came around 9:15, sometimes a lot later.

He pushed me off the bench with his knees and sat up.

I sat back down beside him. "Rough night?"

"Rough night. Got chased by the police on the ped mall. Fernando's been breaking and entering again and they think it is one of us. Goddamn Fernando. Why can't he go rob someplace else?"

A passing vendor stopped with his thermos of coffee. I bought us two small cups and could smell the sweetness even before it touched my lips.

"Word has it there's a new kid on the Malecón," I said as Francisco took his coffee in sips.

He pulled his head back slightly to give me a look of incredulity, "A new kid? Now why would I know anything about that?"

"Come on, Francisco, I know you see a lot. You know a lot about what goes on around here. You're a smart guy."

My flattery seemed to be working. Francisco just needed some cajoling to be cooperative. He took another tiny sip of coffee. "There is some brat who's raising lots of trouble around the hamburger stands in front of the park. He collects bottles with that old crazy guy, the one with one hand. But it ain't just bottles he's collecting. Looks like some wallets have gone missing, too." I loved how Francisco called him a brat, even though they were the same age.

"Sounds like the kid I know. I met him last night. You get along with him?"

"I don't get along with nobody," Francisco said clearly. "When you start hanging out with others, that's when you get into trouble. People start pointing a finger at you, too. I know lots of people but I don't count any of them as my friend."

I might have lost my opportunity to ask for José Alberto's whereabouts. Francisco, in his attempt to appear tough and self-sufficient, could get cantankerous at times. Even his face changed, his eyes narrowing when he put on his tough-guy act.

"Yeah, I know you are always on your own, Francisco, but that doesn't mean you don't know things. The more solitary the wolf, the more crafty he has to be." He smiled and eased up at that. He liked the thought of being a wolf.

"So if I wanted to find this kid with the bottles, where would I look? He told me he slept around here, around the obelisk."

"No way, man, this is my zone. You gotta check the other obelisk—the masculine obelisk. Down by the round-a-bout, near the water. That's where you'll find him."

I stood up and made a fist with my right hand. Francisco reciprocated and we lightly bumped knuckles together to say goodbye. I left him waiting for the bus and headed down the Malecón.

As if to assuage the blatant phallic nature of the "masculine" obelisk, it is always painted with flowing, full-body portraits of the Mirabel sisters, the three young women who defied Trujillo's dictatorship and fought to rid the country of his tyranny. The obelisk was clad in a light blue, the color of the Caribbean sky on a clear day. The three sisters—Patria, Minerva, and María Teresa—were depicted in ethereal white gowns, more like angels or sea nymphs than liberators from tyranny. It is a welcome change from the cult of Duarte, Sanchez, and Mella, the three founding fathers of Dominican freedom. The feminine repossession of the obelisk is the only visible insistence of the role of women in the making of the modern nation, and then as a corrective force against masculine tyranny.[2]

I rounded the obelisk on the ocean side and looked out to the small grassy expanse between the Malecón and the cliff edge that stood above the sea. But for a few palm trees and trash, there was nothing there. I stepped off the sidewalk, behind the high cement benches, and out onto the shelf that leads to the ocean. The rock was porous basalt and the holes created sharp, jagged edges. Even in shoes, I could feel the shapes beneath my feet. I knew there was a natural stairway leading down the five feet to a low shelf where shoeshine boys and some of the street kids we worked with would go to bathe and swim in the ocean. Although it was certainly dangerous, given the basalt and the strong current and lack of beach, the water was clearer and cleaner here. I peered down into the half-hidden bathing area and saw nothing but the spume and jets of water meeting the land.

I turned away from the water and headed back up to the Malecón. A palm tree near the corner bench caught my eye. It was the only one bent over, the branches peeled down from the trunk as if it were a banana. No storm would cause the tree, even a small one, to be bent like that. The folded fronds hid the base of the tree. It was a perfect place for a boy to sleep and hide out.

If he was there, I didn't want to scare him or startle him from sleep, so I decided to approach the tree from the bench. I went back to the sidewalk and sat down on the gray cement. I didn't want to draw attention to this hiding place either. Secrecy and safety go hand-in-hand. I turned my head to the left, as if I were looking down the Malecón, peering between the palm fronds. Near the base was a collapsed cardboard box and a crumpled up t-shirt. Someone had been sleeping in plain view. If I wanted to meet him— or them—I would have to come earlier in the day.

The next morning, I arrived early to what I had started calling the tree house. I decided to follow the same protocol as the day before and sat myself quietly down on the bench next to the makeshift shelter, trying not to draw attention to either myself or to the tree. My fear was that the tree was actually the sleeping place of one of the adults that roam the Malecón. The majority of the adults on the street either have a high consumption problem (usually crack) or some form of mental illness, or both. At any rate, they can be unpredictable and unstable, not the kind of thing you want to face alone, or the type of person you want to disturb waking up early in the morning.

It amazed me how well that little palm tree did its concealment job. From a distance it beautifully obscured the contents within and barely looked out of place. Up close, it masked what was inside. I looked from the corner of my eye through the small openings in the individual fronds. There was what looked like two small lumps curled up around the base of the tree on top of the same cardboard I had seen the day before.

I checked the time on my cell phone: 8:20 in the morning. Not too early, really, as most of the city would be up and running, scurrying off to be at work by nine. How could I make my presence known to the sleeping kids without giving away their position or frightening the living wits out of them by some strange gringo alarm clock?

I got up from the bench and walked toward the cliff. An approach from this side, when I turned back, might wake them without my having to do anything.

A movement to the left interrupted my reverie, someone climbing up from the rock base below. I was not mistaken; it was José Alberto, shirtless and shoeless, clambering across the jagged basalt. He hadn't seen me yet. I placed myself in his path.

I remained looking out at the sea, but removed myself slightly from the cliff. He was going to cut wide to avoid me, so, I called to him, "You're up early this morning."

He stopped in his tracks and it took him a fraction of a second, a pause during which time he recognized who I was. "Oh! Oh-oh!" he began, using an expression of surprise that is common in the Dominican southwest—not the worry or nay-saying that it conveys in English, but rather a gesture as if to say, "So, you think you surprised me but I was on to you all along." He wiped the beads of water dripping onto his forehead from the mass of his hair. "You're pretty smart," he said. "I didn't think you'd find me."

"Not as smart as you," I replied, "if that tree house is your doing." A broad grin appeared on his face, out of pride. "You going to introduce me to your friends?"

"I'm going to sit on the bench," I explained as we walked toward the palm tree, "That way your friends can decide if they want to talk. How many of you sleep here?"

He knew I'd seen it clearly, the whole set-up. "Three. Me and those two guys. We've been here about a week."

"Where were you before?"

"Naw, I was down by Montesino"—the large statue of the good friar farther down the Malecón—"And these two guys just got here last week."

"You knew them before?"

"Yeah, they're from San Cristóbal, like me."

San Cristóbal is little more than a half-hour to the southwest. I had seen this before. Kids come to the capital to work—shine shoes, wash windshields—and then one night they don't have enough money for bus fare, or it is late and they are afraid of arriving home because someone is going to beat them for returning late, and so they stay on the streets in the capital. They might have months—even years—of coming to the capital, and then one night they stay. One night becomes two, two four, and then, before they realize it, they've been a whole week out of their home. The fear of reprisals becomes greater. It takes a lot more courage to return home sometimes than it does to stay on the street.

I chose the next bench over from where I had been sitting. I didn't want José Alberto to think I was eavesdropping. He parted two palm leaves and ducked down onto the ground where his friends lay.

Amauris may have been small, but he was restless, shifting back and forth in front of the bench. The other one, Javi, looked like he had woken up hard. I attempted to explain who we were and what we did. Amauris perked up. "I know you guys! There was a lady with railroad tracks in her mouth and a red-headed woman and they stopped by the Malecón one night. I remember! They gave me juice and cookies and we talked. Hey, where are the juice and cookies? I'm hungry! Don't you have juice and cookies?"

I had to think really hard—a girl with railroad tracks in her mouth? Must be Marlenys, a young woman with bright silver braces who worked as an educator with us for a brief spell of three or four months. That put it almost a year ago that Amauris met us, when we had just started night outreach once a week. It meant that, at eleven years old, Amauris had slept on the street before.

"Whew, that was quite a while ago," I said, trying to dam the flood of Amauris's speech with my own. I started to explain that we offered other activities and services besides the visits like the one Amauris had received.

"Oh yeah," he interrupted me, "I told those two women that I was going home the next day. It had just gotten late. And I did go home. My mom doesn't say anything. Like today. I'm going home after I work a bit. Me and Javi are going home. Ain't that right, Javi? We're going home."

Javi didn't reply. I turned to José Alberto. "Does this mean you're going home?"

"Me? Home? Not a chance," he answered curtly.

"You don't have any cookies and juice, do you? No? Well, I'm going to go bathe if you don't mind. Come on, Javi, let's go for a swim!"

I let Amauris go. He practically pulled Javi from the bench and they headed off together down toward the water's edge. I was left with José Alberto.

"Do you believe what Amauris says? You think they're going home today?"

"Probably."

"But not you?"

He shook his head and looked down at his feet. He wouldn't meet my eyes.

"That's OK, José Alberto. I understand there are reasons not to go home. We can talk later about that, when you feel ready. Would you like to participate with us today?"

He looked up from his bare feet.

"You remember Eli the Spanish girl I was with, the dark-haired one, that night in the colmado? Well, if you want to participate I'm going to give her a call and find out where the bus is at so they can come pick us up."

"Is the other one going to be there too? The blond?"

"Núria? Yeah, she'll be there too. You in?"

José Alberto nodded a simple yes. Not too enthusiastic, but a yes nonetheless.

I pulled out my cell phone from the front pocket of my jeans and gave Eli a ring.

"Eli! My dear, I can barely hear you. Sounds like you are in a tin can." The connection was bad, filled with crackly static.

"I'm in the bus. We're just passing Montesino."

"Perfect! You remember José Alberto from the colmado the other night? He wants to join us today for the activity. Let me pass him to you."

I offered the phone to José Alberto who looked at me as if to say, "Me? What am I going to say?"

"Just say hi to Eli," I prompted.

He took the phone in his hand and placed it to his ear. "Hello? Yes. It's me. Pepe. Yes.... Yes.... By the park? OK... Yes.... OK.... Adios."

He smiled as he passed the phone to me. "Come on, we need to cross the street. They're going to pick us up at the corner." I don't know what Eli told him, but he was already weaving his way through the heavy traffic by the time I got up from the bench.

## CRYING WOLF

"Turns out your little friend is quite the monster," Núria told me a week later, a rare afternoon when we all found ourselves in the office at the same time. I was typing some reports at the computer as the drop-in center work team arrived. They looked beat. Even Núria, who never looked it, who always was an orb of energy, looked drained that day. Her hair was a flat mess and the single thin braid she kept near her bangs was falling in her eyes. Héctor followed Núria into the room and plopped down on one of the padded office chairs. He was a big man, tall and wide, the kind nothing should tire out.

"Man, they were all over the place today," he said, placing his hands on his belly and looking ready for a nap. "Thirteen of the buggers of all sizes is a bit much."

"Who's my friend the monster?" I asked Núria, unclear as to whom she referred.

Eli popped her head in from the hallway, a dark grass stain across her light blue shirt. She heard my question. "The monster? José Alberto."

"José Alberto? No way. I don't believe it. He seems so calm, so together."

"Maybe on the streets but he's got a ways to go in the drop-in center. The kid doesn't listen. And it's not like some of the other kids who don't listen and then after like five times and a short discussion finally help you out. No, José Alberto refused to participate in anything. And those are some of the most difficult kids because they don't go with the flow of anything, they always stand against the current.

"Literally, Jon, he just wanted to play with blocks the entire day and when it came time to do the group activity he ignored every voice and continued with the blocks. One of the older kids—Juancho I think it was—went up the stairs to where José Alberto was with the blocks and kicked what he was building, saying it was time for the activity," Núria paused for a sip of water, "I never would have imagined José Alberto a fighter, but man, he has it in him. And then he picked up that rock . . ."

"And Juancho has little fear of getting into a fight," Héctor came alive from the chair, "Had to send them off on foot from the center. Can't have them throwing rocks the size of your head. You know how it is, once there is one fight it always leads to two more. We started with thirteen kids in the bus this morning and came back with seven. I think things were easier when we worked on the street."[3]

At two in the morning the pedestrian mall lost all of the little charm it had during the day. Unlike most of the rest of the city, this part of the Colonial Zone was normally well lit, even well into the early morning. But the street lamps created this artificial halo, this glow that radiated out from the middle where the early twentieth-century style lamps were and faded into twilight on the edges near the storefronts. There were few people out at this hour—some returning home from the clubs, a couple of hamburger street vendors cooking up for those with late-night snack attacks, and small bands of kids. At that hour, the homeless adults were safely on their storefront steps, wrapped in cardboard boxes or blankets or plastic garbage bags. It's the young ones, the kids under fifteen, who roamed through the Colonial Zone in the early morning. The older youth were looking for money in other ways—sex work, drug sales, or finding the right place to rob.

There was a small group of five in the block ahead of me. It was a mixed group. Some were bootblacks with their homemade wooden shoeshine boxes, seated on top where the customer's shoe would go. Although they would say they were going home that evening, the truth was, it was too late for most of them to get back into their neighborhoods. Their neighborhoods were too dangerous to enter at that hour.

The others in the group were two kids from our program, Hilário and Máximo. Máximo was all dolled up. He had on a long mauve-colored quilted women's jacket—a winter coat really. Because he was so short, the coat reached his heels and looked more like a mobster's full-length trench coat than something a snow bunny would wear. Máximo wore the jacket with a pair of aviator glasses he might have stolen from a shop. He was the center of attention. Even Hilário, who normally preferred to lead than to follow, was under Máximo's spell. It was clear they all wanted to try on his new gear. He knew it, too, and kept the costume like it was the golden fleece.

"Hey mobster," I called out to Máximo and the group as I passed by, "careful the tourist police don't catch you horsing around at this hour."

"Jon!" Máximo called back, detaching himself from the group. The coat billowed out slightly and the tails trailed behind him. Jesus, I thought, he even walks like a mobster. This thirteen-year-old knows how to act.

Hilário was right behind him. He was shoeless that evening and had on a pair of pants riddled with holes. His short frame was covered in a shirt that was three times too long, hanging well below the waist. The combination of the pants, no shoes, and the oversized shirt gave Hilário the look of the perfect mendicant child. He met me with a magnificent grin that stretched from ear to ear.

In one swift movement I threw an arm around Hilário's frame, lifted him up and put him under my arm as if he were a newspaper. He got a kick out of that and started laughing as I twirled around with him under my arm a couple of times and set him back on his feet. The young kids were fun that way; you could swing them around, carry them on your back. Not all of them, though. I would never have attempted to lift Máximo off the ground. He was too serious, too much wanting to be in control. As much as I admired Máximo and his natural-born leadership skills, to be a leader—to be a leader on the streets—you can't show the kind of frivolity that comes with letting an adult educator give you a piggy-back ride.

"What are you guys up to?" I asked after having set Hilário back down.

"Look at the glasses I found. Pretty cool, huh?" Máximo offered me the dark glasses to try on. I knew it was a gesture of respect—he hadn't let any of the kids try them yet. I took off my own prescription lenses and passed them to Máximo. The aviator glasses were so dark that my view became pitch black. It was a wonder Máximo could make out anything with them on.

"How do I look?"

Hilário cracked up upon seeing me, letting out a full body laugh from deep within him, "Like a drug dealer! Just like the guy up on Forty-second Street that they call the Gringo. He's got dark lenses like those." Chagrined, I peeled the glasses from my face.

Máximo had placed my glasses on his face and held his hands outstretched, looking at his fingers first and then out beyond them, down the Conde. My prescription was really strong. "Damn! These things are crazy!"

He called out to everyone, "It's like smoking weed. Everything seems so far away. It's trippy."

I'm not sure how I liked having my corrective lenses compared to a drug trip. "Here ya go," I offered Máximo back his glasses, "so you can be a mobster again." He reluctantly handed my lenses back to me.

The shoeshine boys came closer from where they had been sitting, their curiosity piqued at our interaction. I recognized Amauris at the same time he saw me.

"Oh! Look who we got here. It's Amauris. You remember me?"

"Yeah, you're that guy, the Niños del Camino guy. The gringo."

"This gringo has a name. You remember it? My name is Jon."

"Jon! Right. Jon."

He seemed a lot more subdued that evening. Not off the wall like the other morning. I checked out his eyes. Thin red lines webbed the white orbs. He'd been smoking weed. That would explain the tranquillity.

"You been hanging out with José Alberto?" I asked, thinking he might know where he'd been sleeping these days. Shortly after being discovered, the palm tree hide-out was abandoned. I had gone back the morning after José Alberto's striking performance at the drop-in center and there was nothing to indicate the tree was still in use—no cardboard on the ground, and the palm fronds were in careless disarray. The tree wasn't going to hide anything in that state.

"No way, man, I don't hang out with him," Amuaris replied, "I shine shoes. That's how I make my money. I'm not like him. I don't dumpster dive looking for bottles. That's just nasty. That's for palomos and I ain't no palomo."

Palomo. Amauris used a term that has a wide cultural currency. It can mean someone who is inept, constantly botching things up. Someone who is not a smooth operator is a palomo. The other use is to describe street kids, but of a particular variety. You are a palomo if you don't take care of yourself, have a visible drug addiction—that is to say, solvent or glue sniffing with the bottle in hand—and if you do typical street activities like dumpster dive, whether it be for food or for collecting bottles. To be called a palomo a kid must look like he has deteriorated in appearance, wearing rags or dirty clothes. The older kids we worked with, the young men in their late teens and early twenties who have been on the street for over ten years, these are considered palomos. Amauris saw that fine social distinction, recognized the kind of path that José Alberto was on. He didn't want to be mistaken for one of those. All palomos sleep on the street, but not all kids who sleep on the street are palomos. By calling someone else a palomo, Amauris kept up the illusion that his position wasn't that bad.

"Just wondering where I might be able to find him is all," I replied to Amauris. "Oh well, obviously you haven't seen him."

"Naw, he's somewhere around here."

"Alright, *muchachones*, I'll catch you later. Be careful tonight."

I extracted myself from the small group and continued on my way down the Conde, past the male hustlers and the female prostitutes that wait outside of Paco's Cafeteria, the twenty-four- hour joint at the very start of the pedestrian mall. Out of the corner of my eye I saw Carlos, one of the kids in our program, pimped up in his muscle-bound tank top looking so much older than his fifteen years. He sat at one of the tables just outside of Paco's with another young Dominican and two aging, wrinkly Americans who had bought their young sports beers. My heart fell, deflated at the sight of Carlos with clients. It is one thing to know intellectually what kids would do to survive; it is another to see it happening. The two old guys laughed loudly, their silver heads bobbing up and down, proud at what their twenty-five dollars would buy them. Carlos caught me looking in his direction and turned his head away.

Like so many other nights, I turned away and let the indignation and anger wash through me. I was just as upset at my own inability to do anything as I was at those aging men. And the worst part was, Carlos would say very little about it, for shame or embarrassment; he did not acknowledge to us how he was making money. If there is no acceptance of one's behavior, you can't begin to talk about self-worth, protection, and having dignity and boundaries in what one will or will not do. Instead, Carlos's prostitution became the big elephant that nobody would talk about. We all knew it existed, but we ignored it until he brought it up.

Even though it was late, I decided against a cab and wanted to walk home. I needed to clear my head now and the walk, if I walked quickly, would only take me fifteen to twenty minutes. I had a chosen route, one in which the street lights were almost always lit and, if worst came to worst, I could walk down the middle of the street. The key, I've always thought, is to walk with purpose, like you know what you are doing and, above all, without fear. You must project self-confidence.

Past Parque Independencia, I turned up 11 de Agosto. The Haitian prostitutes used that corner by the optical shop for their base. That evening there were three women in heels and high-cut skirts walking back and forth like caged animals on a small stretch of sidewalk. Good Lord, I thought, it's everywhere you look. I ignored them, gave them wide berth as I turned up the street, hearing them call after me, *Ven acá mi amor, qué buscas?* I'm looking for nothing but my own bed, I silently answered.

I crossed to ascend the street. On the next corner, outside a dingy colmado, there was a large pile of trash—boxes filled with detritus and loose agglomerates of food waste and other items shoved under the street lamp. There was something moving in the pile and at first I thought it might be a dog, but when the figure looked up I saw it was human. And not just human. It was José Alberto.

I was going to have to walk right by him, so of course I was going to talk to him, but Jesus, it seemed as if I had caught all of our kids *en flagrante* since I stepped out of the disco. There is such a stigma against dumpster diving I didn't know how José Alberto was going to take it that I had caught him in the act.

"Hey, Pepe," I called out as I got nearer. Better to just make my presence known. He turned his head in my direction, back still slightly hunched and hands holding on to the box he was rifling through. In his pursed lips was the same silly corn-cob pipe that made him look like a sharecropper. Must be his work uniform.

"Oh! Oh-oh!" José Alberto recognized my presence without taking the pipe from his mouth. He was getting good at that.

"What's the what with you?" I greeted him in my best street Spanish.

"Calmer than a clam," he replied, pulling the pipe from his lips. He dropped the box. "Lookin' for bottles. I made 150 pesos yesterday in bottles."

"They tell me you haven't been going to the center lately. What's up with that?"

He straightened up, getting defensive, "That Spaniard said I couldn't come back."

"Eli? Eli told you not to come back? I don't buy it. That doesn't sound like her."

"Well, it's true. After the fight with Juancho she told me not to come back."

At least he was owning up to the fight. "Hmmm . . . well how about if I ask her what she meant by that, all right? Would you like to participate again if you could?"

"Sure, I guess so."

I checked out his appearance and thought, Geez, Amauris was right, he does look like a palomo. His clothes were filthy. Even in the low light of the street lamp I could see the dirt and grime on his jeans, and the maroon t-shirt was more gray than anything. But the worst part was his hands and feet. He wore flip-flops, and the dirt was caked on. José Alberto was fairly dark-skinned but his hands and feet were two shades darker from the filth. If he were going to the drop-in center he could at least bathe regularly and get a clean pair of clothes or wash what he had.

From around the corner came a tall, lean man just as grimy as José Alberto. He had an overgrown beard matted on his face, the once curly, kinky hair laying in rope-like patterns. He carried a sack over his shoulder and looked like a thin, black Saint Nicholas.

"You find anything, little guy?" he asked José Alberto as he approached.

"Naw, nothin' worth anything."

I made to introduce myself, but the man kept walking passed me and muttered, "Let's get goin' then." He turned down the street without another word.

"You hangin' out with him, Pepe?" I asked, a bit unnerved that he should choose that guy as his street companion.

"Yeah. We collect bottles together. He lets me share his spot down by the Cathedral. He's got a way to sneak into that gated park down there."

José Alberto's choice of friends troubled me. Adults usually mean abuse. "You guys sleep together?" I asked, using an ambiguous construction that could mean anything from having sex to sharing a similar sleeping space.

"Yeah, there in the park. There's lots of space. But we're the only two. Only he knows how to get in through the parking garage next door."

The man had stopped at the corner where the Haitian women were still plying their trade. He was looking back at us.

"You'd better get going. He's waiting for you. I'll talk to Eli though about you participating in the drop-in center, alright?"

"Sure. I'll check you later."

He threw his bag of bottles over his shoulder and headed down the street. The bag was so full and José Alberto so short, the bottles dragged along the pavement, clinking into the night.

"That little bugger," was how Eli reacted when I told her what José Alberto had said. We sat in a colmado in the Colonial Zone sharing a beer after work. "So he blames me for not attending? Never mind the fight or the fact that he wouldn't actually participate, but just sit there wanting to do his own thing."

"Yeah, well, I didn't really buy it. I figured he might have misunderstood."

"I told him that if he decides to come to the center, it's to participate in the activities and not to sleep or play with blocks all day. If he's not going to partake in the life-skills sessions than I told him he shouldn't come. I left it up to him."

"José Alberto doesn't really take to being corrected very well. He shuts down, won't say a word. He gets all embarrassed and won't meet your eye." I caught Eli's disapproving look, "OK, all right. No more work. How's the apartment search going?"

It was almost impossible not to talk about work. It pursued us. I was constantly running into kids and street adults I knew after work hours and on weekends. To some degree, I searched it out. I chose to walk down the Conde, knowing full well I would run into a kid I knew; to choose any other parallel street would have felt to me like I no longer gave them preference. We finished our beers talking about other aspects of our lives—home, love, gossip. The sun had set on us, the sky darkening while we sipped our cold drinks from the tiny plastic cups.

"Which way are you headed?" Eli asked, knowing it would be closer to home for me to walk north from where we were, up to Avenida Mexico.

"I'm not ready to go home yet," I said, not mentioning why—that the electricity in my barrio only came on after eleven o'clock at night, and why would I want to sit in a dark apartment trying to read by candlelight? "Come on, I'll walk you home. But on one condition: we walk down the Conde."

Eli smiled, putting her hands on her hips and cocking her head in mock reproach, "The Conde? What about not working after hours, huh? I don't really mind. It's just sometimes you don't want to run into anyone you know. It's not just the kids, you know? The entire world is always out on the Conde."

Parque Colon was still busy at 8:30. The streetlamps were all lit up and the two outdoor cafes were full of people. Around the base of Christopher Columbus's statue sat a group of young hippie wannabes. The green metal park benches in the recesses of the shadows cast by lamplight were filled with pairs of lovers, holding hands and kissing.

We crossed through the park, onto the Conde. The Conde was more normally a thoroughfare. Now people walked slowly, to be seen and to see. Up a couple of blocks at the entrance to the ice cream shop, Eli touched my arm.

"Look who we have here," she indicated the figure bent over one of the plastic trash receptacles bolted near the street lamp. It was José Alberto. "Come on, we're going to settle this here and now."

"It really bothers you, doesn't it, what José Alberto said?"

"Of course it does! It always bugs me when someone puts the blame on me for their inability to take responsibility for themselves and their own decisions. Even one of our kids. To me it's a fundamental part of being a mature person, and isn't that what we are trying to do by working with them?"

If Eli was upset with José Alberto, she didn't let it show in her interactions with him. He had lifted himself out of the garbage can, carrying his plastic ten-pound flour sack of bottles behind him. He didn't see us. Eli put herself in his path, arms crossed across her chest, mocking impatience. Or was it an "I've caught you!" position?

The element of surprise is best, and José Alberto was just that—surprised enough to drop his bag of bottles. I came up behind Eli and joined her. "José Alberto," I said, "How is the hardest-working kid on the streets today?"

Eli righted herself and made her way to the free bench nearby, tugging at the same dirty maroon shirt I had last seen José Alberto in. "Come on, have a seat. It's been such a long time, you and I have some catching up to do."

José Alberto sheepishly joined her on the bench, not really having much choice. I stood in front of the two of them, my left foot resting on the edge of the bench, on the outside of José Alberto. With Eli on one side and my foot up on the other, we had him between a rock and a hard place.

"Remember the last time we talked," I began and immediately José Alberto knew what was up, he knew he'd been found out and would not meet my eyes. His gaze found the grubby cement of the pedestrian mall infinitely fascinating.

I didn't wait for an answer because I knew he wouldn't reply. It was not his way. When he became embarrassed or ashamed he would clam up. "The last time we talked, you had mentioned how you would like to go back to the drop-in center but that because of certain things that occurred, you felt you couldn't. You had said that Eli said you couldn't return." He didn't even look up at that.

Eli turned her body in towards his, placing her hands on his legs, which remained dangling from the bench. "*Mi hijo,*" she began, even using the right Dominican intonation for the phrase. "Mi hijo" showed just the right amount of care and concern; "my child" marks everyone as potential family.

"Mi hijo, you know I would never want you to not participate with us. If I remember correctly, what I said was, if you wanted to come to the drop-in center, it would be to participate fully in all the activities we do there. It is not just to come and hang out, doing whatever you may want to do. If you don't want to participate in all the activities, it's best that you don't come. That's what I told you, isn't that right?"

He sort of mumbled a yes, but kept from lifting his head. "We're not upset with you, José Alberto. We just want everyone to be real clear with what was said."

We stayed in that tableau in silence for a good minute or two, hoping José Alberto would say something. I took the palm of my hand and placed it gently under his chin, raising his head to meet my eyes. "Hey, I want to tell you a story. But I only tell stories when I know people are listening. Maybe Eli knows this story, too. Maybe she can help me. Do you know the story about the boy who cried wolf?"

Eli played off me beautifully: "Remind me how that goes."

"Well, once there was a kid about the age of José Alberto. His family sent him off every day to care for their ears."

José Alberto looked quizzically at me. "Ears?"

"Oops!" I corrected my Spanish, "I meant sheep." *Oreja* and *oveja.* Funny difference. We all laughed at the slip up.

"So this kid, this little—how do you call someone that takes care of sheep?" I invented the word *ovejero,* which elicited more laughter from José Alberto.

"No!" he called out, "Someone who cares for sheep is called a shepherd." Of course it is, a *pastor,* just as a pastor tends his flock, his congregation.

"Oh, right! Well, this young shepherd goes out every day with his family's sheep. But it is boring out there with just the sheep as company. So one day, he wants a bit of excitement and decides to yell out to the village that there is a wolf threatening the sheep.

"What do you suppose happens when he called out 'wolf'?"

José Alberto didn't answer, but kept his gaze on me.

Eli jumped in, "I bet the whole village came to protect the sheep."

"That's right! But you know what? There was no wolf. And when the villagers found out there never was a wolf they got upset.

"Well, the little shepherd kind of liked it. He thought it was great fun that all the villagers came running when he called wolf. So he does it a few more times and each time the villagers come ready to protect the sheep, but there is never any wolf.

"Now, the villagers are pretty ticked off. But then do you know what happened? A real wolf comes along and the little shepherd is very scared, not knowing how to fight a wolf. He calls out as loud as he can, 'Wolf! Wolf!' and what do you think happens?"

"The villagers come to fight the wolf?" José Alberto answered after a pause.

"Why would the villagers come?" Eli commented. "They've been called time and again by the boy when there was no wolf. They got tired and didn't believe the boy."

"Right. The villagers didn't come. The wolf had the family's sheep for dinner."

José Alberto looked surprised, as if the outcome should have been different, "But they should have come! There was a wolf!"

"But because the boy lied time and time again, calling wolf when there was no wolf, the villagers didn't believe him when the wolf actually appeared."

Eli picked up the theme and drove it home, "So let's try to call out wolf only when the wolf appears. What do you think?" She stood up from the bench. José Alberto followed suit. She placed both palms on the sides of his forehead in a gesture of tender care. "So, if you want to go with us tomorrow to the drop-in center you know where to catch the bus, right?"


## GOING HOME

By all accounts, home should be the last place most kids we worked with would want to go to live. The vast majority leave some horrific situation or another—mixed families, abusive stepparents, irregular meals. I grew to sympathize with kids when they chose not to return home. I could not advocate for something that I myself, if placed in a similar situation, would not have chosen. And, even if the home situation was not so bad—a perfect family life, or at least things had changed for the better since the child left—returning home could still be the impossible choice. In many respects, street life can be said to be easy and enjoyable—kids govern themselves, make their own schedules, with no one telling them what to do or when it do it.

On top of the freedom and the ability to lead one's own life, drug addiction also keeps kids from wanting to go home. It is unlikely that a child who is sleeping on the streets, no matter how young, has not tried drugs of some sort. And it is not just the physical, chemical addiction that creates a habit or dependency on the drug. The social importance of consuming, the high priority of expressing group membership through smoking weed or crack together means that when children return home they miss not only the chemical addiction—which can be easily replaced by buying and consuming substances wherever they may live—but they experience a social withdrawal, the camaraderie that chemical dependency on the streets engenders and promulgates.[4] Even the dangers of life on the streets appear to diminish in the face of addiction and relative freedom. Abuse by the police is preferable to chronic abuse by one's stepfather—it is an abuse they choose, although they are just as unable to fight back. They accept the insecurities of everyday life on the streets in exchange for the ability to do as they please.

Yet, all the same, sometimes kids do decide to try going home. Their motivation may be nostalgia, desire to see their mother or siblings, or pursuit by the cops for a robbery they may or may not have committed. Addiction management can be a motivation, too. Returning to one's family provides time and space to detox.

When José Alberto approached Eli after a few weeks of participating at the drop-in center, and told her he wanted to go back to his house, but not alone, I was both elated and skeptical at the same time. Why now? What had changed? If it was precipitated by some crisis—external or internal to José Alberto—would that be enough to keep him there even though the household situation may be slow to change (if it ever would)?

Kids understand very well what the problems and family dynamics at home are, although few will give you a diagnosis in so many words. When asked outright why they left, the majority will give you a laundry list of acceptable items—stepfathers or stepmothers who beat them with electrical wire; alcoholic parents who spend all the household income on rum at the expense of feeding the family; mothers who choose their new husbands over their sons. But the underlying causes come out over time. The partial pictures described by kids must be compared with those same household members and their version of events. It is a slow process to build the trust that first allows kids to communicate with us, and then allows their parents to talk about what are often private or embarrassing situations.

"You sure that's what you want to do?" I asked José Alberto. I squinted at him, barely able to see the features of his face in the glare of the setting sun reflecting off the bricks of the ruins of the old city walls.

"Yeah, I'm sure. I told Eli and Núria. I just wanna make enough money to buy a pair of jeans, some shoes, and take 400 pesos for my mom. Then I'll be ready to go."

"No wolves?"

He smiled at the joke, a broad full-face grin. "No wolves." It's the truth. "As long as you guys go with me, I'll be ready."

I looked down at his flip flops, a sea foam green that had turned brown with a dirt coating, much like the actual color of the sea off the coast of Santo Domingo. "What size shoe do you wear?"

"I don't know. Like 41 or 42."

"What if I were to find you a pair of shoes—nothing fancy, just a pair of canvas shoes. No Jordans, you understand?"

"Like just a plain pair of black tennies?"

"Yeah, black canvas—Converse or something similar. I'll tell you what, I'm going to see if we don't have a pair of used jeans too, back in storage. That means all you need is the 400 pesos. What do you say?"

José Alberto's marble eyes grew wide. "Really? I've got 150 pesos saved up. I gave that to Núria today. I'll have 400 pesos in no time."

It was Núria's idea to start small savings accounts with some of the kids who talked about wanting to visit their homes but didn't want to go empty-handed. It is important for some kids that it appear to their families that they've been doing something on the streets, earning some money for the household, even if that was not the primary objective for being away from home.[5] It lessens the sting of coming home, a gift that might mitigate a beating for having left. It also maintains the expectation that when things are tough, the child will go in search of money for the family.

I offered my right closed fist, which he tapped with his own, "We'll start making plans to visit your home. Where are you going to go, your mom's or your dad's?"

"My mom's." No hesitation. Then, almost like a non sequitur, he looked beyond my face and offered, "My dad's in the military. He's a musician in the regiment's band."

I understood the difficulty; it was almost as bad as being a policeman's son. I knew he wanted to talk about this but he'd clam up if I asked directly. I motioned to the juice seller on the corner, the blue metal bike with the green tinted oranges in the front metal cage. "You thirsty?"

He nodded. We walked over to the shade on the east side of the building to drink our juice. We both stared intently on the sun's brilliant patterning on the opposite side of the street. It would be more difficult if we were to look at each other.

"So you play an instrument, too?"

"Naw. Just a little guitar. My dad taught me some."

"What do you know how to play?"

"Bachata, of course."

"Bachata? That's great. What's your favorite song to play?"

"La Reina." He took a long sip from his juice.

"La Reina? The Frank Reyes song?"

"Yeah. You know that one?" How could I not? It was severely overplayed in every bar, colmado, and disco.

"Sing me the chorus. I love that song but I don't sing. How does it go?"

He sang softly, but audible, into his Styrofoam cup.

"That's pretty good. Your dad teach you to sing, too?"

"Yeah. He plays sometimes with a bachata group in San Cristóbal."

"Where's he stationed?"

"I don't know," José Alberto spat out automatically, then paused, reconsidering. "Here in the capital. At the barracks down by the government buildings."

"You think he's still stationed there?"

"I don't know. I ran into one of the men in his regiment a couple of months ago. He wanted to take me to my dad but I told him no. I used to pass by the building, standing on the opposite corner by the hotel there, to see if I'd see him go in or come out. I never saw him. I don't know if he's still there. I stopped going after that guy saw me."

"How long since you been home?"

His straw made that empty sucking sound when there is no more liquid. "Over a year." He threw the foam cup in the box by the juice man. "I gotta get going. I'll see you later." He pushed off from the wall, "I gotta go look for bottles."

"All right. I'll let you know about the shoes."

The outreach team sat around the long white table in the office for our weekly Monday morning meeting to plan out the activities for the week. These meetings gave us an opportunity to discuss individual case histories. "I think José Alberto is pretty serious," Núria commented as she leaned forward, arms placed flat in front of her on the table's surface, "He has 300 pesos saved up. He has it in his head that he needs 400 pesos to take to his mother. He'll have it this week, for sure."

"We'd better plan to go this week," replied Ana, "Maybe Thursday."

"Héctor, we've got shoes in the closet at the drop-in center, right?" Héctor nodded in agreement. "Could you remember to find him a pair tomorrow?"

It seemed as if we were ready to move on to the next case when Eli's face took on a quizzical look and asked, "So, his parents don't live together but near each other?"

"That's what he says. They both live in San Cristóbal, maybe in the same barrio? The mother has a new man and his father is also with a different woman. There are younger kids from this other marriage, too, but José Alberto is the only one on the streets." Ana spoke rapidly, so quickly I was amazed the words could shoot out of her mouth fully formed. She picked up speed the more excited or upset she became.

"I'd like to accompany you, Ana," Núria volunteered.

"Me, too." I wanted to see how this developed.

In the end, it was agreed that we would go on Thursday afternoon, assuming José Alberto didn't back out due to cold feet or because he didn't feel he had the money to go. Our accompaniment was to reassure him that we would help smooth things over with his parents. It's a fine line because we couldn't guarantee anything. Our very presence could even be false hope, a buoy that disappeared when we did.

Thursday came, and the excitement was infectious. We were on the phone communicating between the office and the drop-in center all morning long, trying to coordinate the trip. Eli called first to let us know José Alberto was with them that day and motivated to go. It was a good sign; he was keeping his convictions.

Later in the morning I called to remind Héctor of the shoes, one of the week's details that got lost among the daily course of things. Núria called around eleven, wanting to know if we couldn't give José Alberto a hair cut before we left. By mid-morning it looked like the pick-up truck would be in use in the afternoon for a different activity. It was either go in public transportation or cancel the trip.

José Alberto arrived at the office with the work crew from the drop-in center that afternoon. You could tell by his face, the constant grin, that he was motivated and ready. There was a subdued nervousness to him. As he sat in the reception area on the hard plastic chair, he shifted his position every three seconds. He excitedly talked of his younger siblings, his friends at the basketball court, how long it had been since he had seen his mother.

"She's going to be very happy to see you," Wanda, the secretary told him. "She must be upset. She'll probably cry, but it is a relief that you'll be home now. Don't you think your mother worries about where you are?"

He didn't answer, just shifted back in the chair and continued talking about playing basketball with his friends.

"I've never seen him talk so much," I commented to Núria as we passed each other in the narrow hallway that led to the back rooms.

"He's been that way all morning long. During his literacy lesson we spent the entire time talking about his siblings. He's ready. I just hope it is a good reception."

José Alberto made it clear in the morning to Eli and Núria that he couldn't go home with the curly mess of hair he had. It looked too wild, he thought. The afro, even packed down on his head, was still an inch high. It looked like he hadn't had a hair cut in over six months. When I tried to run a comb through his hair the teeth snagged on the snarls of curl. I extended a small clump out from the scalp and it reached almost four inches.

Héctor, educator-turned-barber, razzed José Alberto, who sat shirtless on the chair out in the back courtyard, ready for his trim. "Never thought of combing your hair out, huh? You're gonna have to settle for a buzz cut, buddy, 'cause there is no way the razor is gonna be able to do anything else. You're gonna clog that thing up."

Héctor gently tapped José Alberto's head forward and took the machine to the nape of the neck, working forward. A clean swathe through the dark hair, the path shone. It was like shedding skin, a molting of the last remnants of street life. The new shoes, the jeans, and the shaved head had removed the visible traces of his former self. If only it was that easy, if the transformation could be that complete and rapid.

"This is going to take forever to get there," José Alberto said as we climbed on to the bus. "We should take the express. With the express we'd get there in a flash."

"I'm not sure the express passes by here. Don't worry, we'll get there all the same." I should have listened to him. A trip that normally is less than thirty-five minutes in a private car took us over an hour in the stop-and-go *caliente* bus.

I would like to think that each of the three of us accompanying José Alberto to his home played a necessary role. Ana, of course, as the sole Dominican in our party, would take the lead. I often thought, while making visits to kids' homes, what place did I have from which to speak? I am neither Dominican nor a parent; I discovered often enough that there were intricacies within the maze of Dominican family dynamics that were never apparent to me in the moment of meeting and talking to parents or grandparents. Things such as intergenerational conflict and household economics revealed their idiosyncratic patterns slowly. Ana understood the coded messages of mothers who could not express their household problems directly. Much of what was said was innuendo, dots that needed connecting to expose a fuller picture.

Núria brought to any interaction a considerable amount of experience from working with at-risk kids and youth in Barcelona. She had recently graduated from university as a social educator, a position in Spain that is akin to social worker, only with more direct contact and intervention with the target population. Social workers manage cases; social educators manage people on a daily basis. She had tools—simple, practical steps to help mediate conflict causing sore spots between parents and children that, when added together over time, would change the face of family dynamics. Whereas Ana's knowledge came from the years of doing the work and from a personal understanding of Dominican families, Núria could translate many of the suggestions and crucial points made by Ana or myself into tangible tasks.

When I had started doing house visits alone with Ana in my first year, it was mostly to families with children who were relatively established in the home—some having been back with their families for years. I felt I had nothing to give beyond being a kind of organizing force for Ana—her personal assistant, if you will, helping her plan visits, writing notes, remembering promises we had made. But the more time I spent working on the streets, the greater rapport I developed with the kids. More and more of the families that I visited with Ana were kids I had first met on the streets, some of whom I had worked with for many months prior to making contact with their families. I found I understood the individual kids fairly well. I knew how they lived on the streets, I knew what their primary street relations were; I could piece together a child's drug consumption pattern. All proved crucial in understanding how easily a kid would become frustrated or intolerant when things became rocky. I cast myself as moral support for the kid. I would leave Ana to talk to the parent or other family member and go for a walk or sit on the neighbor's stoop with the child. I was there for them in a way Ana could not be: she was the mediator between the family and child, seeking a middle ground for both. I became the listener, to learn how things were from the child's perspective, things they would never say in front of their parents. I would pass this on to Ana, who would filter it back to the parent in such a way that it would seem as if Ana was clairvoyant, reading what went on in the household when we weren't there. If it sounds like a slow and frustrating process, it's because it was. People have a reason for telling you the things they do; they don't reveal their secrets all in one day. Sometimes you have to shine the beam directly on what they most want to keep hidden.

It would have been much easier if we had been able to go in the pick-up truck. Instead, we arrived by slow bus to San Cristóbal. We disembarked at an anonymous street corner and wove our way through the city center, José Alberto leading us. San Cristóbal's only real claim to fame—or infamy— is that it was the hometown of Trujillo. He had lavished economic growth and gifts of housing and public works on his natal city and in honor of his mother while he was dictator, but after the assassination, from the early 1960s on, San Cristóbal crumbled.

The streets were narrow with small threads of broken concrete for sidewalks. José Alberto confidently walked us along for a couple of blocks and then stopped, hesitating. I could tell by the way his brow knitted that he was having misgivings. He stopped us on a shadeless corner by the remains of an abandoned building. The sun was in its full afternoon force. Ana carried her bright purple umbrella high to block out the rays, but I was feeling sticky and sweaty. Núria, too, looked a bit wilted.

"You forget where you lived?" I joked, hoping Pepe would lighten up a bit.

"Maybe I should go to my dad's, instead, while you all are with me."

"Do they live near each other?" Núria wondered.

"Pretty close. I would live between the houses."

Ana pulled José Alberto aside. As Núria and I crossed the street to stand in the shade, she huddled under her umbrella with Pepe, talking quietly.

"The kid's scared," I commented to Núria in our position against the wall.

"Yeah, any wonder? I'd be scared and reluctant too, if I were him. Imagine all the stuff going through him after not having been home for a year."

Ana signaled with a wave that we should cross back over. I hoped she had salvaged the situation, because I couldn't help seeing José Alberto looking a bit like a cornered rabbit now that we were this close to arriving at his family.

"José Alberto is concerned about his father's reaction if he were to show up alone to his house. He doesn't know how his dad might receive him coming home. I told him not to worry, that I would go first to talk to his father," Ana announced.

Núria placed her arms around José Alberto's shoulders and walked ahead of us. I whispered to Ana, leaning under her umbrella, "He's afraid of rejection?"

"Yes, but he's afraid his dad will beat him for having gone away."

We walked about fifteen minutes more when José Alberto stopped again. "My dad lives around the corner, Ana, in the green house. The second door. It's right there on the corner, in front of the mechanic."

"Come on Jon," Ana called the shots. I was going with her. "What's your dad's name, Pepe?"

"José. Don José. I'm named after him."

What José Alberto didn't tell us was that the green house on the corner was actually three separate apartments. Ana and I stood across the street in front of the mechanic's shop—little more than grease puddles and strewn car parts—contemplating the house before us. One of the three wooden doors was open and periodically two small children, naked and barefoot, would run out onto the cement slab that acted as the common patio and then would run back indoors. Ana lowered the umbrella and led the way across the street.

First contact with a family is never easy. Ana would tell stories of having some kids be accepted with open arms, others being indifferently allowed to stay, and still others whose presence was rejected altogether. And after initial contact things become even trickier, as the social worker takes on the role of arbiter and negotiator, not just between child and parent but for whatever family problem might exist. Families are relieved to have someone with whom to share the burden of their lives. I have seen Ana play parenting coach, marriage counselor, economic advisor, and neighborhood liaison all in the same visit.

One of the naked boys ran into the house as we stepped onto the patio. "Can I help you?" came a voice from the door. A large, pregnant woman with a dish rag slung over her shoulder stood in the frame. The two young boys crowded around her, peeking between her swollen legs.

"Is this the house of Don José?" Ana asked.

"Yes," she replied suspiciously.

"The Don José who has a son, José Alberto?"

The pregnant woman's eyes changed at the mention of José Alberto's name. Not surprise, not alarm, but a certain impassive curiosity. "Yes," was all she replied.

"We would like to talk to him, if possible. We have news about his son."

As if on cue, a short man with three day's growth on his face and a beer belly rivaling the pregnant belly of his wife stepped behind the woman. "I'm José. What do you mean you have news about my son?" His faced pulled anxiously at the question.

Ana asked Don José to sit down and when he brought out four broken and beaten plastic chairs to the patio, Ana began with the much needed preface, "Pepe is well. Do you know where he has been?"

It is a tough question to ask a parent. Some were slow to admit they had no knowledge or control over their child. Others were surprisingly blunt about the whole affair, showing little concern and cursing their ill-behaved child. Others made up stories: He's at his grandmother's, cousin's, neighbor's, father's—someplace else, where the parent is not responsible.

But Don José didn't do any of the usual excuse making. He looked at his pregnant wife sitting precariously in a three-legged plastic chair across from him and then dropped his head in his hands. "I don't know. I don't know where Pepe is. He's been missing for over seven months. Please tell me you know where he is."

"We work for an organization called Niños del Camino," Ana continued, "We work with kids who live outside the home."

"Like in a center?" Don José's wife asked.

"Sometimes," I replied, "But we ourselves have no center or sleeping facility. We work with kids directly on the street."

"We do educational activities, accompany them when there is a medical problem, and help motivate them to come back home," Ana finished our collective spiel.

It didn't seem to have sunk in, no recognition between what we do and where we found and met José Alberto. "We met Pepe a couple of months ago." I had to spell it out so that they understood. "On the streets where he says he has been living, in the capital, for about a year." That seemed to do it, as with the weight of the phrase, Don José's head shook heavily, bowed even farther.

"Every day since Pepe left, I would go to work early. I worked at the barracks on Independencia in the capital. I'm military. Every morning I would go in early on my motorbike and drive around looking for him. I would go all along the Malecón, up to the new market and back down or sometimes I would go up and around the length of all the major streets. But I never saw him. I must have spent well over 10,000 pesos in gas looking for him. Just ask my wife. Isn't that right, Segunda?" He turned to seek confirmation from her, sitting in the door's frame. She returned his inquiry with a placid look. "For almost two months now I've been unable to work. I've done the paperwork for disability from the military. But I still would go looking for Pepe every chance I had, every time I had money for the gas. Oh God, where is he?"

The man was on the verge of tears. His unshaven face turned blotchy and puffy. His tiny mouth quivered, like he wanted to say more but couldn't get the sound out.

"We have José Alberto with us," Ana told them, "He's up the street with another educator, waiting. He asked to come back, wanted us to come with him. He would like to come back to live here."

"Jesus Christ! Yes! Please! Where is he?"

Ana gave me a slight nod. I made to go get Pepe. Don José sat with his forehead down, examining the patio floor while Ana continued to talk. I had seen that pose before. It was what José Alberto did when he was ashamed of something he had done.

I could tell they were anxious because the minute I came into view both Núria and José Alberto came running down the street to meet me.

"So?" José Alberto asked. From behind him, Núria's eyes echoed his question.

"Your father really wants to see you," I told them, "He's very emotional and has missed you very much. He has been very worried about you."

"Pepe!" a small voice called out behind me. I turned to look at the older of the two naked boys who had been at the house. I hadn't noticed I was followed. "Pepe!"

"What are you doing out of the house without shoes on, Josué?" José Alberto asked as his stepbrother threw his tiny arms around the legs of his missing sibling.

"Where have you been, Pepe?"

José Alberto scooped Josué up. The kid buried his face in his brother's shirt. It was all the encouragement he needed.

"Come on," Núria said, "Let's go meet your family."

As he rounded the corner, naked sibling in hand, José Alberto slowed down. Don José didn't see him at first. My hand rested on Pepe's shoulder, as if to give him stability, to prevent him from falling over. There was this pause, a few seconds, really, in which time it took for full recognition to set in. Segunda stopped mid-stroke in brushing her daughter's hair. Don José, red-eyed, wore a look of expectation as he would his best button-down shirt. Even Pepe's two young stepbrothers were still, Josué looking into his father's eyes and the younger, snot-nosed kid staring unbelieving at José Alberto. Only Ana seemed to be the capable of moving, reaching her left arm around the chair, motioning for Pepe to come forward to greet his father for the first time in many months.

That broke the spell. Pepe released his brother to the ground, coming to stand beside the safety and comfort of Ana.

"Pepe! Pepe!" Don José repeated, eyes pooling and then releasing tears in a steady cataract. "Where have you been? Thank God you are ok, unharmed!"

José Alberto was still unsure of what to do. He stood by Ana's chair, watching his father cry. Even when his father had opened his arms to receive him, Pepe stood back momentarily. It was a minute hesitation. He went to his father, letting himself be taken in by his father's display of emotion. He started to cry in wordless sobs.

"Pepe, I would go look for you every day, Pepe. I drove all around the capital thinking, if I could just see you, tell you how much I love you, and how much we miss you. Every day your siblings would ask, 'Daddy, where's Pepe? When's Pepe coming home?' I never knew what to tell them. It has weighed so much on me these past months, not knowing where you were, if you were safe. Oh God, Pepe!" Don José held Pepe near his lap, Pepe half standing, half leaning on his father's thighs as if Don José was afraid to let him leave the sanctity of his arms.

"I'm very happy to see this, this kind of reception of Pepe. It proves to me that there is space where we can work," Ana daubed her eyes with a worn Kleenex. "But we also know José Alberto didn't leave home for nothing. We need to work that part together. Pepe kept his agreement with us—despite how hard it was to come back, he told us he was ready and followed through. We, too, kept our agreement and brought him here with us. Your willingness to take him in shows your willingness to work. We work fifty-fifty. As long as you and your family do your part, we will do ours. Our agreement is to visit once a week for the next month, to follow through.

"What do you think you can do, José Alberto? What do you think was a reason your father would get upset with you?"

"Oh, Papa," he answered after a drawn-out silence in which you could tell he was thinking through what the consequence of his answer would be. It is never easy to admit one's own faults, and to have José Alberto recognize his own behavior as causing some of the stress in the household was key. "I know I would stay out late and you would wonder where I was. I would work late and sometimes not come home."

"Pepe, I don't want you to work. I provide what I can but I am not one of those parents who send their children out to work while they get fat on their child's labor." Pepe's face fell visibly at this but he made no move to counter or argue with his father.

"You know," I interjected, "even though you do not need the income provided by José Alberto, working is something he enjoys doing. He likes to have a few pesos of his own." I searched Don José's eyes for his reaction. You can't rescind all the freedom a kid had on the streets and expect him to conform and enjoy it. I was acutely aware of the irony. Here we were, an organization founded on protecting child rights and we were advocating child labor, encouraging a kid to go out and work. But the truth was, work brought worth and dignity and extra income. It depended on the type of job.

"Your son is a very hard worker. I know a lot of kids who are in similar conditions as Pepe was and none of them work like Pepe—your son strove very hard. He didn't want to return home without some money. He worked and saved so that he could buy shoes and a pair of jeans. I think we should think about what kind of work he could do and maybe reasonable hours, eh?" I lied. I didn't want Don José to know how much his son had saved because that money was for his mother, not his father's household.

José Alberto didn't look at his father while I spoke. His chin down, he searched the floor for comfort or answers. "Dad, I want to work some."

"Well then, you can work with Segunda's brother selling bread."

Ana broke in, "Maybe we should ask Pepe what kind of work he wants to do? Pepe, your father has offered you to work with your uncle. You talked to us about shining shoes on the bus over here. Which would you prefer?"

He remained silent, unwilling to contradict his father to his face. Don José, taking the silence as hesitation and reconsideration, said, "I know what you want. You want a bike. I'll buy you a bike and you can ride around all day. You don't need to work because I am the man of the house, I provide for my family."

This man was not listening. I turned my head to exchange glances with Núria, whose face was bunched in frustration. "I don't think anyone here thinks that José Alberto needs to work for economic reasons," Núria couldn't keep quiet. "It has more to do with filling time and allowing Pepe to do something he enjoys. Plus, working, Pepe can continue to show responsibility like he did in saving money to come here. I strongly urge that you reconsider and allow Pepe to shine shoes."

"That's just it. He would leave in the morning with his shoeshine box and not come home until ten or eleven o'clock at night."

"That's why we need to talk about some rules," Ana motioned at José Alberto with the palm of her right hand, "Why do you think your father said that?"

"Because I would not come back all day long. He didn't know where I was."

"So, I'm hearing two things," I smiled as reassuringly as possible to José Alberto, "One, that maybe we should set a work schedule and a curfew for you this week and see how it goes. And two, think about where you can go to shine shoes, what area you should stay within." As the words came out, I realized I discarded completely the idea of working with his step-uncle. His father seemed to want to exert immediate control over everything. That wasn't going to work. It would push José Alberto away again.

It was much later than we expected by the time we had ironed out as much as possible between José Alberto and his father. The sun was starting to sink over the houses and the orange glow of dusk settled like a mantle in the sky. We had been there for over three hours and had spent nearly four and a half with Pepe. We weren't ready to leave, either, for there still seemed to be a lot of unresolved issues hanging in the air. What was decided was that Pepe would shine shoes in the morning until one in the afternoon, when he would come home for lunch. He could only shine shoes around the central park area, the nearby post office, and the local government buildings—all in central San Cristóbal. At night, he had to be home by nine. He could spend the afternoon playing, visiting his mother, and doing chores around the house until school started in a couple of weeks. Núria drew up a simple graphic of faces in columns, separated out in days of the week. Don José and Pepe were to fill out the schedule together, circling a smiley face if Pepe made it in before the nine o'clock curfew or a frown if he did not. A month of mostly happy faces and he would earn the opportunity to go on a field trip with us. All this was, of course, the ideal. We knew that Pepe, gone in the morning to work, would probably go where he pleased and work as little or as much as he would want to work. But, it gave the illusion of a schedule, which was a start.

We agreed to come back in a week and continue with weekly visits for at least a month. That first thirty days is always crucial because any little annoyance can set a kid packing. Knowing that we would come every Tuesday would give them something to hold on to, to say, "Ok, I can wait till Ana gets here to talk to her." It also gave us the ability to get to know the parents.

With Don José, we asked that he start the process of enrolling Pepe in classes at the local elementary school. The new school year would begin in less than a month. Although Dominican education is compulsory, if a school says it is filled up, it can turn away students. It may have already been too late for day classes. At the very least, Pepe could go to night school— not ideal, but better than nothing.

"Don't worry," Don José assured us, "I will go tomorrow and get him enrolled. I'll buy his uniform next week and he'll be ready to go." In all, we felt we were leaving with a solid base from which to start work with Pepe and his family.

We walked with José Alberto back toward the bus stop. Ana had her arm around his shoulder the entire walk, whispering encouragement.

"My dad's a big talker," Pepe told us as the bus arrived to take us back to the capital. "He makes a lot of promises, says a lot of nice things but doesn't do much more than that. You'll see."

"You gotta give him the benefit of the doubt. He received you well and was very relieved to have you home. Not every kid gets that kind of reception."

"Yeah, I know. You're right. I'm glad to be home."

## THE FIRST HURDLE

The following Tuesday came and it was uncertain whether we were going to be able to make the time to visit José Alberto. The day-to-day activities would pile up and we would often find ourselves without enough time and resources in the day to get everything done we intended to. In many ways, the organization was spread too thin, between the drop-in center's morning activities and the afternoon outreach activities that also included home visits like those with the family of José Alberto. Núria and I knew we couldn't skip the visit, even if it meant a longer day. The light was fading by the time we arrived, the concrete houses of San Cristóbal bathed in a purple twilight. Núria and I stood on the corner where the bus dropped us off, trying to get our bearings. As night came upon us, everything about the unfamiliar city looked more hostile and alien. It was one thing to be in part of a city that we knew well, even if there was no electricity, but here, we were at a loss, minimally guided by the occasional streetlamp. I was having second thoughts, but we were already there; we might as well go through with it.

We arrived at Don José's house. The electricity in this part of the city was out. The pinprick lights of candle flames were the only welcoming presence. On the patio two small figures crawled about the cement, playing.

"Josué," I called, hoping it was really him and not some other little kid.

The silhouette looked up at the calling of his name.

"We're the ones who came last week with Pepe. Is your mom or dad around?"

Josué scrambled from the floor, disappearing into the gaping cavern of the door. Segunda's pregnant profile soon came out, holding a small candlestick to the darkness.

The flame of the candle flickered, the light licking at Segunda's face. Her features were half-lit, half in darkness so that her lips emerged from the blanket blackness around her, her cheekbones sloping off into nothingness. "Pepe's not here."

In that instant, my heart fell heavy like lead shot in the ocean as I leapt to the inevitable ending: José Alberto had left home again, was back on the streets. The pause was minuscule, not even long enough for a breath.

"He is with his father tonight. Don José is playing at a birthday party."

The tightness released itself, the heaviness dissipated. I could feel Núria, too, ease up, the proverbial collective sigh shared between us.

"How did José Alberto do this week? How was it having him home?"

"Fine. He came home on time every day this week and helped me out around the house some, ran errands. So far so good, but that will wear off. It's just because it is still new and he doesn't want to upset anything."

"You're right, it takes time to change behavior, but that's why we are building up from a good foundation like this positive week, no?" He was not her son. She had no obligation toward him, but it would only harm the process if she were not supportive.

"Men don't change," she said firmly, almost spitting out her truism, "they only hide what they do. I am not so naïve to think it otherwise." She must have seen Núria's face and my own visage, the way her pessimism was a brutal blow, because she added quickly, "We are glad Pepe is back home. Having him home makes some things easier. But there will come a time when it all returns to how it was before, and then what?"

"That's why we are here," Núria stepped in, trying to save the situation. "We offer you and your family tools to work out the situations that gave you trouble before. If a person has the will and desire to change, they can. We believe in José Alberto and in you and Don José too. Otherwise we wouldn't be here."

She didn't look convinced, only bobbed her head in a slow, weary nod. Ignoring Núria's response, she called out to Josué who emerged from just inside the door.

"Get sandals on and lead these two to Magda's house," she eyed us, raising her gaze from her son who ran back in the house looking for something to put on his feet. "Josué will take you to where José and Pepe are. Pepe has been waiting all day for you."

Núria took a hand offered by Josué who, even for being five years old had the uncanny ability to lead us through the streets of his neighborhood at night, in the dark. The party was not close by. We kept winding down street after street, turns revealing narrower avenues until they shrank to footpaths as we headed toward the river. It occurred to me the absurdity of being led by a five-year-old in a neighborhood I knew nothing about but could guess wasn't the best. Poor didn't always mean unsafe, but poor, at night, during a blackout, and near the river was not the gold standard of safety.

I didn't want to be the Doubting Thomas of Josué's abilities, but after fifteen minutes of following, I was getting worried. "Hey little guy, are we getting close?"

Josué stopped and looked up at me with impatience. Even in the dark I could see his features set in a defiant jaw clench. "Yes, it's just over there." He pointed to another street of wooden boxes that looked the same as the ones we had passed. His voice was so sure, even evidenced of slight exasperation at having to have been asked, that I relented.

Further down, the houses became punctuated by milling groups of people, standing around in anticipation of some event. A larger concentration sat on their plastic chairs in front of the house second from the far corner. "This must be it," I said to Núria.

"Josué, find Pepe, ok?" He pushed through the legs of the crowd, unnoticed.

Toward the back of the house arose the tinny sounds of an electric guitar being played acoustically. The plucking of a melody, tentative in its keeping of time, was vaguely familiar. I pointed in the direction of the melody. "What's that song?"

Núria cocked her head, trying to make out the music above the murmurs of the crowd. "I think it's Frank Reyes. I think it's 'La Reina,' but played a little slow."

"'La Reina'?" I smiled. I knew who was playing. "Come on!" I took Núria by the arm and we wove our way unannounced and uninvited into the backyard.

Wooden planks that may have been pallets at one time and an awning made from a plastic tarp made a small stage. Still no lights, but a field of candles burned along the edges of the makeshift stage. Through the heads of the crowd I could see it was José Alberto playing the guitar. He sat on a stool, head down, concentrating attentively at the movement of his fingers along the frets. Josué stood by his side, unwilling to disturb his older brother, waiting for him to finish before telling him we were there.

I nudged Núria, "Does that guitarist look familiar?"

"I didn't know he could play!"

"His dad taught him. Look how intent he is."

We pushed further, coming to the edge of the stage. Núria placed a hand on Josué's shoulder. He started at the touch and was about to speak, but Núria bent her head down, index finger to her lips. We were going to wait for Pepe to finish, too.

"Bravo! Bravo!" Núria and I called out when Pepe had stopped playing. We clapped wildly, over-enthusiastically, as you do at times to encourage kids.

Pepe looked up from the guitar strings, surprised to see us standing before him. A sheepish grin waltzed across his face. A bit embarrassed, he averted his gaze from ours. It was unclear if it was being caught playing the guitar or our improvised fan club act that made him so shy. He slipped off the stool and set the guitar in the open case behind him, careful to shut the case and set it by the amplifier.

"I was just fooling around. My dad and his bachata group are supposed to play, but the electricity hasn't come on yet," he paused, torn between expressing his doubts and his obvious joy that we arrived. "I didn't think you were coming. I was waiting all day. I thought you had forgotten."

Núria put her arms around Pepe's shoulders and explained why we were so late. "But we kept our promise, even if we arrived a bit later than usual."

"Besides," I interjected, "we'd have missed seeing you play if we'd come earlier."

"I have all smiley faces!" José Alberto obviously had this on his mind as well, "I arrived home on time every day last week if I wasn't out with my dad."

We offered more praise. Reinforcement was what he needed at this phase, while he was still eager to please. "We'll make you another calendar for this week, all right?" Núria explained, letting Pepe know there was an upcoming fieldtrip at the end of the month and he'd get to go if he kept up his curfew.

I made my way to the edge of the stage and sat down on the low platform, motioning for Núria and Pepe to follow. Pepe sat between Núria and me. Josué had disappeared into the crowd, tired of waiting for us.

"How'd the rest of the week go, José Alberto, besides the curfew?"

And here he became tight-lipped, responding with a simple, "fine," as if all that happens in a week can be summed up in a mono-syllabic and flat tone.

I looked at Núria, "That 'fine' doesn't sound all that convincing."

"I think you are right. I wonder if it is fine, things were great or fine, things went all right, or fine, it has been a tough adjustment."

José Alberto looked down, "It was just fine . . . I don't know. They treat me well and it is good to be home, but different. I wanted to buy a bike with the pesos I brought with me and my dad said no, that he would buy me one. He hasn't done it yet."

"Ah. . . . See, Núria, that 'fine' had a deeper meaning than we were going to know," I nudged José Alberto in the ribs with my elbow, to show it was in fun. "If you want we can talk to your dad about the bike."

"The thing is, I believed him, you know? So I gave my mom most of the money I saved and now I don't have enough to buy a bike. And I can't work because my shoeshine box needs to be stocked."

"You did something noble by helping your mom out. Did she need the money?" Núria asked.

Pepe shook his head yes. "She's not working right now and she needed to buy school uniforms for my younger brothers. She was really grateful."

"Did it feel good to give her the money?"

He paused, as if trying to excavate the feeling from deep within, conflicted between his own personal desires and his family's need. "Yeah, I suppose. But what do I do about a bike? I know my dad. I shouldn't have believed he would buy me one."

"Well, how much did you have left of the money you saved?"

"A hundred pesos."

"Can you fix up your shoeshine box with a hundred pesos?"

"Probably."

"Well then," I said, clapping my hands together once, "You saved up all that money before. You can do it again by shining shoes. You'll get your bike in no time."

"And," Núria added, "It'll feel good because you earned it yourself. We can even set up another savings account for you if you want."

"I suppose you are right. I could even save more and buy a better bike."

"That's the spirit! It's good you help your mom."

"Yeah. She's got this boyfriend, but he doesn't work much either and he's not responsible for my little brothers. They aren't his."

"Come on," I urged, "It's late and Núria and I should be getting back to the capital. Where's your dad? We should see him before we go."

"Next week," Núria reminded us, "Ana will come and we will meet your mother, ok? We just don't have time today."

Pepe seemed relieved we weren't going to his mom's place. "My dad's over there," he pointed to a group of seated men with the dark silhouettes of beer bottles guarding their feet.

"Why don't you tell him we're here and would like to talk to him, ok?"

Don José was drunk. Not slur-your-speech-have-trouble-keeping-balance drunk, but well on his way to that state of inebriation. Even in the dim light I could see the unfocused eyes and ruddy skin. He greeted Núria and me profusely.

"Oh! My son's gringo friends! You made it. You know Pepe has been waiting and waiting all day long. He kept saying, 'They'll come. They'll come.' And here you are, in time for a party."

Pepe looked embarrassed, his face imploring us to leave as his father talked.

"We had some difficulties that prevented us from arriving earlier," I said. Don José wasn't going to assimilate details. "Listen, Don José, it is late and we didn't mean to come in the middle of a party. We just wanted to make sure you knew we had stopped by and talked with your son. Ana will be here next week, at a more decent hour."

"What? You can't leave yet. Stay for the party. As soon as the lights come back, we're going to start playing."

"José Alberto said he made his curfew every day this past week," Núria brought us back to the task at hand. "We want to do that same sheet for this coming week."

"Oh yes! That's my boy. He came home on time every day. Not a single problem. He helped Segunda out around the house, too. Surprised me, you know? I didn't know he could be such a good kid."

That stung. I put a protective hand on Pepe's shoulder and firmly replied, "That's because your son is a good kid."

Telling parents that they needed to be supportive of their children, that they needed to offer positive reinforcement, was one of my least favorite roles to play. More often than not I would tell parents that their own children were worthy, that they were intelligent, hard-working, kind, capable human beings. It was not that they did not see this themselves—I refused to believe that they were blind to their children's own qualities—but they would not express it, did not know how to put it into words. And if they finally did, it came out like a backhanded compliment. I could see that Don José was no different. He did not see his son for who he was. I felt my ire rise at his insensitivity to his son's needs and abilities. I think he, too, sensed that he and I had entered into a new antagonism over his son. I hadn't meant it to be that way, but I had lost respect for the man before me.

It was Núria who diffused the situation. She eyed me with a gaze that told me to back down and said, "Don José, we will also want to talk to you about Pepe's school enrollment next week. I know you understand how important it is that he keep studying."

"Oh yes, of course. I didn't get to go this past week but no need to worry. I will go and talk to the principal myself this week. I'll get that uniform, too, for Pepe and he'll be ready for school."

"Good, because we don't want inscriptions to fill up and he be left out of school next year. I know you understand how important this is."

"Oh yes, yes. Leave it to me. I take care of my children. I see to it they get what they need. Like this bike. Pepe was going to buy a bike and I told him 'No, don't go spending your money on a bike. I'll go and buy you a bike,' I said. I said, 'I'll buy you the bike you want. That's what fathers do.' And this week I'll go buy my son a bike."

At the mention of the bike, José Alberto squirmed uneasily. It was time for us to go before Don José deflated more than he already had in the eyes of his son. It was not our desire to unearth the inadequacies of his father. "Don José, we really should be on our way. Please, enjoy your party and we will see you next week." I was back to my cordial self. The anger I had felt melted away to pity. Don José was trying the only way he knew how to show his son he loved him. I would vacillate between these two emotions—anger and pity—for the rest of the time I knew Don José.

"Pepe," Don José commanded, "Take these two to the bus stop, ok? And then come on back. I have a feeling we'll be playing soon."

We wove through the purple blackness of the unlit streets back to the central park. Pepe walked between Núria and me. All the excitement and enthusiasm of seeing us, of the party, of playing the guitar, had seeped out of Pepe. He kicked invisible rocks every so often, scuffing along. We arrived at the buses. As we prepared to board, José Alberto spoke for the first time since we left the party and his father. "He's not going to buy it, you know. He talks big but he won't do it."

"Now, José Alberto," Núria began, "If he doesn't buy the bike we already said how easy it will be for you to buy one for yourself."

"Not just the bike. He won't buy the uniform either. Nor will he go to the school. He just talks big, puts on a show for you all but then forgets when no one is around."

I crouched down on my heels, having to look up into Pepe's eyes from below. I wanted to look up at him, to see into his eyes. "Sometimes parents have the best of intentions, Pepe. They want to do the best for their kids, but they don't know how. All we can do is give them the opportunity to do what they can. Give your father another week to see if he comes through. If he does, great. If not, it doesn't mean he loves you any less. It means he really wants to do the best for you but doesn't know how."

"Sure. I know. I'll wait and see. But I'm just telling you now it won't happen."

"Is that going to change what you do?" Núria asked.

"What do you mean?"

"Well, you've made certain promises to us and we've made certain promises to you. Will that change?"

"No, of course not."

"Good," I interjected, "Because regardless of whatever your father does, we continue to work with you, Pepe. Remember our deal—fifty-fifty, right?"

"Right."

"All right, you'd better get going. Maybe the lights will come back on and you'll be singing tonight." I stood up and ruffled his bald head. Núria gave him a big hug and we boarded the bus.

## TELLING THE TRUTH

Epifanio pulled the truck into the side streets, twisting through the paved maze to Don José's street. He pulled up on the opposite side of the street, seeking the shade of a tall, broad avocado tree. On the front porch sat a large black rubber tub, circular and glistening wet in the sun. Pepe's two younger brothers splashed about, slapping the water in wide arcs and wetting the cement floor of the patio. Before we could get out of the truck they had bolted out of the bath, shoeless and naked. They ran toward us excitedly. I could hear them yelling in their approach, wanting to know if we had any cookies to give. The asphalt should have been scalding hot, but they showed no pain on their calloused feet. Epi rolled down the driver's side window in their approach.

"You got any of those cookies? Any of those crème-filled chocolate cookies?" Josué asked us without offering even a greeting.

"What do we look like, the cookie salesmen? No greeting, not even a welcome, just wanting to know about cookies?"

Josué wasn't to be deterred. "Sorry. How are you? Do you have any cookies like last time?"

Epi reached out of the car and tweaked Josué's ear lightly, "Cookies, huh? Only cookies. There might be a cookie in it for you and your brother if you go tell Pepe that we are here to see him."

"Pepe's not here. He doesn't sleep here anymore. He's staying at his mother's."

"Is your dad around?"

"No, daddy's out at work. I can get my mom." Josué made to run after his mother, in hopes of earning the promised sweets.

"No, that's all right, Josué," I said, digging two packages of cookies from the plastic bag at my feet, "We'll find Pepe at his mom's. Make sure you tell your dad we stopped by." I passed the packages and watched their greedy eyes widen in anticipation. They snatched the plastic wrapped goodies from my hands and hurriedly ran back to the awaiting tub, as if they feared we might chase after them and take back the cookies.

Epi rolled the window back up. "That's great," Ana said with a sigh, "We made the trip out here for nothing. Something's going on. We're losing José Alberto."

Epi moved to pull the truck back out of the neighborhood. "Where are you going? Aren't we going to find José Alberto?" I asked. "I'm pretty sure I can get there, at least get to the street. Pepe showed Núria and me his mom's place during our last visit."

We made only three wrong turns, none of which were so off track that we were not able to find our way back. With persistence, I was able to find the colmado that stood directly in front of the alleyway that led into Pepe's mom's place. The colmado was recognizable by the eerie half-shark half-man hand-painted sign announcing the name proudly as *El Tiburón*, teeth on the shark portion of the figure protruding a solid white like a vampire's.

It was a narrow street, the last thin ribbon of concrete before the flow of footpaths and shacks that lead on to the river below. Epifanio pulled high up on the curb and still the truck blocked access for any vehicle that may have wanted to pass. As it was, we would not be able to turn the truck around. This was not a neighborhood designed for motor vehicles but, then again, the poor were not to have cars. The rich among them drove their motor-cycles with pride and bravado. Cars were the envious dreams of others.

We entered the alleyway. The contrast between the hot, open street, baking in the early afternoon sun, and the cool darkness of the alley was disorienting. It wasn't even quite an alley, more a spillway for water, still damp. Green and black mold splotched the cemented walkway, making for a slick run. Although the coolness of the shade felt reassuring, the closeness proved stifling and propelled pedestrians on.

Three hundred feet in from the main street, the alley broke open into a tiny mud courtyard with six or seven makeshift doorways. If they were ever shut, the inhabitants would barricade them with corrugated tin and scrap wood contraptions that were more booby-traps than conventional doors.

Old women sat in front of their homes in various stages of undress. The large, gray-haired matrons dressed only in their one good bra, barely able to contain the fullness of their sagging breasts. They brushed their own hair, scrubbed pots, gossiped, or readied their grandchildren for the afternoon school session. They made no effort to cover themselves at our appear-ance into their courtyard. We had intruded, had no way of knocking as we tramped into what was a semi-private extension of the cramped quarters where they slept. Most of home life was lived in the patio.

They gave us curious looks, but did not address us; as the unfamiliar we were the ones that needed to state our affairs. Ana and Epi showed no signs of discomfort, although I was uncomfortable. It would have been differ-ent had it just been a street and we found a door on which to knock. These old women and their enclave tucked off the street were another intimate domestic world altogether.

Ana greeted the old women respectfully and asked if the mother of José Alberto lived nearby. The women responded jovially enough, happy to steer us toward the right doorway at the far end of the circled houses. The dwelling was a mix of wood and tin from various sources—scraps brought together to form the frame. The floor was cement, however, and, looking into the open doorframe, I could see the small living area crammed with a dining room set in a deep lacquered ochre. It was the forlorn gem of the place, well-kept and cared for and definitely hard earned.

Ana called into the home from the courtyard, her voice strong and confident. Despite the door being open, there were few signs of movement or activity. The lights were off and there was no music or television sound. Ana called two more times. After the third time, there was some rustling from within the room we could not see from the entrance and a reply that the occupant was on his way.

José Alberto emerged from his house in surprised disarray, like he had just woken up. He wore the same pair of blue jeans we had bought him for his triumphal return home. He was shirtless, his long arms crossed against his bare chest. Sleep hung about him like a robe. "Ana!" he exclaimed, moving to greet her with a hug.

We sat around the table in the good chairs, which ended up not being in such good shape after all. The one I sat in was not as solid as it looked, creaking and wobbling as I shifted my weight. I figured we should start with the obvious question.

"So, how long have you been staying at your mom's?"

"A week now. After you and Núria came I started staying here. It's just easier. Living with my father makes me uncomfortable," José Alberto mumbled to the floor.

"Hey, Pepe," Epifanio got the young boy's attention, "We're up here, not down on the floor. You have no reason to be ashamed. You can talk to our faces."

The kid looked up and held Epi's gaze. "Things are just uncomfortable at my dad's. He has his new family and you know how it is, he says he will do something and then doesn't."

"So no school uniform?"

"No. My mom enrolled me in classes. They started this week. I go at night, but she can't buy me a uniform."

"Where is your mom, dear?" Ana asked.

"She'll be back. She went to find something for dinner." It was now nearing one in the afternoon and there was nothing cooking.

"Does your mom work?"

"No, not now. She did work in a factory but left that. Her boyfriend sells bread but he doesn't live here," which meant he wasn't responsible for the household but could still make certain demands. That was probably for the best because he would have less control over Pepe.

I reached into my pocket and pulled out twenty pesos. "Do you have any oil?"

"Yeah, there is some."

"Go run to the colmado and buy a couple plantains and some salami, all right? You'll need to eat something if you're going to study."

Pepe slipped the bill into his jeans pocket and ducked into the side bedroom, hidden by a sheet hanging in the doorway. When he emerged, he had put on a red t-shirt and a pair of flip flops. He smiled, eagerly telling us to wait, that he would be right back.

"His father seems to always have plenty of food. Obviously he doesn't support José Alberto's mother any," I said after Pepe had left.

"You can't expect him to, Jon," Epi corrected, "if she has a new man in her life."

"Yeah, well this new guy isn't supporting them either."

A shadow fell upon the doorway. "Can I help you?"

José Alberto's mother was a short, thin woman. There had once been a beauty to her, before life had gotten the better of her. She was not an old woman; late twenties or early thirties at the most, but with an aura of weariness that warded off any youthful exuberance she may have once had. Looking at her, it was obvious she was Pepe's mother: he shared her high cheekbones and broad nose. Ana did the talking, introducing us. Epifanio and I rose from our seats to greet her, awkwardly showing courtesy while already comfortable in her house. She showed no embarrassment at having us in her home, but did not join us sitting down. She entered the house and stood leaning against the doorway leading to the bedroom.

Marcía was how she introduced herself, and when Ana addressed her with the obligatory honorific of Doña she merely replied, "No, not Doña. Just Marcía." She may have had children, but that didn't make her an old lady.

"Marcía, has José Alberto talked about us to you?"

"Oh yes, you are the ones who brought him back to his father's. He had been staying with you in the capital in the shelter you run."

Ana and I exchanged glances. It was not uncommon for kids to mislead their parents, letting on that they had been staying at a shelter run by our organization when the truth was we had no shelter and they were on the streets. There was a great stigma to having been on the streets and telling their mothers where they had been. It was shameful to admit that they had not done nearly as well as they had led their mother to believe. Ana didn't have a chance to correct Marcía's misconception; José Alberto came back carrying two plantains and a chunk of salami wrapped in rough butcher paper. He placed the goods on the table and dug into his pocket, fishing out a few coins, which he returned to me. He was expectant, his body wound rigid.

I looked again at Ana. This was why we tried to work in pairs. I understood it would be best if she talked to Marcía alone. Epifanio rose, saying, "I'm going to check on the truck."

"Come on, Pepe, let's go with Epi." I got up from my chair and placed an arm around the boy's shoulder, shepherding him out of the house.

The sun was brutal, shining full force on the streets. The three of us maintained our silence to the truck. Epifanio unlocked the doors and started the engine. Pepe and I climbed in the back seat. The first hot breath of the air conditioning washed over us, slowly cooling to icy, stale air. Epi contorted his body in the front seat to get a better look at José Alberto. I pressed myself in the nook between the seat and doorframe, angled vaguely in the kid's direction. Pepe spread out, waiting for the luxury of coolness.

I eyed Epifanio and he indicated with a rise and fall of his eyebrows that I should begin. The same question would be on both our minds.

"So you haven't told your mother what you were doing in the capital?"

An extra bow of the head. He didn't think we would find out and hadn't wanted us to. "It's ok," I quickly added, "You know, Pepe, it's nothing to be ashamed of."

He mumbled into his chest and played with the seat pocket in front of him.

"What was that?" Epifanio asked.

José Alberto repeated what he had said, audible but still incomprehensible. I reached across the back seat and gently cupped his chin with the palm of my hand, raising his head to see us. He did not resist. His eyes implored us to understand. "You try telling your mother you were on the streets," was all he added to the look.

I released my hand. He didn't move.

"Why is it different with your mother? Your father knows. Segunda knows. Why should telling your mother be more difficult, Pepe?"

"Because it is. Because she's my mom." He paused, looked out the window to the alley that led to his house. "I was supposed to be helping her, but I never did."

"Did she ask you to help? Did she send you out to work?" Epifanio asked.

José Alberto turned his head to look at the front seat. "No. I went on my own. She's never asked me to work. I just know I need to. You don't know what it was like. You don't understand. She wasn't working and my father had his new family. I was ok, I could go to his house, but she couldn't. Things got really bad. I didn't want her to do what she was doing." It was an oblique reference, one that José Alberto wasn't going to elaborate. He had taken to exploring the pocket on the back of the driver's seat.

My gut reeled. I had a sense of what Marcía had been doing that would make her son ashamed. She was still an attractive woman, despite the weariness. She wouldn't have too much trouble finding clients—maybe not the very wealthy, especially in San Cristóbal. It would explain her uneasiness with titles of respect, wanting to diminish her age. I didn't dare ask if she was still doing what he hadn't wanted her to do. It obviously weighed upon him.

"You know, people think it is easier than it is," I said. "It's a common misconception. They think it's easy to make money on the streets and save it. Think about it. No house. You can find food easy enough, right? So all that money you make shining shoes or selling bottles you can save. That's how it is, right?"

Pepe perked up. "No way man. Sure, you earn some money, but it's day-to-day. And whenever you've got some hidden or saved someone always knows how to steal it."

"How many times were you robbed?"

"Whew! Lots. Too many to count."

"So you see, you really didn't have a lot of opportunity to send money back to your mom, did you?"

"No," he bowed his head again, "but you don't understand."

"What's not to understand?" Epifanio interjected. "It's not that you couldn't send money back, is it? It's that you sometimes enjoyed living on the streets. You forgot about her. That's it, isn't it?"

The poor kid looked tortured. He wiggled uncomfortably in the seat and twisted as to hide his face from us. Epifanio had hit the truth. Pepe was ashamed at having lived it up on the streets while his mother struggled at home. He may have been on the streets, but that had more dignity than what his mother did back home.

"It doesn't matter, Pepe. You know that your mother is not going to be ashamed of you." I reached out, placing a hand on his shoulder. Pepe didn't turn to look at me. "Your mother, she understands what we have to do to make ends meet. She'll understand what you did and why.

"Besides, you can't hide the truth forever. At some point she will talk with your father and then it will seem like you lied to her."

"It's like the boy and the wolf, huh?"

"Just like the boy and the wolf. You want people to believe you and trust you, right? The only way for that is to tell the truth.

"But it's up to you. No one is going to force you to tell your mother where you'd been living. But we won't lie for you, either."

I knew that this was a bigger deal for José Alberto than it would be for his mother. I could tell how in his mind, Pepe had worked over the shame of whatever he had done on the streets, polished it until it glared at him whenever he examined and scrutinized it. It would be an ugly trinket to show to others by this time. He needed to let it go, give it up. It would be difficult to build trust in his family otherwise. His father had already failed to earn Pepe's trust; he needed to have a solid relationship with someone other than the three of us who came every two weeks to visit.

Epifanio indicated the digital clock blinking on the dashboard. It was getting later than I expected. "We ought to get going if we are to stop by Doña Tita's this afternoon." He cut the engine and out we went, back into the cruel heat of the street. It pushed down upon us, a weighty, material thing to trudge through.

Ana and Marcía were still in the darkened interior of the home. It looked like they had not changed position in the minutes we had been away, Ana seated in one of the worn wood dining room chairs and Marcía leaning against the entryway to the bedroom. Marcía's cool eyes watched her son approach the doorstep.

The shaded room gave little relief from the heat. Ana's face sparkled with sweat. She must be baking in those polyester pants, I thought. Marcía, on the other hand, appeared at ease. Her white tank top, although damp, was less stifling.

At the sight of his mother, José Alberto must have known that she already knew. Her demeanor was striking, like what she had expected to have been the truth all along had been revealed. To her credit, she did not say anything to Pepe. Whether this course of action was her own, or advised by Ana, I did not know. It did provide the space for Pepe's own confession, however. There was no prodding. Eager to get it over with, Pepe left off any preamble, merely filling the silence that opened up as we arrived.

"Momma," he began in a low voice. He was opposite his mother, leaning his back against the table, eyes fixed on the floor out some inches from his feet. "Momma, I didn't tell you everything. I wasn't always at a shelter in the capital. I lived a lot on the street, too. Niños del Camino doesn't have a shelter. I met them on the streets." As an afterthought, he added, "I'm sorry." It was an ambiguous addition that could have meant he was sorry for having lied or sorry for having gone to the streets to begin with. He bowed his head further and waited.

Marcía was not upset, but rather resigned to the truth. "Come here, my son," she called to him and Pepe went, looking for reassurance. Marcía wrapped her arms around her son's head and back and Pepe buried his face into her chest. "It's ok. I understand. I understand." She didn't cry and neither did he. It was much more a statement of the obvious, calling attention to a common element of the landscape, like a tree you see every day but don't realize is there until someone tells you to look at it.

## BACK ON THE CONDE

Eli and I left work late Friday afternoon and headed to the Conde for ice cream. The Conde was bustling with the flow of people. There seemed to be more tourists than normal—gaggles of them clustering together as they wove in and out of shops and grazed from souvenir stalls. As groups of Europeans and Americans walked down the cobblestoned streets, entourages of bootblacks followed in their wake.

We sat down, cones in our hands, and quickly devoured them before the Santo Domingo heat melted them to a puddle of cream and emulsifiers. Our seats looked out to the flow of pedestrians, the push-and-pull movement of life. The crowds were thick and it became difficult to follow individuals as they moved through the scene. Instead, I found myself staring at the motion, the mass as it passed by. I didn't hear Eli's question.

"I thought you said he wasn't supposed to come this far anymore."

"Who?" I asked, tongue full of ice cream.

"José Alberto."

"He's not. Just to the park in San Cristóbal."

"Well, he's almost to the park, but the one here in the capital. That is him over there, near the bench, right?"

In the middle of the ped mall, placed every couple of hundred feet, were park benches back-to-back. I couldn't see what Eli was seeing for the people passing by. On the park bench facing the storefront sat a group of young white folks, possibly American college students by the look of their State U t-shirts. The group were engaged with something at their feet, looking down and commenting every so often to each other.

There was a break in the flow of the crowd and I could see three kids sitting on shoeshine boxes at the feet of the Americans, necks craned to look up. I recognized not just one, but two of the bootblacks from the unmistakable jitteriness and elephant ears of Amauris and the bald dark head and stilted movements of José Alberto. I couldn't quite tell who was enjoying themselves more—the kids or the Americans.

"Damn it!" I bitterly commented to Eli, "He knows he's not supposed to be here."

"When does that ever stop a kid from doing what they want to do?"

"So what do we do?"

"Well, we could just let it be, pretend we don't see him and then ask him next time we see him in San Cristóbal how the capital was." Eli read my reaction, "You're not just going to let this one go, are you?"

"Well, no. We've put a lot of effort in Pepe, a lot of time. I don't want to see him screw it up."

"You mean you don't want to see him back on the streets."

I didn't answer, but Eli was right. It had less to do with my wanting José Alberto to be as successful as he could be, although I did, than it did with my feeling like he was putting himself at new risk. The truth was—and I'm not sure I could have articulated it this way at the time, knowing how such feelings could cloud over judgments and make us less "objective" in our work—but the truth was, I loved the kid. I loved him for his tenacity, his quiet mutinies, his oversensitivity to the world, his vulnerability that he tried to hide with just enough bravado to make it obvious what he was hiding.

I wasn't enraged. I didn't feel duped. It wasn't my place to discipline him and false threats—like telling his parents or cutting off working with him and his family—were unproductive and mean-spirited. What was I going to do? What could I do?

The kids were hoping for money from their new American friends. Amauris kept holding the index finger of his left hand up and beseeching the girls with alternating mashed English of "un dollar please," and "mucho hungry." The girls laughed in response, one even bravely reached out and patted Amauris paternalistically on the head.

Eli could see the conflict swelling within me. I sat half poised on the plastic chair, somewhere between sitting and going.

"If you want to go and talk to him, we can. Just make sure you know how you are going to react." She shot me a reassuring smile. It was all the support I needed.

I tried to put on my best lighthearted and carefree attitude. I told myself I was going to play this one as if I had run into any other kid I knew. I crept up behind the three boys. Neither they nor their American quarry paid me any attention, being too wrapped up in the game of give and take. Taking my two index fingers, I poked them lightly into the sides of Pepe's sitting body. The kid jumped squarely off his shoeshine box and looked wildly around him to see who the culprit was.

I stood grinning before him, forcing the artificial smile to rush across my face. "What a surprise to see you here," I said in fake jovialness, "I thought we only saw each other in San Cristóbal now, but look how lucky we are, Eli, we get another visit in."

Pepe's surprise quickly turned defensive. It was no sheepish cat-who-ate-the-canary routine. His normal posture of turning off—when he'd look to the ground and not reply whenever found with something he did not want to answer for—was gone. He stood defiant before us.

"I'm out shining shoes."

"Oh, shining shoes, is it? I must have gotten confused. I thought we had agreed on staying in San Cristóbal, not all the way to Parque Colón."

"Yeah, well, it's just for the day. I'm going back tonight. Aren't we, Amauris? Aren't we going back tonight?"

Amauris disengaged from a hand jive with one of the jocks to look in his friend's direction. "Yeah, man, in a bit." Recognition swept across his face as he looked up at Eli and myself. "Hey, I know you two. You got any crackers?"

"Sounds good, then, that you'll be going back tonight. What do you think, Eli, he must have his school shirt tucked in that shoeshine box somewhere, 'cause I thought classes started at six."

"Classes were cancelled." Pepe was fast to reply. It had equal chance of being truth or lie, knowing the Dominican school system. Especially night school, as it was dependent on the vagaries of things such as electricity and whether or not the teacher had something better to do.

José Alberto knew he wasn't supposed to be there in the capital, knew he had been caught. I couldn't tell if this was the first time or not he'd come in since we took him back several months ago. It made me angry to see him there, back in his old turf as if not much had changed in the intervening months, as if we hadn't been investing so heavily so that he might succeed.

"I didn't know his mother and we went to all the effort to enroll him and get him a uniform so that he could be truant. Sounds like a fine deal to me. Come on, Eli, let's leave him to his shoes." I turned away. Eli, following, whispered at my side, "Don't you think you're being a little harsh, Jon?"

José Alberto called out into the street. He was ready for the low blow. "You aren't my dad. You can't tell me what to do."

That was exactly what I didn't want, what I feared might be coming. I turned around and walked back to where Pepe stood. I wasn't going to let words spoken in anger and frustration hurt our relationship. I crouched down to be lower than his eyes.

"No, you are right, Pepe, I'm not your dad. And even if I were, I still couldn't make you act in a certain way. It hurts me to see you back here on the Conde because it reminds me of when you lived on the street. If this is where you choose to be, then this is where you are. We'll talk more on our next visit to your house, next week. Or, if you aren't there, then we'll talk here."

As I straightened my legs, coming back to full height, I added, "You are right, I am not your father. But your welfare concerns me nonetheless. Now, go back to Amauris. We'll talk later."

He had expected to hurt me, and in truth, he did, but probably not in the way he intended. Pepe reminded me that I was dangerously close to crossing that line between concern and being overbearing. We were not there to police behavior or mete out punishment or even to be an authority figure. Those were lessons parents needed to learn—how to be fair and just, how to correct behavior without force, how to accept and love and demonstrate that love and acceptance in healthy ways. We were not to be substitutes, even in the meantime, while parents tried to grasp those skills. Many parents never would. All the same, we were just guides.

I turned and walked away, tempted to check over my shoulder but not daring to show the weakness, either to him or myself.

## COMMENTARY

Effective outreach work with homeless populations is achieved when social service organizations understand the complexity of the lives of their clients. Street cultures have deep internal divisions, even if they appear relatively homogenous to outside observers. Some of these cleavages are based on territorial differences, in which children and youth sleep and work in particular areas of the city. There exists, however, a nexus in which social identities on the street are the combination of territory, drug consumption habits, occupational niche, and biological age (or perceived biological age). Thus, in the constellation of street identities in Santo Domingo, there exists crucial internal division between those individuals labeled palomos and those who feel they can pass as working class. Palomos denote deterioration of appearance and mental faculties due to prolonged solvent use, like glue and paint thinner. They are marginalized even among other street youth, mostly because of the stigma of being dirty and sticky that is associated with solvent use. Youth who exhibit signs of mental illness are often lumped in this category as well, but it is a division used to police the borders of acceptable behavior even by those whose situation may not be very different. Thus, when Amauris labels José Alberto a palomo, he is critiquing his former friend's appearance and means of making a livelihood (collecting empty bottles). Never mind that a few short weeks previously the two had been buddies or the fact that José Alberto was not a solvent user. Amauris's new reference group, consisting of Hilário and Máximo, smoked marijuana and, sometimes, crack, and used their ability to pass as bootblacks as cover for petty theft. For them, the division between how José Alberto was living and their own street existence couldn't be clearer.

Other occupational niches on the street also carry moral overtones. Thus, teenagers and young men like Carlos who engage exclusively or periodically in sex work occupy a morally ambiguous place in street hierarchies. On the one hand, because they attract primarily foreign clientele, such youth must take special care of their appearance, including personal hygiene and dress. They have an easier time moving through dominant society even while they periodically sleep on the streets. They also have more regular access to material goods and cash. While they may consume crack, they must take care that their habit doesn't become so great that their physical appearance marks them as drug users. They may also have periodic access to higher end drugs such as cocaine and ecstasy that are provided by clients. On the other hand, youth who rely exclusively on hustling run the risk of having their masculinity questioned. Teenagers who, like Carlos, make the move into regular sex work exist without the support—and constrictions—of larger street cliques like those represented by Hilário and Máximo. Their ability to reinforce their differences from other street youth is part of their livelihood strategy.

The trickiest distinction for outreach programs like Niños, however, is how to define the line between a working child and a child living on the street. Javi, Amauris's friend under the palm tree, and especially Amauris were both in a situation in which the street offered excitement and the opportunity to earn money. The fact that Amauris had been contacted by the organization on a previous late-night outreach trip is telling—he had undoubtedly been in a transition between home and street for well over a year. Yet, it is possible that he would never come to spend a protracted time sleeping away from his home. Indeed, it appears as if Amauris had the security of a regular place to sleep, a family that welcomed him, and the flexibility to come and go as he pleased. José Alberto, however, was in a different situation. He found living at home untenable, even as much as he regretted his decision. In his case, altered family dynamics, in addition to the straitened economic situation of his mother, are what made the street look like a more attractive place to be than either household of his parents. In particular, it appears that part of the reason José Alberto took to the streets to begin with had to do with his father's lack of economic support and concern for his mother, leading Marcía to turn to prostitution as a means of sustaining the household. José Alberto partially justified going to the streets to work as a means of helping his mother out financially, even as it was a way for him to be ignorant of what Marcía was doing to survive. Likewise, Francisco's turn to the streets had much to do with a combination of extreme poverty and strained family relationships. There was little for him back in his mother's house in the country, in terms of economic possibilities. Why stay in a cramped shack with little to do when he could eat better, earn money, and enjoy more freedom on the streets of Santo Domingo? The distance from his country home to the capital was too great for him to make sporadic trips like those of Amauris and Javi.

Thus, approaches to offering assistance depend upon the social and personal characteristics of each client. Outreach is necessarily inefficient work in this regard because while there exists a "best practices" guide, each client comes with a unique history—differences in street habits, family background, and personality all alter possible outcomes. The diversity of types of children and youth living on the street was one of the major challenges facing Niños. Teenagers like Carlos, for example, have very little sympathy for and little in common with youth like José Alberto. Even Amauris's distinction between his social group of Máximo and Hilário and his former friend José Alberto demonstrates how divisive social differences can be on the street. Outreach workers need to develop both a general sense of the heterogeneity of various types of street situations as well as understand how the personality and social relationships of a particular child are limiting factors as to the types of services available.

Thus, in any new encounter, there were several things educators wanted to be aware of. First, as with making initial contact with José Alberto, most kids will not own up to the fact that they are sleeping on the street. This is because of both the stigma associated with sleeping on the street and the secrecy of the specifics of an individual child's life. In many ways, this makes perfect sense—why would you divulge your life's story to a stranger, even a stranger who professes that he or she is there to help? For outreach educators, real work can only begin once rapport has been earned. This is initially difficult, given the fact that street populations are very mobile, moving throughout the city. It may take several weeks of chance encounters to speak to a new contact a handful of times, especially if the contact isn't part of an already known or established group, as in the case of José Alberto.

There is also a concern by outreach educators to make sure that an initial contact meets the requirements for the type of services the organization can provide. Economic and time resources are scarce and, unfortunately, organizations like Niños are very aware of their limitations. For this reason, aid organizations often narrowly define their target population to concentrate resources and efforts where there is the greatest potential for change. They know that their funding agencies want to see results in order for support to continue. Outreach workers are on the front lines of vetting potential participants in programming. In the case of José Alberto, we could tell he fit the profile for intervention set forth by the organization and its funders because of some prominent characteristics. First, initial contact was made later in the evening at a time when bus service would have made it nearly impossible for José Alberto to make it to his home outside of Santo Domingo. Second, the type of work he was doing, collecting bottles, was more associated with sleeping on the streets than that of working children in Santo Domingo, who are more often associated with shining shoes and selling candies or other small items. Outreach workers learn to make judgments about whether or not a potential case fits the profile even before in-depth investigation can take place.

Some of the concern with ascertaining fit with a potential client relates to finding the right kind of assistance for a given child or youth. Granted, social services are scarce in the Dominican Republic, but given the narrow definition of the agency's target population, the fear was that the organization's focus could shift if we were not vigilant. In the constellation of NGOs that professed to work with street and working children, only Niños took on the hardcore cases of accompanying those children and youth who had been living on the streets for a relatively long period of time. There also existed the fear that, if we did not properly vet a potential participant in our programming, we would "create" a street child. For instance, Javi and Amauris were in a different street situation than José Alberto, with much more constant contact with their households and with a greater tendency toward work that sustained the livelihood of their families. Outreach workers could actually interfere with that balance by inviting them to take part in programming. Going to play baseball in a park and getting a free meal could be incentive to have a kid move from consistent contact with their families and only spending nights on the street sporadically to being more fulltime on the streets. Offering assistance, food, and fun, in addition to putting different kinds of children and youth in contact with one another, has the potential to sway a child to the streets.

Social service organizations require a clear ideology justifying their work. This is especially important for organizations like Niños that provide social services to a clientele based on their own moral compass and not because they have been court ordered to do so or because they receive primary funding from state agencies. Outreach work is more than just social work, which can often be justified as being in the best interest of the client. This "we are doing this for your own good" approach that borders on paternalism is particularly prevalent in social services provided in conjunction with institutions such as prisons, orphanages, and mental hospitals.

Outreach work, on the other hand, can be a radical approach to understanding the lives of the marginalized. For Niños, the founding ideology was borrowed from Catholic liberation theology's belief in the preferential option for the poor. This means that instead of a "working for" attitude of social services, the ideology is one of "working alongside of" marginalized populations. In other words, in the language of the organization, outreach work is about accompanying others in their life, understanding the reality in which they live and the opportunities and impediments to changing their circumstances. Ideally, outreach workers should suspend their moral judgments about the lives of the people they work with and see the world from their point of view. The emphasis on accompaniment also entails following others on their path, even if that path goes in a direction you know to be unfavorable. Through accompaniment, regardless of the circumstance, outreach workers are able to work with marginalized populations to develop plans of action, work for justice and dignity, and strive for mutual existential recognition of the humanity in us all.

In practice, what accompaniment meant for me as an outreach worker was purposely putting myself in situations where I knew I would come into contact with the kids and youth with whom our organization worked, even if I would have rather slipped away unnoticed at times. In Santo Domingo, a city of over two million residents, being an outreach worker with street and homeless populations was still a public identity. There were few places within the city that I did not run into children, youth, and adults that I knew from doing outreach work. I quickly learned that the ethos of accompaniment upon which the organization was founded meant that we were always "on duty." This sense of obligation came partly from the ideological underpinnings of the organization, but the longer I spent doing outreach the more I sensed that it also was derived from long-term outreach workers' own desire to be present in the lives of kids and youth whom they had worked with over many years. It is hard to divorce oneself from the quality of the relationships being built in order to provide services for a clientele. Outreach workers are not immune from growing attached to the people they work with through the process of accompaniment, be it from nostalgia, to frame the work they do with meaning, or because of developing a genuine affection for them and friendship with them. Accompaniment, as we shall see, is messy, emotional work. Investing in relationships means you have to get involved with your whole being.

The messiness of accompaniment is highlighted for outreach workers when a child or youth moves from the street back to the home environment. Partially this has to do with reading the cues of household dynamics and ascertaining where the child fits in relative to other people in the household. In situations where the child has signaled that physical, emotional, or sexual abuse has occurred, how can returning to the family be advocated or condoned? Yet, because of weak social service protections, and despite progressive pro-child rights legislation, we were often placed in the position of advocating for the right of a child or youth to live in his or her own home even as we knew the situation was not ideal. When compared to the forms of harm that could happen on the street, abusive homes were often the better prospect. At the very least, we would rationalize such decisions with the hope that we could work on changing parents' behavior through periodic visits and counseling. We did have success with this method, especially in cases of physical and emotional abuse that stemmed from other stressors than a deep dislike of the child.

Outreach workers, then, are placed in the awkward position of being an advocate for a child in his or her own household. The child has grown to trust the outreach workers' abilities to mediate conflict, provide counsel, and be a sounding board, a process that has lead to the child feeling safe enough to visit their home. In some cases, children view outreach educators as the most caring adult concerned for their well-being that they have encountered, more understanding and communicative than their own parents, as became evident the more we worked with José Alberto's family. In particular, the discrepancy between Don José's actions and his attitude toward his son was an impediment to improving family dynamics. Our presence accompanying a child to his or her home revealed an embarrassing situation for the family that they were no longer able to ignore, mainly that some dynamic in their household produced a situation where their son or daughter sought refuge on the street. For some families, this created more embarrassment than for others. Don José obviously felt chagrined at the fact that his eldest son had taken to the streets, especially when this fact was brought to light by our presence at his house. José Alberto's mother, Marcía, on the other hand, appeared to take that revelation in stride, with a display of acceptance of her son that, at least for me, demonstrated greater authenticity than Don José's reaction. Even though the initial reaction may not change behavior or attitudes in the long term, it does bring to light several fault lines within the household. Parents began rationalizing and justifying the outcome by laying blame, often on poor economic conditions and the "wild" nature of their son or daughter. It was our job to push away these surface explanations to get at the more underlying causes. As with the initial contact with their children, this was a process that took time and depended upon the disposition of household members.

As in the case of José Alberto, children on the street grow to rely on the presence of outreach workers and educators—they have become a means of support. As children move back into their own household they lose the excitement of the street, their street networks, the chemical dependency and social behaviors associated with their drug use, and regular (often daily) contact with street educators. These multiple losses are a shock. The tenor of the initial months of returning home are crucial for the ultimate success of a child or youth finding comfort and a space of acceptance within their family. It does not take much to upset the uneasiness of a child who has taken refuge in the street before—he or she already knows that a practical solution to household conflict is to leave. Outreach educators, once they begin to work with the entire family, must provide the tools for both caregivers and children to communicate effectively with one another.

Even then, despite all best efforts, children and youth may still find the street the more attractive option. Accompaniment is predicated on working with children and youth wherever they are, on whatever path they may be on, even if it is not the path you would hope them to choose. This is the hard emotional lesson of doing outreach work, learning how to accept the choices and will of others in a nonjudgmental (but not necessarily noncritical) way. It stung when I discovered that José Alberto was spending greater amounts of time in the capital. I knew I was supposed to be detached from the choices children and families made, but not from their lives. The paradox of outreach work is to believe in self-determination yet still develop close rapport and even friendship with others. How do you not become invested in the outcomes of their lives?

# 2 · STRUCTURAL CONDITIONS

## FINDING PANCHITO

The word on the street is always garbled, mangled, never pure and unadulterated news. In a climate of suspicion and scarcity even the most basic of information—for example, when someone changes territory—is wrapped in double-talk and deliberate misinformation.[1] There tends to be a kernel of truth, a tiny seed of real events, in every piece of gossip that circulates, but having to peel back the layers of the fantastic or malicious to reach that seed is a daunting, if necessary job.

Three months previously we had received reports from a number of different kids that Blue Eyes had been shot at Montesino's in a drug deal that went sour. He had just turned eighteen. He and his best friend Alejandro, a tall, gangly Haitian with impossibly large hands, disappeared completely. I went to police stations and even the main Homicide Department, where the nearly illiterate, toothless detective let me rummage through old reports. There, on the sticky plastic chair in the airless, windowless room about halfway through a three-inch stack of typed reports, I found the paper that turned me cold despite the infernal heat. "Malecón and Montesino," it was headed in anonymous typescript. Two bodies found, one shot in the temple, dead; the other wounded in the back and taken to the hospital. Both bodies unidentified, but the one shot in the back had (adolescent) inserted in the description. I didn't have to be a forensic scientist to read the scene. One guy shot point blank in the temple, the other one gunned down as he ran away. There was the kernel, the part of the story that was, morbidly, true. We had no way of knowing if it was Blue Eyes or not. Even though the report was over a month old, there might be a chance the kid was still in the hospital. I convinced Héctor to go with me to the hospital to see if we could find him.

Blue Eyes was not a well-known youth to most of the new team. He no longer did daily activities with us and only seemed to find us when he had a problem needing to be fixed. I had seen him and Alejandro almost daily for five months straight, always sitting on the same green metal bench in front of where the collective taxi dropped me off from work. We had a conversational relationship. When Blue Eyes noticed I had once had both my ears pierced, he invented his version of who I was in my younger years—some streetwise womanizer and heavy marijuana smoker. He couldn't have been further from the truth, but his erroneous projection of who I was cemented our relationship.

Héctor and I arrived during the last half hour of visiting hours, which was lucky, because trying to enter a public hospital on off-hours could be like trying to see the queen. Darío Contreras is the closest thing Santo Domingo has to a trauma-one hospital.[2] It is where all the victims of gunshot wounds and motor accidents go in this city of over a million inhabitants. If you have a broken bone or had a round of lead unloaded into you, you must come to Darío Contreras; the other hospitals will turn you away.

"Who are we looking for again?" Héctor asked as we climbed the wide cement stairs to the men's wing. A smell of antiseptic could not mask the bouquet of decay: odors of urine, sweat, and the metallic tinge of old, dried blood.

"Blue Eyes. You know, Alejandro's friend. Quiet, calm, always high on pot?" It wasn't ringing a bell. I hated to do it, but I had to resort to Dominican color codes. "You know, the white one who looks like he's from the Cibao but is really from Baní."[3]

"Víctor? Always hangs out with Alejandro down in Hostos Park?"

There were twelve rooms for men at Darío Contreras, separated along three corridors. Each room held between ten and twelve beds. Besides the patients, the rooms would also have the designated caretaker for each patient, usually a woman family member, who stayed through the night. Without a personal caretaker, patients would not receive timely checks and needed care. No one would bathe them or take them to the bathroom.

We started in the first room, stepping just inside and looking at the faces of patients to see if Blue Eyes was somewhere among them. The room was like a macabre chorus line: all the patients were flat on their backs with one or both legs extended in the air, held in place by a grisly pin inserted through the knee, rope tied on either protruding side of the pin and then connected to a counter-weight and pulley system.

About three-quarters of the men looked under twenty-five. They lay listlessly on the mattresses, wearing only underwear in the hot, stuffy room. Even the bare cotton sheets some had loosely tossed on top of their bodies seemed too much. Their immobile legs hung like specimens. No one bothered us, or even registered our entrance or exit from the room. It was easy enough to do a quick survey of the faces and look for the bed without someone waiting beside it.

We moved on to the next room. Héctor was telling a story about his younger brother who had broken a leg in a motorcycle accident and sat in a cast for six months. He even had to be in Darío with the pin through his knee, waiting for surgery to put a steel rod in the femur. So that was it. All these beds were filled with patients waiting for surgery: literally dozens who were waiting for the correct combination of available money, doctor, anesthesia, and medical supplies.

"My brother waited three months in Darío for the rod they were going to put in his leg. And then he lasted four months in a cast, had surgery again to take the rod out and another two months in a different cast. And he walks with a limp today."

Héctor's story had taken us through the entire corridor; the four rooms yielded nothing but bodies anonymous to us. Down we went to corridor number two which, by the looks of the inhabitants of the first room, was devoted to a hodgepodge of patients. Gone were the semblances of medieval torture; these patients nursed gunshot wounds or had plaster casts hugging various portions of their bodies. The patient at the left of the doorway, a shirtless grizzled man in his sixties, slept on sheets stained crimson, the dark spot radiating from his lower back outward. It looked slightly wet.

I was transfixed by the sight. Héctor tapped my shoulder, "Doesn't that one look familiar?" He pointed toward a sprawled figure in the back corner, the black skin of the body offsetting the stark white cast that ran from the hip to the toe of the right leg.

"That's not Blue Eyes. I told you, he's light-skinned."

Héctor laughed at me, "I know it's not him. But what I am saying is I know that kid. Don't you recognize him? I think it's Panchito."

Sometimes, by accident, by blind chance, you end up where you are needed most, even if your original intention had been different. We wove our way among the beds toward the sleeping figure. A young woman was giving a sponge bath to her boyfriend in the neighboring bed, dipping a tattered rag in a shallow bedpan of tepid water. "You know him?" she asked protectively of the kid we could now plainly see was Panchito. Héctor started to explain how we knew him but the boyfriend interrupted, "Well, he's been here for almost a month. No one's come to visit him and the hospital officially discharged him weeks ago. He's still here 'cause he can't walk out."

The girlfriend gestured to the occupants of the room. "We've been feeding him, too, when we can. He's no longer a patient so the hospital doesn't care for him."

He was sleeping deeply, the shallow breaths inflating his shirtless chest in a steady rhythm. There was a slight, acrid smell of old body odor rising from the sheets. They had not been changed in a long while, probably since he arrived. Despite the cast, though, Panchito looked comfortable, oddly at peace. I glanced at Héctor, "You want to wake him?" He nodded and tapped the fourteen-year-old lightly on the shoulder, repeating his name three or four times.

He woke gently—no great startle—and as his eyelids fluttered, adjusting to the light in the room, he merely said, "You guys came." And then he smiled broadly, a grin that stretched the sides of his mouth and revealed white teeth and a bad case of halitosis.

"It's a surprise to see you here," Héctor commented dryly. "We didn't know we'd find you lying about."

"Yeah, I've been here for a while," Panchito replied in his faintly accented Spanish, stuttering over the words as if he had trouble finding his voice. Although he had lived in the Dominican Republic for many years, you could still detect the Haitian lilt to his r's, which came out soft. "I didn't know the number to call. I couldn't remember it."

"That's quite a cast you've got," I said.

"It goes all the way up to the hip. I can't walk. I have to pee in a cup."

"So what happened?" It was Héctor's turn to ask. Ignoring the root of the question, Panchito replied, "I've got three bullet wounds in my leg. One here"—he pointed to his upper thigh—"one here"—and then to just above the knee cap—"and one back here"—his hand went behind his thigh. "Shattered my bone. The x-ray is under the mattress."

I lifted up the corner of the bed gingerly. The mattress was well worn and yellowed. There was a large manila folder stuffed onto the wire frame. I pulled the x-ray out and held it to the light. It pictured a long bone that, clearly, even to my untrained eye, was split in pieces. There even looked to still be a piece of shrapnel or shot embedded in the upper thigh.

"Looks like you did a good job breaking the leg." I passed the x-ray onto Héctor. "You want to say anything about the bullet holes?"

For the moment, Panchito was silent. The story would come out in fragments over the next several days. He was never a big talker, whether from a sense of privacy or embarrassment, I never knew for sure. "I was down at Montesino and saw something I shouldn't have seen." That was all he was going to say, but at the mention of Montesino my ears pricked.

"Montesino? About a month ago? We will need to talk at some point, Panchito." I fought off the urge to hound him with questions. He wasn't going to answer them with all the people who had taken care of him for the past month around, eagerly listening. He had a certain image to keep up— that of the innocent orphan.

Panchito was one of the few kids we worked with who could claim to not have family. Or, I should say, not know where his family was. They had come to the Dominican Republic from Haiti when he was a young child, his father working as a seasonal agricultural laborer, his mother as a maid. Like many Haitians living there, they were in the country illegally, looking for better conditions, a better chance than Haiti offered them at that moment. One morning, Panchito, about ten years old, went out to play baseball with some friends. When he returned that afternoon, the house where he lived was deserted and in shambles. The National Police had made a raid and picked up his entire family—mother, father, and siblings all gone, all deported back to Haiti to some town Panchito could not remember. He didn't even know his family name; he was "given" the last name of neighbors who let him stay with them for a few months. Finally, feeling he had worn out his welcome, he came to the capital and began living on the streets, shining shoes. That had been four years before.

"Hey Héctor, can I see you out in the hall for a minute?" It dawned on me that we had no place to take Panchito. What were we going to do with him? We had no one who could provide him with the needed care. He couldn't get around on his own yet. Normally we would have used such moments as opportunities to finesse a reunion with a kid's family, but Panchito had nowhere to go.

Héctor followed me out the door. "I didn't want to say anything in front of him, but where are we going to take Panchito? He can't stay here and that cast is going to be on for a long time."

"I was thinking about that, too. They're not going to let him stay here now that we've been to visit. I can't believe the hospital discharged him with no place to go. Let me call the office and talk to the boss. Maybe she can make some phone calls."

In the small world of Dominican social services, there were only three residential options for kids who had spent any length of time on the streets, each with a very distinct profile and limited capacity. Quédate con Nosotros, where Héctor had worked for a number of years, had only fifteen beds and viewed itself as a rehabilitation center for kids under twelve years old who had spent less than six months on the street and had (supposedly) no addiction to drugs. At the first sign of difficulty or deviancy, they encouraged the kid to go back home, which usually led them back to the streets. Yo, Tambien was for older kids—preteens and adolescents. They were always at maximum capacity, over twenty kids, with little adult supervision. Some had spent years living at the shelter; others would bounce in and out whenever things got too difficult on the street. Finally, Hogar Crea was a drug rehab center for mainly adult men. They had a number of houses scattered throughout the country. The program was designed around a modified twelve-step residency program lasting three years. It was cold turkey, no drug replacement therapy, and only group auto-critique sessions that bordered on Soviet-style self-abasement before one's peers. It worked for some people, but rarely for the young men who were used to the freedom of street life, of doing things on their own whenever they wanted. There was no leniency in Hogar Crea; you were asked to leave if you couldn't follow the rules.

Back in the room, Panchito sat with this expectant, "now what" expression on his face. I reached into my yellow backpack and pulled out a packet of cookies. "You want some?" I extended the plastic pack in his direction. He nodded eagerly.

The attention in the room had shifted from Panchito's visitors to the old guy bleeding at the entrance. The blood had started to drip on the tiled floor, a slow leak, and splatter with each droplet. Someone had advised the on-call nurse, who had finally arrived to discover the mess. Everyone—from conscious patients to their attendants—had an opinion about the situation, some taking the anger of their own medical inattention out on the situation and cranky nurse.

Ignoring the spectacle, I tapped Panchito's torso to get him to scoot over slightly, and sat down by his waist. Looking him straight in the eyes, I gave him the most serious face I could. "Listen, Panchito, I need to know what happened at Montesino. We were told that Blue Eyes was shot and probably killed there about a month ago."

Panchito interrupted me. "Blue Eyes? The guy that hangs out with Alejandro? Shot at Montesino?"

"Yeah. The very same. That's why we came here today. In hopes of finding him here. Instead we found you and you say you were down at Montesino. I need to know what happened, if Blue Eyes or Alejandro was with you. I know someone else was shot at while you were there, Panchito. I know someone was killed."

His eyes narrowed and he painted a stern grimace on his countenance. "It wasn't Blue Eyes. It was some old guy, some Haitian who was selling. I was there, just walkin' by," his voice hissed in a whisper, "just walkin' by when I see this Haitian selling to a car and hear the shots and the Haitian falls back on the weeds. I knew the guy in the car saw me—I turned and ran but he got me in the leg before he sped off."

I placed a hand on his arm as if to calm him, and extended the corners of my mouth into what I hoped was irony. "Just walkin' by, huh? Pretty bad luck to be caught in the middle of that."

He didn't get defensive, but rather returned my smile. "Just walkin' by."

"We stopped by the Colombian woman's burger stand last week. She said you'd eaten some bad food and were recuperating at a friend's house in El Farolito."

He got upset again, a rarity for Panchito who was normally so even-keeled. "What does she know? There are people that send a person out to do a favor—a dangerous favor—and then they don't come lookin' for that person when things go wrong. I don't want anything to do with that woman." Now that was interesting, I thought to myself. Deliberate use of the third person impersonal couldn't really hide the fact that Panchito was speaking of himself.

Héctor lumbered back into the room, giving the nurse and the bleeding man a wide berth. "You know, Panchito, we don't have a place where you can stay while you recuperate. And you don't really have any place else you can go."

Panchito nodded blankly, as if to say, "Tell me what else is new . . ."

"So," Hector continued, "It looks like we've found an option for you. You know the program Yo, Tambien? It sounds like they'll give you a place to stay, but we are waiting for the final word. At any rate, we can't do anything until tomorrow. You're gonna have to sit tight here until tomorrow afternoon. That all right?"

Panchito took the news in stride. "Not like I'm gonna walk outta here."

Out in the hallway, on our way out of the maze of hospital corridors, Héctor told a different story. "No one wants to take him if he is in a cast. Too much work—they say they don't have anyone to do it. Estívaliz is calling the priest who is in charge of Yo, Tambien. María Dominga wouldn't give the go ahead without the Father's ok. Sounded reluctant. It's 90 percent sure he'll be at the shelter tomorrow, but you never know."

"Come on," I said, a bit incredulously, "It's Panchito. The kid has never been trouble to anyone. He'll win them over once he's there. I can't believe he's never been to Yo, Tambien as long as he's been on the streets."

"So Panchito says he was just passing by on the Malecón when he saw this drug dealer get shot at by a client in a car and the client, seeing that Panchito had witnessed the whole thing, shoots at him, too. At least that is one version." I then told Héctor the surprising outburst, so uncharacteristic of Panchito. "He got angry—his face got all red and he put on this grimace I had never seen before, talking about the Colombian when I asked if she knew he was in the hospital. You know, I was thinking at the very least she'd come to check on him.

"So here's what I think. I think she sent him to make a purchase down there at Montesino. I've always thought she sold more than just hamburgers and hot dogs from her cart. I think she sent him to buy her more marijuana to sell and Panchito walked into a bad deal. That woman is such a liar! We just talked to her last week asking after Panchito and she gave us some story about how he was sick with food poisoning. Food poisoning! Ha! More like lead poisoning. You don't mind if we make a detour, do you? I'd kind of like to double check she doesn't know anything about where Panchito is."

"It's not a detour if it's on the way," Héctor laughed. "You know, you're right. We could use this to help Panchito leave that woman once and for all."

The Colombian's real name was Inés. I would never have called her the Colombian to her face, just like I would never have told her it was morally and legally wrong for a sixty-plus-year-old woman to be sleeping with a fourteen-year-old boy. Panchito was not the type to talk a lot about anything personal; it took over a year for it to slip out that his relationship with Inés was much more than maternal. And even then, it was mostly conjecture. He had told Ana, innocently enough, that "that Colombian lady" had a large piece of skin and hair on her upper inner thigh. He called it a wart but described it as the size of his fist. Ana, I suppose, off-handedly commented something to the effect of, "How would you know she's got something that big and ugly on her inner leg?" Because he'd seen it many times, he said. And then he never returned to the subject of Inés's hideous mark.

It was just after five in the afternoon as Héctor and I pulled the truck around the plaza where Inés had her cart. It was a great location, as this particular park was filled in the evening with Santo Domingo's young hipsters—rockers in their leather, punks with their Mohawks, the occasional transvestite, rough and tumble lesbians in their butch best. Even at one hundred pesos a chimibuger—outrageously expensive for anywhere else, for anyone else's burger—Inés always had a line of customers milling around her metal cart. But it was still early and it looked like Inés had just pulled the cart out of storage. She was cleaning the grill with a steel-wool pad and a spray bottle. That was something she would have had Panchito doing. She must be missing him for that, too.

I let Héctor do the talking, as I could feel the anger and indignation slowly rising in me. Héctor greeted her cordially.

Inés lifted her eyes only from the grill, head and back still bent over the metal surface. "Good afternoon. I'm not quite open for business yet." She gestured with her head to the cleaning process. We had been there enough times—I knew she recognized us, that she knew full well who we were.

"It's a bit early for a chimi," Héctor replied, "We were passing through to see if Panchito was here. We haven't seen him around here for a couple of weeks."

"Panchito got food poisoning, like I had told you. He and I both—I was laid up for a couple of days. Couldn't even open the cart for business I was so sick. Panchito went to stay with a friend in El Farolito, one of the Haitians that hang around the plaza. That was over a week ago. I haven't seen him since. The worst is," and here, I thought, might be real emotion, as she choked ever so slightly on the bleach smell rising from the steel wool and grill, "I don't know where this friend of his lives. I've never been there. And I don't know his number, so I can't call. I hope Panchito is all right."

"I'm sure he is doing fine," Héctor assured her, without even the smallest hint of irony in his voice. "He's probably having a good time with his friend. Living at someone's house would be a good change coming from where he has been living."

Inés became defensive. "You know he rarely sleeps on the streets. I always pay him for working for me—pay the *pensión*, buy him new clothes. I take care of him like he is my own. He never lacks anything."

Back in the truck, I turned to Héctor, "I don't know how you can do it, be so cordial like that. Oh she makes my skin crawl!"

Héctor was the voice of equanimity: "You know, we deal with a lot of unsavory types in this job. Some of them are our own kids. You just have to try to treat everyone with the same sort of respect. It's not like she would force Panchito to do the things he did. She offered certain things and, he, out of necessity or desire for those things, deciding he didn't want to get them through other means, he agreed. Is it right what she does? Of course not. But as much as we like Panchito, remember what his role has been, too." Héctor paused, turning the ignition, and then added, "Besides, maybe he was in love." His uneven teeth flashed in a wide, mischievous grin.


## ENTERING REHAB

Panchito—after Héctor and I fireman-carried him out of the hospital, down the flight of stairs and along the corridors because no wheelchair could be found—had adjusted well to the controlled chaos of life within Project Yo, Tambien. He had been given his own room and the other kids took it upon themselves to entertain and care for him. Indeed, the gunshot wounds made him an instant celebrity and gave this otherwise unassuming adolescent more street cred than he probably deserved.

It was still unclear—at least to me—why he couldn't stay, even if the shelter was "going on vacation" for a week. When we arrived to move Panchito, the shelter was almost empty. Only two kids were left, Panchito and a twenty-something member of the parish's youth pastorate who would be house sitting for the week.

Epifanio and I went to the main floor bedroom, just off the foyer, where we knew we would find Panchito. It was a windowless room, but it had a bathroom connected to it. The low-wattage bulb shone a wedge of light into the hallway. I made a perfunctory knock but didn't wait for an answer before I walked through the open doorway.

"You ready for the big move?"

The leg in the cast was elevated slightly, resting on a bunched up blanket. They had even given him his own TV to watch, a small black-and-white set sitting on the dresser opposite him. The picture flickered low-quality images of music videos. Women in hot pants gyrated on the screen. Panchito was singing along to Don Omar; when he saw us he stopped singing and grinned sheepishly.

"I'm ready to have my cast off, I know that. It's itchy all down my leg. Am I going to be able to walk soon?"

"You've got an appointment this month. It all depends on what the doctor says. How're the gunshot wounds? Are they healing?"

"Almost gone—look." Panchito pointed to where the cast had been cut away to allow the round, pursed-lipped wound to dry where the bullet had exited the flesh. They were still a tender pink set off against the rich brown of his skin, but the oozing and infected puss—a mash of green and yellow discharge—had finally cleared up. It only took three months.

"You got your stuff?" Epifanio asked. Panchito indicated the large black garbage bag at the side of the dresser. He rotated his body off the low-lying bed, reaching for the single crutch by the head of the bed and pulled himself up. "I'm ready to get out of here," he said enthusiastically, "They've been kind and everything, but good Lord, the guys here screw around a lot. Always messing with each other or with your stuff. One can't be left alone here, you know?"

"Oh, look at you, my love," Ana popped her head in the doorway, "Up and about on crutches. You'll be walking without a cast in no time. Come on, let's get going. Hogar Crea takes all morning."

Núria was waiting for us at the central office when we arrived. She sat in the small waiting room, twisting the thin blue paper with Panchito's number on it between her fingers. She stood out, this dishwater blond in a sea of Dominicans. It was easy to pick out the addicts in the room. They were the jittery ones, nervous twitches sprung without warning on their faces. Some were fading figures, so thin they were ghosts of their former selves. Missing teeth, scarred faces, tattooed arms. These were bodies that had been artificially eroded, time accelerated through magic powders and liquid dreams. Núria was the most whole-looking person in the room; the rest were fragments, including family members accompanying each addict. They had been worn down by proxy. Addiction is corrosive. Eyeing the men in the foyer—for they were all men—I thought to myself how out of place Panchito looked. Even with the bullet holes and cast there was still enough of him left that he didn't look like these shades haunting the sunlit corners of the room.

We got Panchito comfortable in Núria's seat, propped his leg up on another. His presence brought interest to those around him. Suddenly there was something else to focus on in the room besides their own anxious mental pacing. What was this kid in the cast doing with two gringos?

Ana took the well-mangled slip of paper from Núria's hands and ducked her head behind the folded screen where the office coordinator sat. She'd been through this many times before, knew the heavyset woman who called the shots like the Wizard behind a different screen.

"We have to wait for the consultation and then go get the blood work done and then come back for the placement. It might take a while." It was 10:30 in the morning. I had never seen the central office so packed. Sending a kid to Crea was not an efficient process and would often take a whole day of waiting—waiting in the Crea office, waiting in at the clinic for blood to be drawn and the results to be presented, waiting in traffic, waiting to meet with the head of the Crea house where the youth we were accompanying was going to live.

The blood work, for me, was always the most harrowing part of sending kids through the Hogar Crea process. Not because I'm afraid of seeing a pinprick and a couple of vials of blood. The main purpose of the blood sample was to test for HIV/AIDS. Hogar Crea had had a policy of not accepting HIV-positive patients into their drug rehabilitation centers. It was a discrimination policy justified with a simple reply, "We don't have the resources to care for that kind of patient." Mandatory testing is illegal and so is discriminatory treatment for people who are HIV positive, according to Dominican law, but rarely does that stop it from happening. Enough AIDS-rights groups had spoken out and some of Hogar Crea's international donors threatened to cut funding if the practice continued. In short order,

Hogar Crea opened its first center just for HIV-positive men. They continued to screen, however. We all knew that if a kid was being sent to Sábana Larga, their test had come back positive.

That was why the blood work always had me anxious. Here we are, with a kid who wants to try a program to get off the streets, and the possibility that he'll find out he's HIV positive can derail whatever motivation he had. He could also return to the streets with a vengeance, deliberately targeting others with whom to have sex and infect. It was not unheard of. In the Dominican Republic, HIV is viewed by many as the end of the road, a definite terminal case. Believing you will die can cause you to do irrational things. Seeing Panchito with that round Band Aid sent this pinprick feeling to my chest. Oh God, I prayed, please come back negative.

Panchito sat patiently through it all. Finally, he and Ana received the call. It was getting to be late afternoon. The minutes ticked. Time dragged while the two of them were in the other room. Panchito was not the last one to be called, but it was getting close. There were only two other possible patients waiting, sitting in opposite corners of the room. One slept, head against the wall. The other stared off at the blank wall, standing every five minutes and exiting to smoke a cigarette.

I was getting impatient and fidgety. Ana and Panchito had been in the back room now for over a half hour, which was not normal. Usually this step in the process was a quick call to the director of the center where the patient was to be sent and then some printed instructions read out verbatim: You have to arrive to the center by the end of the day. If you do not arrive by the end of the day you will not be allowed in and must start over again, including new blood work. Núria, too, was anxious. We had to drop Panchito off to wherever he would be going and still make it to visit María and it was almost five. There was just too much to do in any given day!

Panchito came hobbling out of the screened area, supporting himself with the wall and his crutch. He was getting better at moving himself around like that, a scurrying, almost sideways movement like a crab. Ana hovered behind, her back to us, repeating thanks to the back office. When she turned around her face told of what more weariness was to come after a full day's waiting.

"Well, Panchito is off to the countryside," Ana said, "He's going to Monte Plata."

"Monte Plata? So far?" Monte Plata was a good hour and a half north of the city, if the traffic was good, which it never was. The traffic on the only road north out of the city center was always a thick, turbid river of cars.

"They had a difficult time placing him. Not a lot of spaces available in the city and, with his leg, not many centers wanted to take him. So, it's Monte Plata or Dajabón. We choose Monte Plata." Of course. Dajabón was seven hours away.

Panchito took my shoulder as support as we made our way to the truck. "Monte Plata? You'll like it there, Panchito. They have a farm and in the back of the center they raise ducks and rabbits." Panchito looked skeptical. "What, you don't like the country?"

While Panchito and I were arguing the merits of country life, Núria pulled Ana aside. I heard an audible, "Diablo! I forgot all about that," come from Ana's mouth. Núria had reminded her about María. There was no way we were going to go visit María—there would be a massive tangle of traffic to get to where she lived and then to get out of the city to take Panchito to Monte Plata.

I turned Panchito over to Epifanio, who was waiting by the truck for us, waiting for instructions. I joined the two women.

"I know we promised," Ana was saying, "but there's just no way we can get there today, not now that we are going up to Monte Plata. You know how bad that road is. We'll be looking to get there by seven, as it is."

"I'm with Núria on this one, Ana. I don't want to disappoint María. What if Núria and I went and took the medicine to María. You up for it, Núria?"

"I think it is important we go. Let's do it." She didn't hesitate.

So it was decided. Núria and I said our goodbyes to Panchito, wishing him well, promising to go and visit on a weekend. We waved as Epifanio maneuvered the pickup truck into traffic and headed for the countryside.


## MARIA'S CONDITION

There was no good way to get from where we were to where María lived with her two teenage sons underneath the 27 de Febrero viaduct except to walk from the Colonial Zone north, fifteen or twenty minutes. The walk was familiar territory for me, as the route passed through the neighborhood I called home. Where I lived was an agglomeration of cement multistory apartments and old wooden homes on the verge of collapse. The neighbor-hood looked deceptively two-dimensional, but behind buildings, off the main streets and on the little alleyways scrunched between buildings, there were more houses layered. From my fourth-floor balcony I could look upon the hidden world behind the building fronts, where the poor lived in crum-bling shacks and cooked on charcoal fires while the relatively wealthier, like me, kept up appearances in our cement boxes. I told Dominicans where I lived and would inevitably get a look of surprise and worry. "You live there? That's no place for a gringo."

The traffic island María called home was located just up the street from where I lived. It was not unusual for me to see her come down my street in her slow, dignified shuffle as she made her way to the Colonial Zone, beg-ging from the houses and corner stores as she went. In fact, María wasn't the only street person I would see around my neighborhood. Where I lived was centrally located for many of the older kids we worked with, the ones who had been on the streets for a very long time. The ones who were the true palomos—glue and solvent sniffers, dirty, aggressive, the most disen-franchised. The ones who were contemporaries of María's two sons. If Eli and Núria worried about running into kids where they lived in the Colonial Zone, I, too, felt like early morning walks to catch the bus to work was dodg-ing through a sea of familiar faces. Sometimes I literally almost tripped over them, as they lay sprawled out on the sidewalk where they had collapsed asleep. Sometimes, if I was running late or had no small change on me to buy them something for breakfast, I, too, would find some way to avoid encounters, detour from where I saw the young man up ahead of me.

27 de Febrero is the main east-west corridor for the city. If streets are akin to the circulatory system, 27 de Febrero is the aorta and, like many arteries, this one was choked with residue—the human plaque that gunks up any system. As the broad boulevard flows into the heart of the city, traffic creeps until it stops altogether at the conjunction of Duarte and 27 de Febrero. Few Dominicans would want to claim this intersection as the heart of the capital—the heart should be the emotional center, its beauty reflecting the grace of its people. The heart should be the Colonial Zone with its orderli-ness and clean lines and old-world grandeur. But I knew better. The heart, the beating mass, the dirty hub—it is chaos. Where 27 de Febrero ends at Duarte there is a fetid flow, like a lazy river choked in too much green. The

overpass casts this part of the boulevard in perpetual twilight, always the color of grey and exhaust. Horns from impatient drivers blare in a cacophony, the high pitch ricocheting between the building walls on either side. Those buildings aren't particularly tall—it's not that they are skyscrapers dwarfing humanity and creating an urban canyon. They are at most three or four stories high, concrete blocks set on the asphalt. But because the overpass acts like a cover to a pot, fitting neatly between the opposing buildings, it feels like a tight cave, long and cramped. The boulevard went on covered like that for a good five miles.

Núria and I picked our way gingerly along 27 de Febrero. Large boxes of rotting vegetables and plastics from the street venders punctuated the street every so often. The boulevard arched in a slow curve before arriving at the traffic island where María lived with two of her sons and her boyfriend, Leandro. At this point, where the street arcs like a river bend, the ancillary blockages on 27 de Febrero thinned out. We plodded along the crumbling sidewalk, walking high up on the incline near a small cement driveway that served as a launch pad for buses heading to the southern border with Haiti. We skirted a large miasma of sewer water, about ten feet in diameter, pooled in the road. None of the passing cars slowed down; their wheels sprayed out fan-shaped expanses of murky water. The place smelled like shit.

On the opposite side of the street was a small park with a cement gazebo and low-lying benches overgrown with weeds. That park—nameless even to those who lived in it—was the smoking and dealing ground for María's two teenage sons, Coqui and Negro, and Leandro. There was a whole cadre of young men who gravitated toward María as a kind of mother, and the park was their crack house. As far as I knew, María didn't do crack and she didn't sniff solvents, but she was willing to watch over those who did.[4] The young men would tell her where they were, what was happening. She was the conduit of information for all things within that world, the nucleus that held all the frenetic electrons in orbit.

Núria and I, having given the putrid lake in the middle of the street a wide berth, waited for a pause in traffic to dart across the four east-bound lanes to María's island home. I had made the mistake once of calling the area an *isla*, in Spanish, assuming that, as in English, the term would be the same. Instead, a traffic island is an *isleta*. Núria had laughed heartily at the inaccurate translation. By calling it an *isla*, I had elevated its status to near-country proportions. Explaining the difference, Núria joked, "Yeah, it is María's island for sure, her own republic—the Republic of María."

That's how I like to think of it, then, María's own domain. She had, throughout her street career, carved out a number of niches that she could call home, where she could raise her family. She had lived in the caves along the Malecón, in a dilapidated shack in the floodplain of the Ozama River, and under a hidden viaduct where the elevated road's supports were unseen. She had even set up home in one of the most notorious parks in the city for a while. But her island home was probably her most stable since leaving the caves over five years earlier.

It wasn't that they had erected structures—María, her sons, and occasional other young men who were longtime friends all slept in the open on smashed cardboard boxes placed on the dirt. But she had been able to collect certain items that she used to store her possessions: a broken stove, a plastic hamper, and, most prized of all, a large aluminum box that had a lock, the key of which María wore around her skinny neck. She even tried to maintain a certain logic to her residence—cooking fire on one side, sleeping area on another, and the scraggly bushes on the far side used to relieve oneself in the night. Her boys were not ones for maintaining this order. They slept near the fire and didn't worry about picking up after themselves. María, when not out begging or searching for food, would spend hours sweeping the bare ground with a balding broom. It was important to her to keep an orderly home.

A metal fence, two feet high and with ornate spikes, marked the edge of the island. The length was the distance between two of the overpass supports. Núria and I stood on the sidewalk that crossed the width of the island at the base of one of the supports. María could be seen, bent over the cooking fire, her back to us but unmistakable in her purple floral print dress. We knew better than to enter without knocking first. The dogs would bark and growl and the park in front had eyes and ears.

I cupped my hands around my lips in a natural megaphone and called out María's name as loud as I could. My voice was drowned out by the rumblings of trucks, buses, and public taxis. I called out a few more times before María, still hunched down over the cooking fire, turned her head and looked over her shoulder. Núria expectantly waved, and María rose from her flat-footed crouch and ambled toward us. She walked stiffly bow-legged in lumbering steps, like a woman much older than she was. In one of the several trips to the doctor's office with her, I sneaked a peak at María's national ID card because I couldn't tell her age for sure, and it wasn't polite to ask a lady how old she was. Only forty-eight years old. She looked twenty years older. Hard times had left her prematurely aged. And a hit-and-run accident six or seven years before left her legs akimbo and her gait shuffling.

As María advanced toward us, so did five of the dogs—a fraction of the pack that shared living space with María and her family. The dogs strolled alongside her eagerly. They were lean and sleek canines—all short-haired mutts in a collage of earth tones, some no more than pups. Directly alongside María walked the Grand Dame herself, ears pointed in alertness, head held regally. She wasn't going to let anything pass her by.

We stepped over the barrier and onto the dusty earth of the traffic island. We closed the distance between us and María, coming up about halfway to the camp itself. Núria gave María a hearty hug; I offered a more restrained cheek kiss. María was, as always, delighted to see us. "Come on, you guys arrived just in time. I'm making some beans and rice I scrounged up this morning."

My stomach sank. I had seen poor women pick around stalls on Duarte before, hunting for the discarded or split bean and rice grains off the sidewalk. It would have been an activity that the resourceful María would have done.

Before I could find the words, we were walking toward camp and the cook fire. Sure enough, María had one covered beat-up old pot on the coals, large plumes of steam emitting from where the lid did not fit securely on the pot. She crouched down and gingerly removed the lid, allowing the steam to mushroom up.

"Coqui is out collecting bottles and Negro is begging from passing cars farther up the boulevard," she explained as she stirred the contents of the pot with an aluminum spoon that had been resting on one of the stones that ringed the fire.

"How are you feeling these days, María?"

"Well, I've got this sharp pain here," her hand, palm-side facing her, went down to just below the stomach, "that's no different. Sometimes it is so bad I can't get out of bed. But it passes." She picked a bean from the spoon to test its firmness, popping it in her mouth. "Not ready yet," she informed us with a smile, "you guys are going to miss out on dinner." She righted herself, emerging to standing slowly.

"How were the painkillers we brought last time?" I asked.

"Not bad. They didn't last very long, but I take them when I have sharp pain."

"Well, we brought you some more," I slipped my backpack off my shoulders and rummaged through the contents, pulling out the box. I opened the packaging and took out the ten silver-foiled pills. If María had the box there was greater chance one of her sons might sell it for drug money. María took the sheet of pills I offered her. "There are only ten," I commented on the obvious, "but they should last you until next week. We're going to the doctor's office a week from today. Maybe the doctor will be able to prescribe a stronger painkiller. These are as strong as we can buy from the pharmacist." They were nothing more than 800 mg of ibuprofen in large yellow horse pills. I didn't know the source of María's pain, what kind of pain struck her in the uterus and how it related to her cancer, but I doubted ibuprofen was going to do anything. She needed a narcotic, but opiates could not be bought over the counter.

The doctor's appointment would be for the official results of her cancer screening, although María was clear about her illness. She didn't need a doctor to tell her she was dying. At the initial exam, the tumor had been visible. The doctor had pulled Ana aside while I waited with María in the hallway. "Her cancer is well advanced. Even without a biopsy," he had told Ana, "I could clearly see the tumor in the uterus. Now we just wait to see if it is benign or malignant."

"We'll stop by Monday afternoon to give you the details of when we'll pick you up for the appointment."

"They're not going to do another test, are they?" She meant the biopsy, the excision from the inside of a piece of the tumor. Ana said María howled in pain, that the doctor offered no local anesthesia.[5]

"No, the tests are all done. We're going to find out the results and hopefully the doctor will tell us what we can do for the pain, ok?"

"So Ana will come and pick me up next week?"

I exchanged a worried glance with Núria. Ana would not be picking María up. Ana had asked if she could step away from the case. It had been a long time coming. Sitting through the biopsy had taken Ana to the edge of her abilities to accompany María. There were too many parallels with her own life. Ana's grandmother, the woman who had raised her, also had uterine cancer, also malignant and inoperable. She couldn't keep following both so closely. Emotionally, it was too much. "While I was there with María," Ana had cried after we had dropped María back to the streets, after the biopsy, "all I could think about was my own grandmother, how I had gone through two such moments now, Jon. Two! When María cried out all I heard was my grandmother's cries. I don't think I can go through two of these, Jon."

"For sure Jon and I will be there with you, María." Núria covered it up as well as possible, "We won't know until Monday when we make the schedule for the week whether Ana can come."

"That Ana. You know we've known each other for a long time. There's not another woman like her in the world."

Yes, I wanted to add, but we all need help sometimes, even Ana. Especially Ana. It was too long on the frontlines, of meeting the emotional and physical challenges of the street head-on. The cycles of stress and anxiety made those of us who worked in direct care live in a constant state of emergency preparedness. The little crises of every day built up over time, and, when the inevitable emergency did occur, we would be thrown into crisis mode for an indefinite amount of time. Most of what we did was react—not act—to any situation. Finding our equilibrium in the midst of emotional challenges was our work life. But ten years of it would have been too much for anybody. I broached the subject with Ana after some of our more difficult moments. How much longer do you think you can continue to do this, Ana? Her answer at first was five years. Then three. Then maybe two. It all depended, she would say, on the support she received around her. There were days she felt she could go on for ten more years, and others when she wanted to quit right there and never come back. I kept encouraging her to plan her exit, because it wouldn't be easy for her or for the organization. Sometimes I thought she was waiting for the older kids, the ones she started with ten years ago—María's kids and their cohort—I thought she was waiting for their cases to resolve themselves, for the kids to disappear, be imprisoned, go home, or die. Otherwise the guilt of having abandoned them after so many years would have weighed too heavy. No, she wanted them to abandon her. She wouldn't have to say goodbye. Until then, she would continue to visit them on the streets, in their homes, or in prison.

While we were searching for better options for María, I was starting to lose hope that we would ever know the fate of Blue Eyes.

## GOING TO PRISON

"Jon! Oh Jon!" was called after me as I walked through the office. I turned and saw Liduvina's excited face pop out from the break room.

"I have a favor to ask of you, Jon."

"A little late to be having lunch, isn't it?" I asked, entering the break room. Liduvina was picking through a Tupperware container with the remnants of *moro*—beans and rice mixed together—and fried plantain. Epifanio sat across from her with a tiny plastic cup of coffee, almost the size of a demitasse. It was so sugared, I could see the sludge sitting at the bottom through the opaque plastic, a sweet sediment.

"I was at the Justice Palace all day long," she replied. "This is the first chance I've had to eat. I don't like eating in the streets, you know?" What she didn't add was why—she was a Seventh Day Adventist and tried to keep a strict vegetarian diet. Yet, even this habit had begun to loosen when she was out on the job with us, as we would order plates of fried chicken to eat with the kids. She had started to pick gingerly at a wing or leg after one of the kids we were with gave her a hard time, saying, "What, the lawyer doesn't share with the rest of us?"

"So what's going on? What do you need?"

"Well," she began, placing the fork in the plastic container and wiping her mouth with a napkin, "I was at the Justice Palace trying to work on Nico's case. But there are some things I need to know from Nico. I've never met him before."

"You've never met Nico?"

"No. I don't know who he is or even what he looks like. Everything I know about him I learned from Ana, you, and his girlfriend. I went to follow up with the magistrate to see why they are keeping him in La Victoria without charges. I couldn't find much out without talking to him directly, first."

"You mean you're going to La Victoria? Can I go?" I eagerly asked.

"Oh goodness! I was hoping you would say that. I don't want to go alone."

To call La Victoria a prison is an understatement. La Victoria began its life as a detention for political detainees and criminal prisoners during the changeover from Trujillo's hard dictatorship to Balaguer's "soft" autocratic rule. For many years, it was the only federal prison on the island. Infamous, every Dominican is familiar with the myth of La Victoria.

"You ever been there?" Epifanio asked.

"No, I've never had to go before," Lidu admitted uneasily.

"Well, you are in for a treat," he laughed. "You at least saw the movie, right?" Earlier in the year, a Dominican filmmaker had released a movie about a man who voluntarily enters La Victoria to find and seek revenge on his son's killer.[6] It had been extremely popular and, because it was filmed inside the prison, had been heralded as realistic and frank. The kids we worked with, in their fascination with anything that could depict part of their reality, endlessly discussed its cinéma vérité quality. Most had snuck into the theater multiple times to see the film.

"I couldn't sit through it." she said, "It was too violent for me."

Ana walked in on the conversation. "What? La Victoria? Oh, I agree, honey. Way too violent. What an awful movie."

"Sure, but that is what La Victoria is like," Epifanio commented.

"Don't try to scare her, Epi. Listen, I've been to La Victoria many times. On visiting days, everyone is on their best behavior. You'd be surprised. Plus, you never know who you'll see in there," Ana laughed. "The last time I went, I ran into a cousin of my husband's in there."

"If you could come too, Ana, I'd greatly appreciate it. I'm going next Wednesday to see Nico."

"Nico? Oh, sure. I'd love to talk to Nico. It's good to go visit the young men when they are in prison. You know Nico doesn't have family. It's just his girlfriend Luisa and us."

It would not be the complete truth to say Nico ended up in La Victoria through no fault of his own, but for the record it was not for robbery or drug charges. It was street revenge that put Nico behind bars.

Plaza Güibia was a hotspot for criminal economies and, by all accounts, has had this reputation of being a locus of the underworld element for at least a decade. Boys from poorer neighborhoods of the city would flock to the ramshackle plaza to squander an afternoon, swimming on the polluted beach. In the morning, aspiring teenage baseball players would use the beach sand to run drills. And at night, the cement kiosks would come alive, serving beer and rum and blasting the latest in merengue and bachata out onto the Malecón. On the surface, all appeared innocent, or, if not innocent, at least within the normal parameters of life in the city.

There was another layer to the Plaza. Below the crumbling kiosks and the broken pavers, right on the trash-filled beach were the abandoned businesses, the physical support for part of the plaza above. As part of my work, I developed the double vision to see beyond the surfaces of things, beyond the mere appearance. I didn't just see the plaza and the dilapidated buildings below. It was a different sort of double vision. I saw the teenagers swimming on afternoons, but I also saw the older men looking greedily at their wet bodies from the overlooking plaza, hoping to arrange a trick with the right combination of cash or consumer goods. I saw the hopefuls running on the beach in the morning and the homeless kids sleeping in the crevices under the overhangs that lined the sand. I saw the nightlife on the plaza, the good times as young couples strolled along or bought food and I saw the covert sales, the drug and prostitution transactions taking place in the darkened niches. I knew too much to not have this double vision. It tainted every tableau I saw in the city. Nothing was ever what it appeared to be, as though I was trapped in a permanent state of suspicion.

But Plaza Güibia was the worst, a place I knew too well. The majority of the kids we worked with slept or hung out in and around the plaza. They were intricately linked to the underground economies of theft, drugs, and prostitution that webbed the plaza. Linked, but they were without any real power. Far from the hub, they were the last node, free falling without a net.

Nico, in his early twenties, was very much a part of the inner workings of the denizens of the plaza. There was a group of "homeless" adults who were the controllers, the ones that moved the goods and services—both illegal and legal—for the more distant owners of the plaza's businesses. These owners, in turn, hired their representatives to watch over the controllers and enforce their will and regulate the commerce. These adult controllers were not "homeless" in the true sense of the term. They had chosen, at some point in their street careers, to make the plaza their home. Some had arrived, lured by the drugs and easy access to sex, first feeding their vice and later, deciding to stay on, gaining either power or trust within the plaza's upper echelon. Others had been homeless or at least tied to other street economies and came to the plaza because business was good. They outfitted the abandoned buildings "given" to them by their patrons—crumbling edifices retrofitted with wood plank doors and padlocks, putrid mattresses and suitcases or duffle bags for clothes. Each controller would, in turn, exert influence over groups of the boys and adolescents who lived on the streets, offering protection, shelter, jobs, and drugs in exchange for work, sex, or drugs—the rate of exchange always changing depending on desperation.

Everything was up for negotiation at any time, everything driven by the market of immediate needs.

Nico had been making a transition, slowly moving from the outside toward the inner circle of the plaza. He had the right reputation of being violent and threatening that had him being used as one of the enforcers of order on the plaza, regulating business of who could sell what in the area through intimidation. Freelancers were not tolerated: all drugs had to be okayed by the owners of the business establishments and the ultimate "owner" of the plaza, who was rumored to be a high-ranking army official.

The trouble with Nico, however, did not come from this side of his life on the plaza. Like all good survivalists, Nico had more than one avenue of support. Since he had been fifteen, Nico had cultivated what could best be termed a "love" relationship with a wealthy Puerto Rican client. I am not sure what Nico's history in the remunerated sex economy was, but by the time I knew him, he had given up prostitution for the role of area bruiser, except for this one long-term client. For whatever reason, Nico kept this man as part of his life.[7] It could be for the extravagance of the Puerto Rican's gifts, the opportunity for large sums of money whenever he came to visit, and the fact that the patron didn't live in Santo Domingo and thus the relationship didn't become a burden to Nico's masculine image. It is hard to say. Nico's relationship to this man was well known. Asking after Nico one afternoon, his girlfriend, Luisa, had simply replied, "Nico? He's with his man. That Boricua picked him up last week and Nico hasn't been back since."[8] Nico would return from such trips with new shoes, new clothes, a cell phone, and even a gold necklace for Luisa, purportedly a gift from the Puerto Rican, just for her.

A couple of months before, as we stopped one afternoon to drop off the kids from that day's activity, Luisa came storming up to the mini-bus. The look in her eye was piercing as she disregarded traffic on the busy Malecón and ran at the bus, weaving in and out of the passing cars, making them stop for her.

Luisa stood on the street on the driver's side and pounded at the chauffeur's window. Kennedy and Luisa had a good relationship—he knew how to talk her down from her violent temper by being unfazed and using the right street slang, as if he knew what he was talking about. Ken motioned that Luisa go around to the side door. At the pneumatic hiss of the door opening, Luisa burst upon the scene.

"They got Nico in custody! That bitch got the cops to take Nico away last night!" No greeting, just the torrent of words ejecting from Luisa. She was agitated, standing at the ledge of the bottom step, her skinny body expanding in her ire to fill the doorframe.

"What's going on, Luisa? You've got no proper greeting for us? Is that how you treat people like us?" Kennedy spoke the idiom of respect.

"No man, I'm just pissed at that bitch." And a bit high, I thought. I could see the red lines veining her eyes and even though she was upset, the jittery movements and increased agitation was for sure caused by some substance.

"Why don't you tell us what happened, Luisa, from the beginning," I urged.

"I'll tell you what happened. That transvestite whore Débora ended up being a rich motherfucker, that's what happened."

At the mention of Débora's name, Ramoncito, who had been talking to Héctor in the back of the bus, spoke up, insolently and bravely crossing Luisa. "You take that back! She's in bad shape because of Nico."

"Yeah, you just say that because you're her bitch." Ramoncito had been under Débora's spell for months. All the kids had been talking about how they had started living together in Débora's cubicle of a room down on the beach. What a sixteen-year-old kid like Ramoncito saw in an aging, mid-thirties transvestite I didn't really know. Ramoncito was taking a risk with his street identity by shacking up with Débora, getting into more fights and taking more shit from all the other kids. It wasn't that he was receiving sexual favors from Débora—most of the young men who slept in the plaza had utilized her services on occasion. It was that Ramoncito expressed it in such exclusive terms. He had spontaneously told a stunned Héctor, "Man, I feel so much better now that Débora and I are married.[9] So much more calm, you know?"

I placed my hand lightly on Luisa's shoulder, partly to keep her from springing up from where she stood and going after Ramoncito and partly to get her attention back to Ken and myself. "Tell us what happened between Nico and Débora, alright?"

"Last night, we're sitting around the kiosk drinking beers—me, Nico, Mamey, Débora, a whole bunch of us. And we're drinking, right? Nico's buying because he's got money these days, he's got some cash." Luisa left out that Nico had cash because the Puerto Rican had been to visit. "Everything is cool. We're joking and laughing and drinking. Then that bitch says, 'Well, here's to the Boricua and Nico's hard work.' That doesn't sit well with Nico but he lets it go, you know? He doesn't want to ruin the good vibe we're on because of her. But she doesn't let up. Every new bottle she's like, 'Here's to the Boricua.' And then she goes too far, man. She says, 'Here's to the Boricua and Nico's hard-working ass. How much does that ass of yours cost, Niquito?' And that did it, man, Nico lost it. 'Cause you know Nico doesn't give up his backside for no one. That's not what he's into. He's no faggot.[10]

"So Nico let her know it. Hits her face—bam!—right in the nose. And Débora, she takes those nails of hers and gouges Nico's face and arms. He's got these long, deep nail tracks here"—she points to her cheeks—"and here"— forearms. "Nico's had enough and breaks a bottle and goes at her with the bottle, cutting that ugly face of hers, beating her up. Mamey and Gambao had to pull him off her and send her to the hospital. Seems she squealed to the police. This morning the cops from the Justice Palace came and picked him up. The Justice Palace! The bitch has some uncle that's high up.

"She's just jealous, you know? Because Nico has a rich and steady client while all she ever gets are the 20 peso suck jobs from the palomos." Luisa indicated Ramoncito. That took Ramoncito to the edge. He bolted from the back seat and sprang down the aisle to attack Luisa, who stood at the front of the bus in triumph. Héctor interposed his large frame, leading with his gut out, into the aisle, restraining a furious Ramoncito.

"That's enough, Luisa. You can get off the bus. We'll have the lawyer make inquiries at the Justice Palace." Kennedy said, getting Luisa to step out, back to the sidewalk. She walked the short distance to the rear windows and began egging the struggling Ramoncito on.

"What, you want to go out and fight?" Héctor asked.

"Let me go, man. Let me get out there." Ramoncito repeated.

Héctor's voice boomed, "Take it to the plaza, Luisa. We don't want a public spectacle here on the street."

Luisa got one more taunt in and darted across the steady traffic. When she was halfway across, Héctor removed his body from the aisle and released Ramoncito. His wiry figure and teased out afro charged out of the bus and across the street, where Luisa waited, tough as nails.

Kennedy put the bus in gear. "Let's get outta here before the rocks start flying."

The damage to Débora had been worse than Luisa let on. While she had unleashed her version to Kennedy and me, a sullen Ramoncito had related to Héctor what had happened. Kennedy pulled onto the Malecón and headed toward the office. I kept a keen eye toward the plaza, hoping they wouldn't hurt each other too much. By the time Ramoncito had crossed the street I could only make out the two blurry spots begin their rumble against the intense halo of the sun.

"Well, the kid's feelin' bad. I don't know why he tells me these things," Héctor laughed, "The kid's screwed up, hookin' up with that kind. You know they've been livin' together for a couple of months now?"

Kennedy looked at us from the rearview mirror, "Love's blind, as they say."

"Ha! More like love's a bitch for Ramoncito. Hookin' up with Débora's meant he's marked out by Nico. He's the one who's been beating up so bad on Ramoncito. Anyway, according to him, Débora's in really bad shape. Nico did a lot of damage—broke her nose and cut her up bad with the bottle. Sounds like he was going for the throat. One of the taxi drivers who hangs out at Güibia and likes the boys took her to the hospital. Ramoncito said he had to give it up in exchange for the free ride."

"That's rough. Are there no good Samaritans anymore?" Kennedy intoned.

"The taxi driver wanted compensation," Héctor replied. "Poor Ramoncito just had no money to pay. I told him that, despite the cost, it was noble what he did. Probably saved her life, getting her to the hospital. You know his reply? 'I couldn't let her die,' he says. 'I couldn't leave her there 'cause I love her.'"

La Victoria lies on the outskirts of the capital, even as the northern suburbs have expanded over the years to meet the city. In its early days, the prison must have felt isolated, surrounded by small hamlets and agricultural fields. The narrow two-lane road curves idyllically through the countryside, oblivious to the fact that it heads to a notorious prison house. It is as if the road to San Quentin were a country lane.

The prison complex rises out of the flat expanse of green that surrounds it before you arrive to the eponymous town. The buildings lay in one continuous section behind the razor-wired concrete walls with armed sentries perched atop periodic watchtowers. The first time I saw the walls of the fence I couldn't help remember that the first prisoners had been political prisoners, not criminals. It altered the vision before me, changed the significance of the isolation of the complex, the segmentation of the fence by the watchtowers, the slits in the tower windows for a rifle's barrel.

The turn-off to approach the prison widened to a four-lane promenade separated by a grassy median. It was not for aesthetics, this low approach, but for the clear visibility, the ease of seeing what comes and goes. All along the walls a wide swath had been cut, almost to the bare brown earth, for easy viewing.

Epifanio parked the truck in the designated clearing a good distance from the first checkpoint and entrance. There was almost a carnivalesque air, or, at least the breezy confidence of commerce. Vendors strolled about, carrying all the imagined goods loved ones were deprived of on the inside—toothbrushes, deodorant, soaps, and shampoos. Boxed treats and homemade Dominican specialties like the sickly sweet dulce de leche held pride of place. But the most popular items were the cigarettes, whose vendors didn't even need to move around to make a good business: people came to them and bought up the packs and half-packs of Marlboro Reds and the cheaper knock-offs.

It was going to be a steamy day, as already I was sweating in the damp air that hit us as we opened the truck doors and emerged from the chill of the air conditioning. I think we all made a collective groan at the heat. It was only mid-morning.

"Remember to leave behind your purse, Lidu, you don't want to carry anything in you won't need, just what we are taking for Nico in the plastic bags."

The line broke into two to enter the prison, men on the right, women on the left. "We'll see you on the other side," Epifanio joked. There were many fewer men than women, most being older—much older than either Epi or myself. We would be on the other side long before Ana and Liduvina.

In front of us sat a young man at a manual typewriter on a rough-hewn wooden table. The young policeman wore the same tan uniform, but he wore it badly, a sloppy carelessness to his dress that one rarely finds with the military. Behind him, as if in contrast, stood his superior, sharply dressed and well put together, the polyester of the uniform molding to his wide physique. His largeness and excessive neatness would be what would make people fear him. He maintained and assured order without actively looking over the typist's shoulder.

I handed the typist my passport. I expected some comment, a question as to my purpose of coming to the prison. Surely it couldn't be every day that an American would show up for visiting day. But no comment issued from either the typist or his commander, not even a raised eyebrow. He entered my name on the growing list, deftly pecking away at the keys of the old machine. In exchange for my passport, which he filed in an open rectangular box next to the typewriter, the cop gave me a well-worn piece of cardstock with a number written in thick black marker.

"Take the number to the door. You'll be searched there." He indicated the line of three men waiting outside a wooden door that led to a small enclosure. I placed myself behind the last man while Epifanio went through the registration process. The door shortly opened and the four of us in line were ordered into the windowless shed. I turned to look at Epi, who was still waiting for the typist to enter his name. My hesitation was met with another bark to enter the building. I followed the older men inside.

It quickly became apparent what was to happen. The room was tightly packed—the four of us visitors plus two policemen. The other visitors, without being told, removed articles of clothing—shoes, belts, and finally, their pants. Not having any grounds to make an objection, I followed suit, watching to see how much clothing these gray-haired, grandfatherly figures were going to take off. They stood in their shirt tails and underwear, waiting for inspection. I fell in beside them, half naked, holding my jeans out in mimicry of the other three.

The cops rummaged through the pockets and cuffs of the jeans, examined the waistband for contraband. I knew from our kids how easy it was to create stash holes in clothes for hits of crack and marijuana. I was surprised at the thoroughness of the job and the docility of these three old men as they were searched.

The police didn't stop with the jeans. They patted the waistband of the underwear, the sides, and then asked us to spread our legs, lift out on the leg bands of our underwear and shake up and down to see if anything fell out. I was relieved that this was as far as the search went.

Satisfied that the four of us were not smuggling drugs or weapons into the facility, the policemen signaled it was ok to put on our clothes again. The funny thing, though, despite the great demonstration of searching for contraband and the seriousness with which they did their job, it was well known that a healthy underground prison economy existed, whereby drugs and knives (or things that could be fashioned into knives) made their way inside. Members of the prison guard, for sums of money, would pass these items into circulation. The visitor search was not to prevent illegal substances from entering, but rather, to control access to this commerce.

Upon exiting the shed on the opposite side from where we had entered, our forearms were stamped a deep crimson just above the wrist. This would be our only assurance that we would not be mistaken for a prisoner once we walked through the door.

I waited alone in the courtyard between the shed and the main entrance gate for a good five minutes. The guards seemed to be taking their time with Epifanio, and I knew the women were even farther behind because of the longer line. I wasn't about to go through the main entrance by myself. I could wait.

A stream of women came out from the adjacent shack about every five minutes. They carried tins of cooked food and assorted care packages that had been rummaged through and picked over by the guards—cookies, tooth-brushes, toiletries. These women were brave family members coming to visit their sons, brothers, lovers, in prison. Visiting days were twice a week, Wednesdays and Sundays, and these women would be there, ready to enter with new items. I am not sure if that is from devotion, dedication, or uncondi-tional love. We, those of us at Niños, would go visit the kids in some unsavory places or when they were in most need, too. We would stand by them in the hospital, under arrest, on the streets. We tried to be present when and where others wouldn't be. But these women who entered prison knew a form of ded-ication—whether out of duty or love—that surpassed anything we could ever do for one of our kids. We could never replace what families do. It just wasn't possible. No matter how many times Ana would justify a visit or an action she did with Nico, saying that a kid didn't have family, that we were his family—it was only partially true. We advocated for our kids, we cared for them, we dem-onstrated affection for them—we even loved them unconditionally—but we were not family. Indeed, I do not think it was ever desirable to assert that we were in any way close to being like their families. The difference between us and the women arriving to visit their loved ones was a constancy and devo-tion even the most dedicated of us could not match.

The others finally joined me, having made it through the screening. We were in the courtyard between the high fence and the main buildings. There was one more set of gates to go through before we were in with the prison-ers. We followed the flow of visitors down the path and to the short cement tunnel through the fortress walls that led into the main building. At the end of the tunnel was a wrought iron gate with another guard. Beyond the gate was a large, bright courtyard lined with the expectant faces of prisoners, waiting for a visitor, any visitor. I could sense the double scent of hope and desperation in the air. We showed the guard our temporary ink tattoos and pushed through the six-foot-tall metal turnstile. Despite being inside the prison facility, there was no evident police presence. The guards ended, it seemed, at the inside of the gate, waiting on the outskirts. They were ultimately useless if there was any sort of disturbance among the prisoners. They could lock the gate, I thought, and let the inmates hash out whatever problem they had among themselves.

We were about to negotiate with one of the many inmates milling around the courtyard to find Nico when a voice from one of the corridors called out, "Ana! Ana!" I kept looking for Nico in the crowds, medium height, built, light-skinned. Nico was Haitian. He'd come from one of the slums of Port-au-Prince as a child and risen to prominence on his portion of the street. His Puerto Rican client had footed the bill for an illegal birth certificate, and Nico had petitioned for an adult national ID card. He was more Dominican now than the scores of poor Dominicans who had never been declared at birth and, hence, were noncitizens.

The voice repeated, calling out Ana's name as it came closer. Ana was not fooled, she gasped, surprised, "Oh my God! Alejandro?"

Coming toward us was a different Haitian than the one we expected, one who had also been legalized through false papers. Alejandro's tall body loomed toward us, ecstatic to see Ana. His long arms encircled Ana without hesitation. At well over six feet tall, he enfolded Ana's short stature. He greeted the rest of us exuberantly, even though of the four of us, Alejandro only knew Ana and myself. When I offered my hand, he pulled me into a quick hug. It was uncharacteristic of this young man to show such enthusiasm. Alejandro, as I knew him on the streets, was laconic and perpetually easygoing, a fact at odds with his reputation of having quick fingers.

As excited as he was to see us, I was even more overjoyed to see him here. It meant he wasn't dead, that he was not the "Haitian" listed on those police reports I had read. If Alejandro was here, in prison, it meant that maybe he knew something about Blue Eyes.

"Oh Alejandro, we had no idea you were here," Ana explained, "We'd come to visit Nico and here you are."

"Nico's here. Dani is here. That glue-sniffer from Parque Enriquillo, the one they call Cocólo, is here. And Blue Eyes is here."

"Blue Eyes is here?" Alejandro nodded his head vehemently yes in reply. "Word on the street was that he was murdered, shot to death," I said, "We've been looking for him for months, worried that we'd never know."

"No, he's here. He's in bad shape. It was his friend who was shot, right next to Blue Eyes, shot just like this," Alejandro mimicked the distance between his body and Ana's, showing how close the friend had been at the time of the shooting, a mere five inches away. "He's just a little crazy, you know? Psychologically he's not good."

"What do you mean?" I could imagine symptoms akin to post-traumatic stress syndrome but I wanted Alejandro to elaborate.

"You know, Jon, he arrived here and wouldn't talk. Got into a lot of fights. He's better than he was, but he spends most of his time high, more than we normally would. Come on, I'll take you to him."

The four of us followed Alejandro down one of the open corridors. Men were everywhere. They hunched down on their heels in what little shade was made by a turn in the walls. They stood in the sun smoking cigarettes. They gambled on dice rolls in small groups. We entered out onto another courtyard, as plain and sun-washed as the first one we had been in. Off to one side, a six-foot-by-six-foot canvas awning had been erected, with folding metal chairs and a podium. In hand-painted letters across the back of the awning hung a crude sign proclaiming that Jesus loved us. Most of the chairs were empty but for a few men with their heads bowed dutifully. I envied their shaded respite. "Hey Alejandro, can't we go sit under there?" I motioned to the shade.

Alejandro laughed. "No way man. Not unless you are ready to find the Lord. See that man in the back row? He's the prison pastor—an inmate but who has become a pastor. And he's a mean son of a bitch, too. There are many churches in here. All of them have their territory."

"So, what, you join a church you get their protection?"

"Exactly. The only one that's not that way is the Catholic chapel. We can go sit in there after I find Blue Eyes."

"You guys who know each other from Niños, do you all stick together, help each other out?" Lidu, like myself, seemed to have come out of the initial shock of being inside the prison. Things had started to take on a normal patina.

"No. Not really. Blue Eyes and I do, because we're *panas full*.[11] Dani's got his own business going on here. He's been here almost a year. Nico, when he's around, hangs with us sometimes, but we never ran around together on the streets, you know? Blue Eyes and I aren't part of the Güibia crowd. And Cocólo, he's got it bad. They're always beating up on him and using him 'cause he's out of it most of the time. I leave him alone. I'm not going to stick my neck out for no glue-sniffer."

"Use him? For what?" I'm glad it was Lidu that asked, and not me.

"Yeah, use him. You know, like a woman." Alejandro replied circumspectly. "It's not worth trying to help him, you know? It just causes trouble for a guy and I don't want any fights. Look at Nico. That guy's been in *la plancha* at least once a month for fighting. He's got a hot head."

"La plancha? What's that?" It was my turn to play naïve. As far as I knew, la plancha was an iron or a metal sheet used as a grill.

"La plancha is where they send you if you cause too many problems in here. It's a small space, narrow, and they put you in there like you were lying on a tomb. It's a slab of cement that's how they got the name because it is smooth like a grill for hamburgers. They put you in there for a few days as punishment. Nico's been in there at least one week every month. Blue Eyes is probably getting high. He's been smoking a lot of weed. Spends all the money his mom brought him on the stuff."

"His mom knows he's here?"

"Yeah, man. She's been here like twice since Christmas to visit. Says she's workin' on the papers to get him out of here. He hasn't been tried. The cops brought him in because of what he saw, but he didn't do nothin' but the breaking and entering. I know where he goes to smoke. I'll find him."

Alejandro left us in the courtyard. He and Blue Eyes had always been well known for their propensity for smoking marijuana. In the early evening, on my way home from work, I would inevitably run into them. They would sit in the little plaza by the YMCA, just in front of the Parque Independencia. It was a cheerless place, despite the ragged multicolored umbrellas of the fruit sellers and deep red tones of the apples and grapes or the bright orange and green, if it was mango season. The two of them would sit on one of the dark green painted iron benches facing the buildings in the fog of a pot smoke high that ran between the jocular and the maudlin. Every time I walked by they would hit me up for money, claiming they were so hungry, so very hungry. I would look them straight in their bloodshot eyes and flatly refuse, telling them they wouldn't have the munchies if they hadn't smoked so much. At first they denied it. Later, as they grew to trust me, they'd laugh and admit it, saying how boring life could be without a little weed now and then. They smoked a lot. I couldn't imagine how much Blue Eyes was using now if even Alejandro commented on the increase.

"Ana!" Another call came from across the courtyard. It wasn't just that they all knew her or that she stood out among the field of young men we worked with. Ana was the organization, the constant presence that interacted with them. They didn't see the people behind her that allowed her to do her job. Indeed, for much of the history of the organization there weren't a lot of people supporting the on-the-ground workers. Three or four women had done it all.

"Ana! What a surprise!" Nico, despite the enthusiasm in his voice, ambled in a controlled pace toward where we stood. He was too self-consciously aware of his tough demeanor to do otherwise.

He wore a pair of clean khaki slacks and a rayon button-down Hawaiian-style shirt with Japanese anime characters. On his feet was a clean but worn pair of flip-flops. He looked like he was out for a moonlit stroll on the beach. If Débora had done any damage to Nico, it didn't show. The nail marks on the face had healed. And if he'd been getting into fights, as Alejandro intimated, he must have been knocking out his opponents before they had a chance to strike back.

He wasn't a particularly attractive young man. His face was hard, angular in the nose and chin, with pockmarks on the cheeks from either bad acne scars or some skin infection, like scabies, which is easily contracted on the streets. He was muscular without being bulky, and he carried himself with a confidence bordering on cocky. But around Ana he softened considerably, to the point of being almost docile.

Seeing him, self-possessed as he was after such a long absence, I doubted he needed our assistance in any tangible way. This was a purely social call. He would take care of himself. We dealt with him on the street because he was such an integral part of the social environment of the plaza, but he was not the type to which you offered support. That would be insulting to someone so self-sufficient. "Did Luisa tell you I was here?" he asked after smothering Ana in a hug and offering the rest of us a sturdy handshake.

"Yeah. We heard about Débora. You really messed her up, you know?"

"Who? That little faggot? She ought to be more careful about what she says. Did Luisa tell you how it was Débora who started it? How she kept hounding me and wouldn't quit? What was I to do?"

"Sure, but Nico," I replied, "don't you think you might have gone a bit overboard? Supposedly her face was pretty smashed up, a broken nose and everything."

Nico dismissed the human damage with a slight shrug of his shoulders. "She's just jealous, especially since I'd never touch her. It's a show, anyway. You know what she did though? She's got some connections in the military. Her daddy is some major or something. Now they've started proceedings against me and they won't let me post bail."

"So what are you going to do?"

"I got a lawyer from my friend." He meant the Puerto Rican, I supposed. "He's gonna help me get this taken care of. I'll be out soon enough. What I need, though, if you think you could do me a favor, is check on what the holdup is, you know? I can't call from here, so I don't know what's going on unless Luisa comes and she can't always find the money to visit, that crack addict. She smokes it all away. You think you could call my lawyer and see what's going on?"

I pulled Epifanio aside, out of earshot, leaving Nico and Lidu to talk about legal proceedings. "Nico doesn't really need our assistance, does he?" Epi nodded agreement.

Alejandro came strolling down the corridor, alone, nobody following him.

"Where's Blue Eyes?" Ana asked.

"He's coming. He needed a minute to clean up."

"Clean up or sober up?" Ana knew better.

"Both. Listen, Ana, he's in bad shape. He's really high right now."

"Then maybe it's better we leave, if he's so out of it."

"No! Ana, he really wants to see you. He just doesn't want you to see him that way. He'll be here soon. Just wait, please."

I'd never seen Alejandro like this before. He was always polite, but this was verging on supplication.

"You're really worried about him, aren't you?" I asked.

"He's my best friend. This shooting has really hit him hard."

So we waited. Minutes passed. The quiet outdoor awning with the seats started to fill with a trickle of inmates. Tambourines were produced from behind the podium and distributed. The service started with smacks on the off beats with the plastic instruments and the deep male voices booming out their love for a vengeful God. The song's chorus spoke of being purified and cleansed of sin by Jesus' blood. I saw Lidu mouthing the words along with the tune. In a few minutes it went from a subdued murmur to a full assault on the eardrums. I couldn't hear anyone unless they spoke in my ear.

The noise enveloped the courtyard. I didn't notice Blue Eyes slouch into the area until Ana tapped my shoulder and discreetly pointed in his direction. He wore a pair of off-white shorts that hung loose around his slight frame, covering his knees. He had cleaned up—face washed and a clean short-sleeve shirt, striped red and white in parody of a prison outfit. He shuffled toward us in his flip-flops, a slow, hesitant movement. It was a relief to see him, after many months thinking him dead on the streets. He may have been incarcerated, but he was alive.

He was too high to cry, beyond emotion at that moment as if he were slipping through a murk that the rest of us could not see. He clearly knew we were there, but there was a detachment about him, like a dreamer realizing he was in the dream and wanting to watch the nocturnal scene. I thought Ana was going to burst with joy. I was ready to cry myself. But Blue Eyes sidled up next to Ana with hands in his pockets, not offering even a hug.

The racket was a so great I couldn't hear the exchange, but Ana spoke to him in visibly admonishing tones. He removed his hands and wrapped them around Ana's body, burying his head in her shoulder. Still, he would not cry.

Alejandro led us through the corridor then, away from the pounding tambourines and prison choir. Ana kept Blue Eyes close, holding onto his hand. We came out into a different courtyard with large openings cut into the cement that had wrought iron gates attached and opened. Some of the openings had sheets hanging for privacy. Others were free of obstruction, allowing a view into the common cells where row after row of mattresses lined the floor. The cells were cluttered, claustrophobic even in the absence of the majority of the inmates. Inside, men sat in their underwear or shirtsleeves. Although shaded from the glaring sun, the airless rooms acted as a sauna with the ambient heat and the mass of human bodies emanating their own energy. Looking in, I was reminded of Renaissance depictions of Hell. All that was missing was the constant lick of flames.

Alejandro led us to one of the open gates on the far end of the courtyard. This one was different—dark, cave-like, a restful dank from the bright and cheerless Caribbean sky seen through prison walls. On the threshold of the chapel, Nico said his goodbyes, thanking us for coming to see him. "With any luck, I'll be out of here and back in the Plaza in a month." (By the time I left over six months later, Nico was still in prison, still waiting for a trial date, and with no possibility of posting bail. Débora's connections were indeed high up. In uncharacteristically blunt language, Lidu summed up Nico's situation after investigating in the Justice Palace about his case: "He's screwed. He may be able to win a trial, but they're going to see that the trial doesn't take place.")

The chapel was lit with one small bulb on an uncovered wire strung up and tacked to the low ceiling near the small altar. There were no vestments, but there was a rough-hewn cross behind the altar. Alejandro and Blue Eyes sat side by side facing the three of us on one bench. They made an odd pair: Alejandro's tall, dark body next to Blue Eye's short white one. Blue Eyes was even more of an anomaly because he was sometimes called Barahonero, or someone from Barahona, a city three hours to the southwest of the capital. In the Dominican Republic, white folks are supposed to be from the Cibao, the north. The darker the skin, the more it is assumed that a person is from the South, especially the Southwest, the implication being that it is closer to Haiti and the Haitian communities that fueled the cash-cropping of the sugar cane plantations. His marbled blue eyes belied his southern origins. Alejandro, on the other hand, although Haitian, came from the North, from near Cap-Haïtien. His mother had brought the family over fifteen years earlier via the northern border crossing. Together, the pair challenged the normal ways of thinking about geography and race in the country.

"Blue Eyes," I said, stumbling over his nickname, thinking that although nicknames express intimacy, it was the wrong kind of fraternity at the moment. I started over, using his full, legal name as I knew it. At the sound of his first name, Blue Eyes looked up into my face. "We thought you were dead. Everyone on the street was saying you had been shot. I went to the Homicide Division and checked police reports. Nobody knew where you were. I really believed you were dead."

"I should be dead," he replied, looking down again at the concrete floor, "They killed Iván, point blank while he hid and I was next to him. I was going to be next."

"Who? Who was shooting at you and Iván?"

"The police."

"Can you tell us what happened, Blue Eyes? Can you tell us what went on?"

He gave a shrug, as if to accede. A lot had happened to this nineteen-year-old man over the years he had spent on the street; I needed to remember that as I reached out and placed a hand empathetically on his knee. But nothing had been as heinous and immediate as this. "You don't have to tell us if you don't want to. We understand it is difficult. This Iván was your friend. Did we know him? Was he from the street?"

"No, man. Iván was from the barrio. He lived in San Carlos with his dad. You wouldn't have known him. Alejandro and I would go up to his house to smoke weed with him. We did some work together." Meaning they orchestrated robberies together. My ears perked up at the mention of San Carlos. That was the barrio where I lived.

"When we broke into the shop, we activated the alarm. I looked around for something to break the alarm but the alarm was way high up and I couldn't reach it." Blue Eyes recounted the scene with a great deal of clarity, despite his drug-induced haze. "I told Iván I couldn't reach it so he climbed on my back and pulled the alarm down. We started looking for money, scrounging around looking for the till, but there was nothing there. I tell him we should go, that there's nothing but he doesn't listen. He says he wants to take some shit then, if there's no money.

"When we get ready to leave, just as we are about to leave the shop, a police car comes by. The car comes by and they stop. Iván, he hides behind one of the chairs. Me, I throw out everything in a box on the floor next to the chair and climb inside, hiding myself. The cops come in and see Iván right away. One says, "I see one, I've got one here. Come out with your hands up." But Iván panics. He's not in his right mind. He tries to escape, running away. And the police shoot him, bam, just like that." Blue Eyes holds his fingers up to his temple as if a pistol and shoots. I don't know if he means that the police shot him execution style or if they had got him from a distance.

"I waited in that box. I didn't move all the time the cops were there. And then the detective arrives to take the body away. He says, 'Hey, what's in this box? It's either gotta be a cat or a rat.' He kicks the box and I'm so scared I jump up. I yell not to shoot me, that I don't have anything. My hands are up in the air and I show them I have nothing. Iván's body is on the floor in front of me, dead.

"The cops take me outside to the car. I can hear them talking about how I saw them shoot Iván. They're saying I will cause them trouble. Then this old lady from next door comes over and asks the detective what's going on, what are they going to do to me. Another cop car comes and they take me away to the station."

"You were lucky," Epifanio interjected, "the police could have shot you."

"You had a guardian angel there," Ana said.

"How do you mean a guardian angel? They shot Iván."

"If that old woman hadn't come out of her house when she did and looked on until the cops took you away, they would have killed you for what you saw. In that sense, she was a guardian angel. Epifanio is right. You should be dead."

Blue Eyes didn't seem uplifted by the thought, but he agreed anyway. "Yeah, you're probably right." I kept looking for any piece of emotion to break through the pot haze he wore like a mantle, but he was so blitzed nothing was going to change the exacting sameness. Not only was he numb from the drug, he was also traumatized from what he had witnessed. But anger, sorrow, a bitter laugh even, would have shown more humanity than Blue Eyes showed in that chapel. In his way, he had shut completely down. I understood Alejandro's preoccupation with his friend.

By the time we left, saying goodbye at the portico from which we had entered, you could tell Blue Eyes was itching to return to his joint and the heaviness it created. That burden made the other burden bearable.

Ana leaned in close to Alejandro as he hugged her good-bye. I could barely make it out, but thought I heard two whispers: hers, telling Alejandro to watch over his friend and Alejandro replying, "You can't watch over what doesn't want to be watched." You can't help who doesn't want help to begin with.

Or, as we were discovering with María, sometimes the appropriate assistance is out of reach and all you can do is stand by the person's side in support.

## OFF THE STREETS

At first she had worried she might be pregnant, that the hardening of her uterus and the pains might be one last miracle child—miracle because María is in her late forties and maybe this could be the child that would lift her off the streets and provide for her. Her other three sons had not been able to, had dragged her back to the streets, or had abandoned her to that life. This cancer, uterine and growing, yes, it may be the child that takes her off the streets for good.

María was not quite ready when we arrived. I left Núria in the taxi and went over alone to the traffic island. María was partially hidden behind some young, scrawny, and sunlight-deprived trees, changing out of her floral print button-down. As I came up to the camp I could see the curved spine and the skin stretched across her back.

"Oh Jon," she greeted me when she had changed tops, "I'm almost ready. Just let me comb my hair." She went over to a blue plastic hamper and pulled out an old purse, some broken sandals, a couple of pairs of pants and, finally, a thick black comb with missing teeth and a gummy spray bottle with what must have been hairspray.

She wet her hair with water from a five-gallon cooking oil container, smoothed it back, and began threading the comb roughly through her mostly graying hair. She didn't have a lot, but it could get straggly and untamable. She stood in front of me, moving her hands over and over her hair. It was rather intimate, watching a woman comb her hair, a private ritual of sorts. I embarrassed easily, so I looked around for something to keep my attention and the only thing that drew me away was her son Negro wrapped in a gray sheet, lying on flattened-out cardboard boxes with three dogs lying about him. Negro's hair was cropped short with patterns almost like a checkerboard. María followed my gaze, saying, "that Negro." She made a crazy sign with her finger at her temple and laughed.

"Coqui got up early today," she explained, putting on the finishing touches. "He collects bottles all day now. That's all he does." She indicated a pile of green glass beer bottles near where Negro slept. As if conjured by his name, Coqui appeared, crossing the broad avenue to where we were. He carried opened bags of oatmeal and two pieces of ham that looked slightly off-colored and with a similar bite mark in each. We greeted each other with a touch of closed fists. He was shirtless and unbelievably thin. His pants were held in place by a worn leather belt but the back loop was torn off the pants, and they sagged around his waist. He wore no underwear and he had no fat around his lower back. All I could think of was famine victims, but his famine was crack and it had slowly eaten away every ounce of reserve his body once had.

Coqui bent down to where his younger brother lay, pushing a piece of ham under his nose, trying to rouse him awake. Negro started and angrily pushed Coqui out of the way. He sat up, his body shooting up like a high-tension wire. María just laughed, not quite a cackle, but not quite good-natured either, and said, "Come on Jon. Let's go. I'll see you later, kids, God willing." We left Coqui and Negro to their breakfast.

The oncology unit—the only one, as far as I knew, in Santo Domingo—was a large pink building located within the campus of the sprawling public university. It was a busy place, even early on a Tuesday morning. María, Núria, and I sat in the full waiting room outside the chemotherapy treatment center's sealed double doors. The aging poly black chairs were filled with a diverse cross-section of Santo Domingo's population: as the only chemo facility for this part of the island, poor and rich alike sat patiently for their turn. Besides me and what looked like an aging husband accompanying his ill wife, all were women. Some wore fancy headscarves to cover their hair loss, coral pink and cobalt blue affairs in rich patterns. Every woman was wearing the best outfit she could muster, as if attending a wedding or Sunday services. María was no exception. I don't know where she had found it, but she was in a forest green velvet and taffeta gown that looked like a 1980s prom dress. The spaghetti straps held the dress on her stick figure, edging into the protruding scapula. It didn't seem to matter, though, what María was wearing. There was a solidarity in the room that transcended class—the first time I had ever felt that on this island where the gap between rich and poor is marked by heightened attention to consumption of material goods. Disease had broken down social barriers as the few rich women in the crowd mixed easily with their poorer neighbors, talking about treatment, residual effects of the chemo, and hopes of remission.

María was immediately drawn into the atmosphere, as women all around her wanted to know what her story was, where she was in the treatment process. I wanted to whisk María out of the room, not for embarrassment but for shame—we didn't think she would be a candidate for chemo treatment, not only because her cancer was so advanced but also because we couldn't afford the time and money required. But that was mainly why we were there, waiting to find out what options María had. María had said on countless occasions that she wasn't afraid of death, but that she was afraid of the unknown, of not knowing exactly what it was she had and what has going to happen.

María excused herself to a small, closet-like bathroom in the corner of the waiting room. How she figured it was there, I don't know. I didn't see it, mistaking it for storage for cleaning supplies. She gingerly tucked herself into the room and shut the door. There must have been no working light because none emitted under the cracks of the uneven door. What a luxury a toilet stool must be for María. Few places in Santo Domingo would allow the indigent in to use their restrooms.

I seized the opportunity to talk privately with Núria. "What do you think?"

"I'm not sure why we are here, you know?" she replied, leaning forward in the chair, "We know it's terminal. She knows it is terminal. We can't afford chemotherapy and even if we could, I'm not sure I would want to put her through that process."

"Especially considering the conditions in which she lives. Chemotherapy destroys the body's defenses, too. She could die of any infection on the street."

"So, what do we do? Why are we here?"

"Because Ana couldn't do it. Because I don't have the guts either to tell María to her face that the options are few. I would much rather have the doctor do it, you know, as some sort of voice of authority that wouldn't come from us."

"In other words, we're here because we want someone to do our dirty work. What if the doctor recommends chemotherapy?"

"I don't know. As much as we love and admire María for who she is, there are limits to what we can do. We have gotten her this far, and no matter what happens, we aren't going to abandon her."

My jaw quivered, "What we should be talking to her about is how to plan for a dignified death, but I'm not ready for that, either."

Núria's reply was cut short. At the sound of the bathroom door, we looked in María's direction in unison. She was adjusting the velvet top, pulling it up into position. I ran my palms over my face, digging the heels of my hands into my eyes.

Maybe she had heard us, unlikely as that would have been halfway across the room and behind the closed door. Maybe she saw the looks we wore, tired and weary. Or maybe she understood, while waiting among all these other women, that despite their welcoming inquiries and inclusive smiles, her situation, her life circumstances wouldn't fit within that room.

She didn't sit down. Standing over us, it was the first time she made use of her age. Like a scolding mother she looked down on us and said, "Come on. I don't need to see the doctor. Let's just go."

She didn't wait for our reply, walking out of the room.

Outside in the parking lot, as we waited for the taxi to come pick us up, Núria asked what was on both our minds. "María, why the sudden change?"

She was circumspect and didn't answer directly. "No, Núria, think about it. I should be seeing to my boys. I should be finding someplace to go. It's time." In less than two weeks she'd be off the streets.

I am still a bit unclear how it was managed, how her boyfriend, Leandro, came through for María and convinced his elderly mother that María could come to her house to die. But, despite all the abuse, the years of battling on the streets, Leandro found a comfortable place for María in her need.

Outside of the city, just past the tollbooth and the airport turn off on the Highway Las Americas is the small community of Las Caletas. There, on dirt roads badly pocked and washed out, was the house of María's "mother-in-law." There was no legal bind between María and Leandro, no marriage contract, although they had endured many tumultuous years together.

One Monday afternoon we had arrived at the traffic island for one of our regular visits. Most of the time we tried to avoid Leandro. He was violent, unpredictable, unstable. We thought we were in luck—María was there and with both Coqui and Negro, cooking beans over a charcoal fire. María had organized some possessions in a bright yellow bag. Negro and Coqui squatted before the fire, shirtless, their many scars and dermatological problems open for view. If it hadn't been for the sweltering heat and humidity, even under the shade of the overpass, you would have thought they huddled around the hot coals for warmth. But it was a ravenous hunger they had. Coqui's spine curved and poked out the skin like the fins of some ancient fish.

Hearing us approach, the dogs—all the pack, the four adults and six or seven puppies—set off the alarm and everyone turned to look at us. Negro bolted up from where he was hunched down and, seeing it was us—Núria, Kennedy, Ana, and me—he started in immediately.

"I need to talk! I need to talk!" Negro said briskly as he pulled at me and Núria with his right hand. His left was immobile against his body. As he came toward us I saw that he had his shoulder wound uncovered. He had been shot three weeks previously, the pellet bullets turning to shrapnel once lodged in the shoulder, just above the pectoral muscle. At the hospital the doctors acted as if they were mining for gold, carving great amounts of flesh, leaving a cavernous wound the size of a softball and just as deep. Try as we might, Negro refused to go back to the hospital to have the wound cleaned, fearing they would extract more from him, thinking himself lucky to have escaped the last time. He wouldn't cover it up, either, but rather walked down the rows of cars at stoplights, begging for money, frightening the old women in their SUVs, threatening drivers with a large rock the size of two or three fists, prepared to break their windshields or their faces.

The wound was horrifying, a pit of greenish-yellow pus. It bubbled, alive, as if the microbes of infection could be seen with the naked eye, pulsating and gyrating within. Núria looked squeamish. I leaned over and whispered in her ear, "Just concentrate on his face." She nodded and then held her head high, chin up, eyes rolled to the heavens. I couldn't take my eyes off the wound. It drew me in and caught me off guard. I missed what Negro was telling us; " . . . he comes and beats her up. You've gotta talk to him, tell him to stop. Mom is sick; she can't withstand that kind of abuse." For a minute I forgot that Negro was nineteen and often violent and that María, when Negro wasn't looking, would make the crazy sign—index finger to the head rotated in tiny circles—and point to him. Instead, I heard the insecure child. It was the most cogent I had ever seen Negro—through the pain of his shoulder, the glue and paint thinner he sniffed, the crack that he smoked—this was what made him the most human, concern for the well-being of his mother.

Núria listened, although she still could not look directly at Negro. "Leandro can be very violent at times," she began but was interrupted by an agreeing Negro.

"Yes! Exactly! That's why you have to tell him to let up. I try to get between him and Mom and Mom tells me to get out of the way! What a crazy woman!"

I called Kennedy over. I, personally, was not about to bring up the subject of Leandro's domestic violence to Leandro himself. Leandro scared the shit out of me.

The first time we met it was well into the night and Kennedy, Ana, and I had parked the pick-up truck and crossed to the traffic island to the camp. In case Leandro was there, Ana told us, we needed to let him know it was us. We called out and María answered, telling us to come on in to the low fenced area that marked her home.

As we stepped onto the island, a figure brandishing a machete rushed out of the darkness and across three lanes of traffic. Kennedy called out hurriedly, the most excited I had ever heard him get, "Leandro! It's Niños del Camino! Leandro, it's Ana!"

As he stepped onto the island, machete still held upright in his hand, Ana said as calmly as she could, "Leandro, it's me, Ana. We are here to visit María. Can you please put that machete away?" As if he hadn't been threatening to chop us into pieces.

The dark scowl on Leandro's unshaven face lightened, "Oh, Ana! Kennedy! Forgive me," he indicated the machete, "but you have to protect your woman."

By the end of the visit this wiry man, smelling of shoe glue and rum, was giving me a hug. The smell stayed with me the rest of the evening's work, like a reminder to be careful, like the smell of fear.

"Kennedy," I began, letting Núria know she could go talk to María or Coqui and didn't need to concentrate on not looking at Negro, "Negro says Leandro's been a bit rough on María lately. He wants us to talk to him."

Negro burst into the same tirade as before. Kennedy just nodded and then said, "Jesus, Negro, don't you think you could cover up and take care of that wound a bit? They're gonna take your arm here pretty soon, leave you with a stump."

"This ain't nothin,'" Negro replied, "So you gonna talk to Leandro, right?"

"Sure Negro, we'll see what we can do if Leandro shows up."

"Good," Negro grinned, "'cause here he comes now."

Kennedy and I both turned to look behind us and, yes, Leandro, shirtless and with a plastic bottle of glue clutched in his right hand, was coming in our direction.

"Right," I said to Kennedy, patting him on the back, "I think I'll let you handle this one. I'm right behind you." Kennedy just laughed.

We set out to meet Leandro on the edge of the camp. Better to talk to him alone.

Leandro was soaring, flying high as a kite. In the time it took him to reach us where we stopped—some twenty-five steps into the fenced area—he had sniffed from the plastic orange juice bottle no less than five times. We wanted to cut him off before he made his way to the camp, expecting there might be fireworks between him and Negro, who stared at us from where we left him twenty paces away.

"Leandro!" Kennedy greeted him, clasping his hand firmly and patting him on his sweaty back, "What's going on?"

Kennedy knew how to talk, knew how to put on the macho façade that Leandro understood. They bantered back and forth for a good couple of minutes, Kennedy priming Leandro, looking for a good entrance into the topic, of which there was none, no smooth way to tell a man he needed to stop beating his wife.

"How's María?" Kennedy finally asked.

"She's fine," Leandro replied, taking a sniff from the bottle, "There ain't nothin' wrong with her. How can there be somethin' wrong? She says she hurts but not enough to deny me my right."

"This isn't like that, Leandro. You have to treat her with kindness, gentleness. Do you know what María has?"

"Naw, she just says she has some water leakin' out. That ain't nothin'"

"No, Leandro, that discharge is because she has cancer in her womb. Do you understand that? That means inside her she has something growing slowly."

"You mean she's pregnant?"

"No, she's not pregnant. It's a tumor, a growth like what you get sometimes on your body, but this is inside her."

"Like a wart?"

"Kind of like a wart, yes, but on the inside, growing inside her. And it hurts. It is causing her a lot of pain. She is not denying you because she doesn't want to be with you anymore, Leandro. She's saying no because it hurts too much. You see how she's wobbling around? It hurts her to walk, Leandro."

Through the fog of the shoe glue there was a slight look of comprehension on Leandro's face, a change that came over him.

"So she ain't lying when she says she's gonna die?"

"No, Leandro. She's not lying. What she has will likely kill her."

"You have to understand, María," Ana said, sitting down on the blue polyester blanket covering the bed. "This woman doesn't have to do anything for you. She has no relation to you. She is honoring the years you and Leandro have been together."

María sat on the opposite side of the bed, legs bowed out. She had on a broad-striped housedress this morning, red, white, and blue. She was far back on the bed, letting her feet dangle off the edge, like a little girl.

"You heard what she said when we brought you here," Ana continued, "She said, 'Well, I'm old and sick too. It makes me sad to know that someone sick would die in the streets.' She's doing it as a favor to you."

"That may be true, Ana, but this woman knows how much I have lost because of her son. Leandro is not an easy man. When Negro's father came back to see me, telling me he was going to buy me a house, what did Leandro do? He threw bottles at him! We were living in the caves at the time, and Negro's father came down to the shore, climbed down to see me. 'María,' he said, 'María, it gives me such pain to see you and my son like this. My papers have come through, María, I'm leaving for Puerto Rico.' He said, 'María, I want to buy you a little house before I leave, some-place for you and Negro. Nothing fancy, just a little wood house so you two don't have to live in the streets. I know you aren't a lazy woman. You are a hard worker. You go out every day looking for what money you can and with that you feed yourself and your family. I know you would wash clothes, iron, or cook to make ends meet. That is why I want to buy you this house.' And what happens? Leandro comes charging down from the street above with bottles in his hand, ready to carve his intestines out! It was all I could do to put myself between the two so that Negro's father could run away. After that, I never heard from him again. He never returned, all because of Leandro and his jealousy. So this woman knows well enough what I have lost because of her son."

"Ok, María, but she still could have said no. You need to value the fact that you are here, with a roof over your head," Epifanio said, indicating the one-room shack with his hand. The house was made of tin and wood beams, but had a cement floor. It was perhaps eight by eight feet, no big-ger. The double bed fit snuggly against the wall. In the left corner, by the doorway, stood an oil drum with a piece of plywood on top, covered in a scrap of cloth. On the wall by her bed hung her clothes on long nails pro-truding from the wood. The room was Spartan, yet you could tell María had taken obvious pride in having a space of her own. It was swept clean. She left her pink floral flip-flops at the entranceway. The bed was neatly made. It all pointed to the fact that, despite the discomfort of living in someone else's property, she was taking care of herself.

María's "mother-in-law" arrived with two plastic chairs for Epifanio and me, which we placed on opposite sides of María. Leandro's mother was a thin woman, much older than María, although they both appeared to be the same age. María's life had been that much more difficult, had worn her features and body to an early grave. At every visit, however, Leandro's mother reminded us that, she, too, was an unwell woman, first drawing attention to an infected wound on her lower left leg, the yellow puss of the scab sprayed white with some sort of anti-bacterial drying agent. She kept the wound open to the air. Once the wound had been pointed out to us, she invariably pulled one of us aside to give us the complete story of her pacemaker and how it was a time bomb and she was not long for this world. It was Ana's turn, as the older woman engaged her in conversation, touching her heart with tiny taps for emphasis. Epifanio continued to talk to María.

"María, I saw that big black-and-white dog the other day, the one who you kept with you there beneath the overpass. She's still there. Looks like she gave birth. She had five or so pups around her." Epifanio's comment drew our attention to the scraggly puppy playing at the foot of the bed. María loved her dogs.

"No, she wasn't pregnant," María answered clapping her hands together and leaning back slightly in a laugh. "She collects puppies that the other mothers have let go, the ones that are abandoned. Look here, young man"— she would call Epi a young man even though he was forty—"that dog is the best bitch there is. She always would bark and alert us when someone was coming—she'd even attack people she didn't know. But all I ever had to do was call her by her name and she'd come running. 'Negra,' I'd call and she'd come just like that."

I couldn't help thinking how much that dog was like María, caring after other's children. Her sons' friends were always hanging around the camp. She'd cook for them, watch out for them. She knew all the news about any one of the young men—all you had to do was ask, or leave a message with her and she'd make sure it was delivered. When Benito had been shot in the leg, blowing apart the back of the calf and ankle, it was María who told us where to find him. "That little thief was at it again," she told us. "They are going to kill him if he's not careful. You must get him out of here. He's over by the supermarket, begging." Sure enough, there was Benito, lying out on the sidewalk, leg kicked out for all the passersby to gawk at, using his misfortune to make a buck. He purposefully neglected the wound so he could continue profiting from it. It looked horrid—like a shark had ripped out the flesh.

It was time to go, as we had other visits we needed to make that day. I gave María the customary kiss on the cheek in taking my leave, but it was a heavy gesture. María and I both realized that we would not see each other again, an awkward recognition that pointed to her mortality. Instead of facing it head on, I mumbled that we'd see each other soon.

"There! Look there! It's Negro," I called out excitedly as Epifanio moved the pick-up truck slowly down Duarte Avenue. It seemed a miracle, this, on my last day of street visits we should be able to run into Negro. In my joy I simultaneously wished it would have been Coqui. Negro could be so difficult at times.

Ever since María had been moved out to Leandro's mother's place three months before, we had lost track of all the young men who had been anchored by María's mothering presence. They all made themselves scarce from the zone where they had been living, not just because of the absence of María, but also because of the invasion of the street island—and its eventual recovery—by the neighbors and business associations. We had only seen Coqui and Negro once in those three months.

María's detailed instructions about who to ask and where to search proved to no avail. Pieces such as, "Go to 30 de Marzo and ask for the old woman in the wheelchair, Teresita. She's an old friend, she'll know," or "Up behind the HiperUno supermarket near the Barahona bus stops," all yielded nothing. Teresita was never around when we passed by, and a thorough search of the HiperUno was in vain. Searching for specific people on the streets, people like these kids who moved so much and even relied on their mobility, was a game of chance.

But here was Negro, leaning against the doorframe of a watch repair shop on the busiest street in the commercial district. Epifanio and I advanced to where Negro nonchalantly stood. Undetected, I placed myself on the opposite side of the doorframe.

"Come on, papá," Negro exhorted the middle-aged owner of the watch shop. He used the common term "papá" not like calling someone father, but in the sense of that flowery speech people use to ask for something or venders on the street use to sell to passing customers. "Come on, papá, give me something," Negro continued begging. "Five pesos, whatever you've got to give me." The man behind the counter shook his head. "Sorry, there's nothing today."

Negro was unaccustomedly docile. "All right, no problem. Another day. God bless you all." The last bit was said without venom or irony. Was this the same young man that rushed cars at stoplights, threatening to bash in windshields? As he turned to leave the store, Negro bumped into me. It looked like he was going to start on the begging routine with me, too, but then he recognized me.

"Oh! Oh-oh! Look who's here!" Negro exclaimed. I reached out and patted him on his good shoulder, "How's it going, Negro?"

Ana and Epifanio came into focus as we exited the shop. We congregated next to a large outdoor display for the department store next door, a bin filled with socks and underwear for sale. The young lady in charge of the sidewalk display eyed us curiously, especially as Negro leaned up against a bin full of white t-shirts with his grubby body.

"Mami was here today," Negro began. "She was here early this morning, like at eight or so. Coqui and I got to see her. She looks good."

"Of course she does," Ana replied, "She's a lot more rested these days. She's eating better and is calmer. It's better she's living there than being on the street."

"Oh, of course!" Negro's eyes opened wide from their normal cat-like slits. "She needs as much peace and quiet as she can get."

"How often do you get to see her?" I asked.

"She's come in like three or four times. I even went to visit her once."

"That's important. It gets lonely out there and she worries about you and Coqui."

"Of course she does. I'm her son," Negro beamed a smile. I had never seen him attempt one before.

"And Coqui's never gone out to visit her?" Epifanio interjected.

"Naw. What for? If she comes here and sees him. He's weird. Says he gets ashamed and embarrassed to go to Leandro's mom's. Me, I don't give a shit. I just go."

It was the most lucid I had ever seen him, even in his motley haircut, bald splotches and unequal lengths mixed together. He didn't have a bottle of glue on him, I thought afterward, as Negro left us, contently heading on his way.

Negro hadn't always been that aggressive, Ana explained. "You have to keep in mind that he has lived on the street a long time, since he was eight or nine. That's over ten years. And a lot of that time he's been consuming. Things got real bad for him though, after Garibaldi's murder. You have to remember they killed Garibaldi in front of him and threatened to do the same to him. It is no wonder he is a bit crazy."

The story of Garibaldi's murder was one of those watershed moments where you know that nothing would ever be the same again. There was a bridge, an overpass really, on Duarte Avenue that we didn't pass under all that often, but when we did and Ana was present, she always, without fail, pointed it out, saying out into the air, "That's where they had placed Gari's body, up underneath in the pylon between the bridge and the support. It was horrible. They had quartered the body and wrapped him in a tarp."

What Ana didn't always say was that it was she and Montse that were led to the body weeks later by the rest of the kids. Negro, no older than thirteen, couldn't hold it any longer and yelled and cried violently into their arms about where the drug dealers had stashed the body of his adolescent friend. Montse and Ana had to identify the body from the decaying, tiny head. After that, after Garibaldi, Negro changed. The same men who had tortured and killed Gari had split open Negro's head like a walnut, leaving the long disfiguring scar from the forehead to the back. It was as if that scar mimicked what happened on the inside, some visible reminder of a deeper trauma. Seeing what Negro had become, I couldn't imagine him as that child witness. He was so forceful, orbiting his own universe, propelled on by the glue and crack and the love of his mother.

The last time is not always the last time. A few weeks after I had said that strained goodbye to María, where it seemed to sneak up on her and seize her, leaving her momentarily still but for the minute crestfallen way her cheeks and eyes had sunk, I found myself back in the pick-up truck with Ana and Epifanio on our way to the airport to pick up a new Spanish volunteer. We stopped off to see María on the way. She was in good spirits when we arrived. The pain was bad, overpowering at times, forcing her into bed, lying in the heat box that was the small room she lived in, but it passed eventually. I almost suggested she start using marijuana to control the pain. At least it was cheap and might curb the nausea, too. But despite the pain, the sonic waves that move through her body at unsteady intervals, she was in a bright mood. She had gone into the capital to see her sons over the weekend.

"I left early on Saturday," María began her story, sitting back on the bed, legs stretched out. "I got enough change for the bus fare into town on Friday—sometimes people are kind enough to give me a bit—and got up early on Saturday. I didn't want to be walking through the streets in the heat of the day. You know how bad the sun can get.

"I get off the bus at Parque Enriquillo and start walking up Duarte. Of course, where was I gonna find my Coqui and Negro? I walked all over the city that morning. I went to the park in front of where we lived—there is nothing there anymore, you know? They've torn down and replanted the island. I saw Teresita, the woman who begs in the wheelchair at the intersection nearby. She tells me she hasn't seen either one of my boys for weeks, that they've got problems with the police. Seems like the businesses around the park have paid the police off to move everybody out.

"So I decide to walk up Duarte to see if they might not be around there. You know Negro has a sister on his father's side that lives around there. Sometimes he can be found nearby. She's a good woman, always gives Negro a little something. But I don't see either of them on Duarte. I'm just about done. It's starting to get warm now. I figure I'll go out on 17th and then come back down to the park to catch the bus.

"When I'm out near the overpass on 17th I see this figure lying on the sidewalk in the distance. All I can see is the way he is curled up with his knees in and I think to myself, That looks like it could be Negro. I go to investigate and when I get closer"—she clapped her hands together for the luck she found herself in—"I see it *is* Negro! Sleeping right on the sidewalk, but in a deep sleep. I tap him awake and he comes to in a start.

"'Mommy,' he says to me, 'Mommy, is that you? Are you dead, Mommy? Have you come to visit me? You always said you would visit but I don't want a visit when you're dead.' I always joke with the two of them that when I die I am only going to visit Coqui because Negro says he doesn't want my spirit to visit him." María threw her head back and laughs in delight at the joke she played on her son.

"I tell Negro, 'Yep, I'm here to visit you. I know you said you didn't want me to, but you don't get to choose.' And me, I'm just cracking up on the inside! It took me a good ten minutes to convince that boy of mine I wasn't dead!"

We, too, were laughing, not because the story was funny, but because María was enjoying herself so. Ana said, "Oh María! You shouldn't joke like that with Negro." "You know Negro is crazy," María replied. "My crazy son thinking I was visiting him when I'm dead. No! When I die that's it, I'm dead. I won't be visiting anyone. While I am still alive I will do the visiting. But when I am dead I can finally rest."

## COMMENTARY

There are hard forces that constrain the life opportunities and affect the well-being of each human being. This lesson from anthropology and sociology is particularly difficult for many from a stable and privileged background to accept, because the structural forces that we encounter just as often open up doors to us as they close off other choices. The social position we are born into, however, and the identity characteristics we possess (or are imagined by others to possess) ensure our future direction. If this seems pessimistic about the possibility of social mobility, consider that, at the very least, it becomes increasingly difficult to make up for detrimental conditions that surround us early in life. Although there does exist some room for maneuver and even, in rare cases, the ability to substantially rise above our lot in life and succeed beyond our expectations, the truth is that there are few Horatio Algers in this world. The more the deck is stacked against us early on in life, the less chance we have of achieving success.

Many theorists and human development specialists describe this phenomenon in terms of social capital, or the ability to leverage economic, cultural, and educational resources to our advantage.[12] The trick is, however, that we usually only have access to the forms of social capital valued and available to the social milieu in which we live. In other words, in terms of brute class disparities, the more excluded we are from the centers of power because of where we were born, the social programs and services available to us, our racial and ethnic background, and our gender and sexual identities, the less chance we have to draw on the same set of resources as those from a more privileged position. It is not even that the deck is stacked against us, it is that the game being played is altogether different. Only exceptional individuals who are astute students of social difference are able to move between games because they've learned the rules of interaction and, possibly, are able to thrive.

For many Dominicans, especially those from more humble backgrounds, the forms of economic and social support available to them from government and nongovernmental sources to aid them in times of need are fewer than in the United States. According to the United Nations' Development Program, the human development index—a measure of the general well-being of a population based on the income, health, and education opportunities available—for the Dominican Republic in 2011 was .689 (out of a possible score of 1.0).[13] This is slightly below the regional average of Latin America and the Caribbean of .731. Although the aggregate income earning potential, access to health care, and schooling have shown a steady increase in the Dominican Republic over the past thirty years, this rise does not reflect the internal disparities of the population, including gendered differences, the rural/urban divide, and the difference between Dominican citizens and Haitians living in the country without documentation.

Such disparities are brought into relief in the characteristics of the homeless population in Santo Domingo. Not only do street populations share obstacles similar to those of the general population of the urban poor but the structural conditions that shape the health and well-being of the general population are recapitulated within homeless populations. Thus, children and youth who have migrated from rural areas to the city to work and live on the street are at a significant disadvantage because they had not previously been exposed to streetwise behaviors. But perhaps the most striking differences that determine the level of care and access to services by street denizens in Santo Domingo are relative age and ethnic background.

Although the last decade in Dominican politics has seen an increasing role for social service protections for vulnerable populations, this has mostly taken the form of bureaucratic proclamations and legal reforms, as opposed to manifesting in on-the-ground programs linked to the national government of President Leonel Fernández. Instead, the Fernández government spent much of the 2000s dealing with macro-level currency stabilization and curbing hyperinflation. While this has encouraged foreign investment, it has resulted in the scaling back of funding for social protections and programming. Nongovernmental organizations working in the Dominican Republic have continued to fill the void, providing needed care, personnel, and training for vulnerable populations. One common pattern in the area of child social services has been private-public partnerships, in which the Dominican government cedes service to NGOs in exchange for nominal oversight. For instance, one of the three juvenile detention centers in the country has been run by a Catholic religious order for over twenty years, with significant involvement by government bureaucratic representatives but relatively few government funds. The government's creation of a federal child protection agency, CONANI, in 2003, has had two simultaneous effects. On the one hand, CONANI has attempted to catalogue and make contact with all of the child social service NGOs operating in the country, to make certain that they are in compliance with federal law. On the other hand, this has allowed the Dominican government to cede greater responsibility to NGOs by giving the illusion of coordination and oversight (when very little actually exists) and removing responsibility from the government to invest more resources into programming. In practice, this means that there are gaps in protections and programming, since NGOs are able to define their target populations and the scope of their work selectively and are able to discriminate against clientele.

Both María's and Panchito's stories exemplify how the paucity of program coverage can leave the urban poor on their own in times of crisis. In the case of Panchito, the hospital dutifully ignored the fact that he had no adult guardian claiming responsibility for his care. Although the hospital did not deny him medical treatment—something that could very well have happened because of his inability to pay for supplies and incidentals (patients and their families are often required to procure their own materials, as will be made clear in the next chapter's story about Eduardo)—they did not contact CONANI to intervene on a case with an unaccompanied minor. Had Héctor and I not shown up when we did, it is uncertain how long Panchito would have stayed uncared for in the hospital. The irony, however, is that the hospital's oversight may have worked to Panchito's advantage. Being an undocumented Haitian, Panchito could have faced deportation back to Haiti had CONANI intervened. The hospital staff may have understood this dilemma and put off action on his case for as long as possible.

As an outreach-based organization, Niños did not have the facilities or staff to provide emergency shelter for the children and youth we served. This sometimes put us in a quandary, especially in crisis situations in which we needed to find alternative locations for a child or youth in danger or in need of immediate care. When we could, we would use a crisis situation as an opportunity to make contact with a child's family, especially if they were located in or around the capital, so we could make regular visits after initial contact had been made. Panchito, however, represented a special case, his family having been deported back to Haiti without him, leaving him effectively an orphan. His age—fourteen at the time—and medical condition increased the difficulty of finding him a place to convalesce. There exist very few social services for street children and youth in Santo Domingo. As a child ages, the number of options—especially for residential and rehabilitation facilities—shrink considerably. The prevailing attitude among the social services for street children is that the older the child and the longer he or she has spent on the street, the less likely will "successful rehabilitation" be—that is to say, integration back into a family setting. Thus, orphanages and some care programs have strict population profiles, none of which a teenager like Panchito who had spent a good number of years on the street, would have matched. If he had been a teenage girl, options would have been even fewer, as the programs that do exist overwhelmingly cater exclusively to male populations. In order to find him a place to recuperate, we had to locate a social service program that was less desirable for Panchito's total care but that would accept him regardless of his residency status as an undocumented minor and with his medical condition. Hogar Crea, a twelve-step-style residency program for adult drug addicts, was the only viable option. It was an ill-fitting match, at best—sending a kid whose own consumption habit was predominantly marijuana to live in a house full of recovering crack and cocaine addicts.

Although finding care for an adolescent like Panchito was challenging, María's circumstances severely limited her ability to receive anything approaching an adequate response to her social and medical conditions. No social service programs existed that would specifically attend to a homeless adult. Niños, because of the organization's history of working with her now young adult children, could step in to offer some care, but our hands were tied by a number of bureaucratic and funding restrictions. The organization's budget was predetermined by the funding agencies that donated money, so funds were already allocated to certain programming, which did not provide much leeway for special cases like María's (no funding agency allows for the creation of an emergency slush fund). María, and to a certain extent her children, were outside our target population because of their age. The cold reality was that our funders expected certain results within a well-defined target population. In order to be eligible for funding in the future, NGOs must justify how the money they receive goes toward meeting certain benchmarks, monitoring the reach and progress of the organization.

International funding agencies are selective in who they support, wanting to make sure that NGOs are responsible curators of their funds. As international monies have grown scarcer with the economic downturn in funder nations (such as the United States and the European Union), NGOs are on notice to justify their services. Whatever care we were to provide María, we would have to do it on our own time and find ways to creatively manipulate some of the budget to include the minimum of services we could provide her. As inadequate as our response was to María, we were the only institutional resource available to her.

María's cancer, although unique in terms of the types of chronic and terminal illnesses we dealt with on the street, is characteristic of the ways in which health and well-being for street populations is affected by unsanitary living conditions, poor care, and chronic social exclusion. A number of the older teenagers and young men with whom we worked on the street—those of María's sons' cohort—were afflicted with chronic and terminal illnesses, including tuberculosis and HIV/AIDS. In all cases, given the dearth of social services, their lack of adequate family or social support, their living conditions on the street, and a persistent drug habit, options for providing comfortable end-of-life care and treatment were few to nonexistent. As they aged out of child social services and were still on the street, their exposure to chronic illness increased at a time when they most needed long-term care. In many ways, such youth represent a kind of failure for organizations like Niños in the sense that prolonged exposure to the organization proved unable to change a child's circumstance, leading to a trajectory of a lifetime on the street. While the principle of accompaniment directed us to maintain a continued presence in their lives, the structural reality was that our limited time and money were perhaps better spent on younger kids who had a better chance of returning home if intervention occurred earlier and with more intensive effort. The ethos of the organization ran up against the limiting realities of money and time management time and again, causing internal strain as staff who had been with the organization for many years were unwilling to let go of youths with whom they had made strong connections.

Inadequate, inefficient, and underfunded services characterize much of Dominican government bureaucracy, especially for social services such as medical care and education. The Dominican police and judicial systems add to this mix a level of dysfunction and corruption that disproportionately affects the poor. Run-ins with the law are an unavoidable aspect of street life. Criminal activity, especially theft and breaking and entering, are income-generating strategies for some street youth, as the case of Blue Eyes shows. Likewise, drug use is woven into the fabric of street life, coloring all aspects of social organization and interpersonal relationships, as the next chapter makes abundantly clear. Both of these characteristics of life on the streets mean that street children and youth have regular contact with police and the justice system. Although there does exist a series of judicial statutes for the protection of minors from being prosecuted and treated as adults, the judicial process is slow. It is not unusual for the accused to languish in prison while waiting for their cases to be brought to trial, as in the case of Nico and Blue Eyes. Without advocates such as private lawyers and concerned family members working on their behalf, the accused can expect to be held indefinitely while the court moves through a backlog of cases. During this process, the accused are detained until trial. The burden of proof is often on the accused. Teenagers like Alejandro and Blue Eyes need to prove they are under eighteen years of age, when their physical size and criminal activity predispose authorities to treat them as adults.

Perhaps the most fundamental flaw in the criminal justice system, however, and the one that most directly and adversely affects street populations, is the level of corruption evident in members of the police force, especially those police attached to particular local police stations. The denizens of Plaza Güibia, like Nico, Débora, Ramoncito, and Luisa, carried on their involvement in the illegal economies of sex work and drug sales (as well as regulation of petty theft in the area) with the explicit connivance of some cops from the local precinct. A number of corrupt policemen received kickbacks from dealers in the area, as well as directly involving street children and youth in theft rings. In such cases, it is impossible for street children and youth to avoid possible abuse from police, especially since the police are a major player in the illegal economies of the zones in which the youths live. The case of Blue Eyes raises the equally disturbing possibility of police vigilantism. According to Blue Eyes's account, officers responding to the break-in had killed his friend Iván, without provocation. It is likely that, had not other officers and witnesses arrived on the scene, Blue Eyes, too, would have been in danger of being a victim of an extrajudicial execution. Although his story is unusual in the sense that extrajudicial summary justice resulting in murder is not as common a feature in the Dominican Republic as in other Latin American countries, it is indicative of the level of impunity that police enjoy. Being poor, young, and on the streets, Blue Eyes would not be making any accusations about police brutality. He did not have a credible identity from which to pursue such a cause.

Perhaps the most pernicious feature of Dominican society, and one that has significant consequence for children and youth on the streets, is the subtle and not so subtle institutional racism in the country. Prevalent across all social and economic classes is a general valuation of lighter skin and a denigration of blackness—including phenotypical characteristics such as skin tone and hair, but also including cultural expression associated with Haiti. In general, blackness is devalued even if not overtly commented on, and those Dominicans who appear more phenotypically (and stereotypically) "black" are subject to soft forms of racism, including the acceptance of cultural norms that mark "black" features as ugly and linguistic terminology that belittles those that are said to possess these features. However, there also exist much more overt forms of discrimination in the country, directed at Haitians or those perceived to be Haitian. Because it is assumed that Haitians display phenotypically African features, there is also an assumption that those people in the Dominican Republic who have darker features are either Haitian themselves or have some Haitian ancestry. While this assumption that Haitians have darker skin does not hold true, it is the principle under which many Dominicans base their discrimination against Haitians.

Thus racism and anti-immigration anxieties combine to discriminate against Haitians living in the Dominican Republic. Many peoples of Haitian descent whose families once crossed the border to work in sugar cane communities or as itinerant merchants, regardless of the number of generations living in the Dominican Republic, are still classified as illegal workers. They are barred from seeking Dominican citizenship, and their children, even though born in the Dominican Republic, are not considered Dominican citizens. Lack of birth certificates prevents children from enrolling in school and accessing medical care. Panchito's story illustrates another feature of life for Haitians living in the Dominican Republic—constant fear of deportation by military and police. Although Nico and Alejandro were both lucky enough to have been able to purchase a birth certificate "authenticating" their Dominican origins, this is an expensive process that is not open to all undocumented Haitians. Because the practice is illegal and corrupt, people buying false papers open themselves up to being taken advantage of. The majority of the children and youth we worked with on the street did not have a birth certificate or a copy of one—they were, in many senses, "non-people" according to the Dominican legal system because of their lack of papers. Poorer Dominicans, regardless of whether or not they are actually Haitian or of Haitian descent, are less likely to have access to official records like birth certificates. During periodic immigration sweeps, in which the military and police deport suspected Haitians, the darker-skinned children and youth we worked with were at great risk of being rounded up and sent to Haiti if they could not prove their citizenship status on the spot.

Since structural conditions segment the kinds of resources available for assistance, populations most excluded from dominant society often have to rely on their own talents and the forms of social capital available to them from their own milieu. Alliances and relationships, however uneasy, with individuals perceived as having more access to valuable economic and cultural resources can mitigate some of the daily stresses and act as buffers against the volatility of street life. These relationships, however, can also be a cause of stress and exploitation, even as they may provide some care, benefit, or comfort, especially in times of crisis. Three sets of relationships in this section demonstrate this tension. All three cases demonstrate the relative limits of social capital on the streets.

The relationship between Panchito and Ines stands out as a complicated mix of sexual exploitation, maternal care, and relative economic advantage, characteristic of the hybrid nature of social relations on the street. The situation is difficult to pin down as a simple case of sex work—indeed, the complex layering of obligations and benefits entangled in their relationship is lost if such stark terminology is used to describe their interactions. Panchito had been involved with Ines for a considerable amount of time. It is unclear whether or not the relationship started out as based on sexual exchanges or if this component was added later, for, from the start, Panchito would do odd jobs for Ines around the park where she sold hamburgers, including being a courier for Ines's marijuana sales. Regardless, as Héctor reminded me, it is important to keep in mind that Panchito was not overtly coerced into this relationship. He was a resourceful youth and entered into the relationship with Ines with the expectation that there would be benefits from such a partnership, as well as obligations. Seeing it from this perspective doesn't make it any less distasteful, nor does it remove Ines from responsibility, but it does allow us to see that there was mutual agreement as to the limits of what each would accept in the other. For Panchito, it is telling that feelings of betrayal—and not "exploitation" per se—are what lead him to reconsider his relationship with Ines. Only when he is injured when buying drugs for her and she makes no attempt to search him out—in essence, leaves him for dead or incarcerated—does Panchito see her as violating his trust. One expects mutual exploitation, indeed it is part of the quality of relationships on the street, but outright betrayal crosses the line of acceptable—and expected—behavior.

While relationships on the street appear to us as dysfunctional and exploitative, that does not mean that they are void of care, support, and concern. María's relationship with her long-term partner, Leandro, demonstrates the Janus nature of affective ties. Like Ines's relationship with Panchito, Leandro's behavior toward María is easily labeled abusive. He was predisposed to violent behavior, especially when under the influence of the quantities of solvents and crack he used. Part of María's successful maneuvering of living on the streets, especially for as long as she had been living there with her sons, was her ability to form alliances with more powerful (and yes, more violent) men like Leandro who could offer protection from other violent men. It was always difficult to gauge María's feelings for Leandro, because she rarely spoke of him in the way that she would express humorous and tender care for her sons. Her comment about Leandro's mother is revealing in this regard. María indicated that, while her relationship with Leandro may have provided some safety, she was also aware of how much she gave up in staying with him. Yet, ironically, it was her connection with Leandro that provided María with a place to retreat in her illness. Social services and government agencies failed to find an adequate response to María's most pressing need—a clean, quiet place to die. Leandro, however, pulled through. Again, despite the abuse and dysfunction, it is only through drawing on the relationships around her that some kind of solution could be found for María. She was reliant on the social capital of her immediate network of friends and relations on the street, while at the same time her involvement in this environment limited her ability to receive other types of responses and services.

Making and keeping alliances with individuals of greater socioeconomic power is a strategy for increasing one's access to forms of social capital from which one would otherwise be excluded. Nico's long-term relationship with his Puerto Rican client is indicative of this calculated move to maintain connections over time for the value they may have in the long run. Again, I am unable to attest to the quality of the relationship between the Boricua and Nico, having never met the man and only knowing of his existence through what I heard on the streets. However, it is certain that he was one of Nico's earliest clients when Nico began sex work, at a time when more of his economic resources came from sex exchanges with foreign clients. For whatever reason, the two have been able to maintain a relationship that is qualitatively different from Panchito's relationship with Ines. Although there is an element of sexual exchange in both, Nico's relationship with the Boricua is overtly couched as a business transaction, at least from Nico's perspective. This may be because of the homosexual character of the relationship and Nico's desire to let it be known that his relationship with his client is not one of mutual affection, out of fear of being labeled a maricón. Indeed, the openness of his relationship with the Puerto Rican and the fact that his long-time girlfriend on the street (who herself participates in sex work) is aware and supportive of his maintaining this connection may be one strategy to deflect concern that there may be something other than business as part of the transaction. This questioning of Nico's masculinity is, in essence, the root of his dispute with Débora. It is even what puts Ramoncito at greater risk on the streets for being romantically involved with such a liminal figure as a transvestite.

Thus, there are a number of limiting factors that put pressure on the opportunities for those who live on the streets. Structural conditions constrict access to the material and social resources necessary to overcome extreme marginalization from mainstream society. Poverty, age, gender, and racism combine, overlapping with one another to prevent even the most capable, intelligent, and crafty from overcoming those constraints. Social connections with more powerful figures, those outside of the social milieu of the street, tend to be predicated on forms of mutual exploitation and rarely offer avenues of escape from one's marginal position. All this heavily infuses the system of cultural values on the streets of Santo Domingo, manifesting itself in a volatile mix of drugs and interpersonal violence. It is the intersection of drugs and interpersonal relationships that is explored in the next chapter.

# 3 · FRIENDSHIP AND EVERYDAY VIOLENCE ON THE STREET

## CONFLICT RESOLUTION

In the evenings, after going through a round of the day's visits, I would normally still be restless, needing some help to decompress. My neighborhood had punctual, daily blackouts from five at night until two in the morning—a consequence of most of my neighbors not paying their bills and having illegal electrical connections. Some nights I would sit in the candlelight, squinting to read, but most evenings I couldn't sit in the dark after a day of outreach. I would eat my dinner of fried eggs and boiled ripe plantains and leave the apartment for an evening walk to clear a space in my crowded mind. I would roam, go visit a friend, or get some ice cream. My destination was always vaguely the same: I went to the Colonial Zone.

It took me at most twenty minutes to walk down to Parque Independencia, even less time if I went at a good clip. Instead of going down the ped mall and Parque Colón, which I would normally do, this particular evening I went to the next street over and walked down to Plaza España, with its clean brick space and the well-lit stone keep of Diego Colon. It was a good place to people watch, to look out over the cannons on the far fortified wall to the Ozama River. It was a popular place for lovers, who would crowd the cannons, enjoying more of each other than the view. I could get lost there, staring blankly at the people and landscape, let my mind settle on nothing but the dim street lamps and shadowed figures exchanging embraces.

I must have stood there a long time, finally coming back to myself as a fine mist settled upon the city. I didn't know if the rain would get heavier, but I didn't want to be caught in a downpour. I walked with purpose, leaving the plaza, turning up to Parque Colón and the end of the Conde. About three blocks from the end of the ped mall, I felt someone come in-synch alongside me, matching me stride for stride. "Crook" flashed before me, irrational as it was, because anyone wanting to pickpocket me would not come alongside me, having me notice them. I turned my head and had to laugh. I wasn't too far from the truth. There beside me, grinning in that sly uncomfortable way of his was Fernando, well known as having some of the stickiest fingers on the streets. At sixteen, Fernando had accumulated quite a reputation. He would steal from anyone and take anything not anchored. He was well watched by the cops, who had started to blame him for any theft in the vicinity. Other street kids loathed him, reviled him. They thought he was too conspicuous, caused too much disturbance in the area. I think they were mostly jealous of his ability.

Fernando was charming and oozed self-confidence. He knew what he could do. He also thought himself better than the other street kids. According to him, he was a cut above. "I'm not an addict," he would claim, ignoring his own heavy use of marijuana. "And look at me. I always go around well dressed and good-looking"—because he pilfered his clothes from the vendors on the ped mall, but he wouldn't mention that detail, either. For Fernando, he was a self-made and self-sufficient man.

"Someone's in a hurry," Fernando greeted me.

"I didn't want to get caught in the rain. You been following me long?"

"A couple of blocks." He turned his red baseball cap around, placing the torn bill to the back. Fernando's fashion tonight met his usual high standards: black jeans and a fitted green t-shirt with a shamrock silkscreened to the chest. With the hat turned back he looked like a misplaced frat boy. His feet were the only thing that betrayed the look. Fernando couldn't wear shoes because of a congenital birth quirk—seven toes on his left foot and six on his right. He had even managed to appropriate this deformation as part of his ethos, going by the street name Seven Toes. He wore a pair of flip-flops, the extra toes overflowing the foam and rubber. The feet were hideous creatures, and not because of the additional digits. They were cracked and caked on dirt and grime found every crevice. He cares so much about his appearance, I thought, yet leaves his feet.

The downpour was going to start any minute. I could feel it, the way a paper sack feels heavy before the bottom rips out. I didn't want to be rude, but I didn't want to be caught in the rain, either.

"Hey, man, I'll check you later, all right? It's gonna dump buckets of water here soon." I made to bump fists.

He tapped my knuckles with his. Then, as I'm turning, almost as an afterthought, he let slip from his mouth, "Oh, you know Shoeshine Boy, right?"

"Shoeshine Boy? You mean Eduardo?"

"Yeah, whatever his name is. Shoeshine Boy. Tall guy. Kind of white."

"Of course I know him. I saw him just this afternoon. What's up with him?"

"They stabbed him in the back tonight. It was Joaquín that did it, although he'd deny it. Looked pretty bad. They dropped him off at Padre Billini an hour ago. I saw them carry him in. He was so far gone he couldn't walk."

The blood in my veins stopped flowing. The sound of the thick droplets of rain beating the concrete filled the air.

"You sure? You positive it was Shoeshine Boy?"

"You think I make this shit up? It's no matter to me. He's not my friend. I just thought you'd like to know."

In a potential emergency there is no reason to panic until you know the facts, until you know what you are up against. I tried my best to remember this principle as Fernando and I walked to the hospital. These kids, I thought, have a tendency to exaggerate, right? Everything is worse than it really is because things are naturally bad to begin with. The only time things are good is when there is enough drug to go around or there's a sudden, unexpected windfall. It's pragmatic pessimism. And, even once you know the facts, I concluded, even once you know how bad it really is, well, then, there is still no reason to panic. You do what you can.

Padre Billini hospital had been recently renovated. Named after a sixteenth-century priestly champion of the poor and founder of one of the first hospitals in Santo Domingo, Padre Billini was once a monastery. You could still see the courtyard, where interned patients wandered around trailing IV's and dirty colostomy bags. The emergency room entrance must have once served as a receiving room for the monastery. The architecture and interior design almost made you forget you are in a public hospital in a developing country. The ceilings were high and decorated with molded plaster. But the utilitarian black plastic waiting room chairs clashed with the religious elegance of the building, the marble columns and mosaic floor. The main foyer was crowded. The ill and their attendants sat, engulfed in the cavernous acoustics. The vinyl line of chairs was filled with the tired yet restless faces of loved ones wondering what was to happen next.

The admitted patients were all tucked away inside the emergency rooms or the hospital beds of the inner sanctum of the building. Fernando and I stood at the entranceway. I was unsure of where to go. I had never done this on my own; I'd always tagged along with one of my co-workers who guided us through the process. They never asked questions of anybody at the hospitals; they never waited in lines. They knew that to talk to staff was to be turned down, told that you couldn't go someplace or do something. Act like you know what you are doing, I thought, if you look lost they'll know the jig is up.

I turned to Fernando, "Where do you think they took him? Emergency?"

"Maybe. That'd be down there," he pointed to a hallway to the right.

We went in that direction, and took the first left door in the hallway. I popped my head in and saw the five beds, occupied and hooked up with IVs. None of the patients met Eduardo's profile. There was another door down further and to the right. This one was actually marked "emergency" in big red block letters. I pushed my way through the swinging doors and almost stepped in a pool of blood. The intern cleaning at the edges of the mass of deep red looked up as I entered.

"You can't come in here," said the elderly man, leaning on the mop. The room was full. There was a team of doctors and nurses ringing one of the beds and a loud cacophony of voices barking orders concerning the patient concealed by the forest of green scrub outfits. My fear convinced me that it was Eduardo on the gurney, that it was his worsening condition that had the medics lose their composure.

"I'm looking for a patient," I wasn't going to let this intern turn me away. I needed answers. I described Eduardo's appearance, his possible stab wounds.

"He's been taken upstairs, he's in line for surgery."

I hoped he wasn't just trying to get rid of me. I had no real choice but to believe him. The metallic smell of the blood was nauseating. "Come on," I said to Fernando whose curiosity had driven him to edge around to take a better look at the impromptu operation going on before us.

Up the stairs we met no one. The corridor was brightly lit, a fluorescent brilliance that verged on radioactive. I didn't know where we should start looking for anything to do with surgery. Choosing a direction, we walked to the left, following the railing of the balcony that overlooked the inner courtyard, searching the signs and marked doors for someone to ask or a direction in which to head. Halfway around, tucked in a corner near a small interior hallway that led to a swinging door marked "surgery," were three gurneys placed end to end, each holding a motionless body. It was hard to tell if they were going in or rejected from the operating room because they were already dead.

The body on the middle stretcher was assuredly Eduardo's. Even with his face turned toward the wall, I knew him from the long shape of his body and the closely shaved back of his head. He was shirtless and curled on his side, a large bandage taped on the low back, the tape yellowing from the flow of blood. The bandage was all red, the thin weave of multiple layers of gauze drenched in the fluid. He was pale, so white that had he not bent the knee in his top leg in a minute twitch, I would have called him dead.

"Shit," was all I could say. Fernando, for once, was subdued by the sight. This was different from the woman in the emergency room; this was someone his age, someone he knew, even if he didn't care much for him.

There was little space between the top of Eduardo's stretcher and the foot of the adjacent patient. I nudged the neighboring stretcher out of the way and pulled my body parallel to Eduardo's head. His eyes were closed, the lids fluttering like rice paper. His breath was shallow, his chest barely rising with each inhalation. He had a hand under his head, acting as a makeshift pillow. There was no expression on his face: no rictus of pain, no grimace. It was blank, not registering or reflecting anything about the state of his body. I took the fingers of his extended hand and ran my hand over them, feeling the clammy coldness. I lightly massaged the fingers, hoping to bring Eduardo back to bodily awareness. I bent my mouth to his upturned ear and quietly said his name. "Come on, buddy. You're not alone here."

Eduardo moaned and his eyelids batted furiously until they opened, revealing large, unfocused pupils in his brown eyes.

I repeated his name. "You know where you are, buddy?"

"Hospital," he croaked back. "Joaquín stabbed me."

"I know, I know. We can talk about that later, Eduardo. You know who I am?"

"Jon. You're here, Jon."

"That's right, I'm here, Eduardo. Is there a family member I can call, Eduardo, like your mom or grandmother. They should be here with you, Eduardo."

"My grandmother."

I took a pen from my back pocket and scribbled the ink to life on my palm. "What's her number, Eduardo?" With some prodding, Eduardo got the numbers out in what I hoped would be the right sequence of digits.

"Eduardo, I want you to know we're here, OK? We aren't going to leave you alone," I rubbed his hand between my palms some more, "You know that, don't you?"

He mumbled a response and closed his eyes again.

The door marked "surgery" swung out with force as a woman in scrubs exited. I looked up guiltily from my position, but she saw Fernando first. "What are you doing here? No one is allowed in here."

I stood up and replied as apologetically as I could, "Please forgive us, doctor, I know we shouldn't be here, but this young man is known to us and I need to inform others about his condition and needs." I explained as quickly as I could who we were, how I knew Eduardo. She softened slightly.

"Listen, he needs surgery. The wound has damaged the internal organs. It is very deep and he has lost a lot of blood. But we can't do surgery until we have two pints of blood, do you understand? We need two pints of blood before we can do more."

"Where do I get blood? Is that something I can buy here at the hospital?"

"No, you need to go to a blood bank for blood, to the Red Cross. Go downstairs and take a right, turning the corner. At the first door on the left is where the hospital's blood center is located. They can tell you where to go to get the blood you need, all right?" She paused, considered whether to say it and then did anyway, "You understand that without surgery he will likely die." I turned from her eyes and looked down at Eduardo's quiet face.

The doctor had not misled us. I rapped on the door clearly marked "Blood Center." It immediately swung open, revealing a heavy-set black woman in a lab technician's coat and a surprisingly comforting smile. "What can I do for you, sweetie?"

The Blood Center was nothing more than a small cubicle of a room with a series of mini-refrigerators against the back wall, a large desk, and a filing cabinet. The attendant barely fit between the desk and the wall. She sat squarely on her rolling chair, holding a vial in one latex gloved hand.

"I need to get blood for a patient who is waiting surgery. It's an emergency." I must have looked like a scared small animal, a frightened rabbit with saucer eyes, because she replied with more care than expected.

"Listen, darling, things will be just fine. You need to go to the Red Cross and buy the blood you need. All the blood here—" she gestured to the mini-fridges behind her with the vial "—is for patients who are scheduled for surgery. We don't have any for emergencies." My face fell even more. "But not to worry. There is a Red Cross behind 27 de Febrero before you get to Gómez. Any taxi driver can get you there. You go get the blood and bring it back and I'll make sure the patient gets it, OK?"

OK. Red Cross. Buy blood because nothing is free. "How much is the blood?"

"Five hundred pesos a pint, because it is an emergency."

Five hundred pesos was a lot of money. I balked at the price. I have no idea how a poor family would be able to afford that price in an emergency. Then I did the calculations, thinking I needed to stop viewing this in terms of pesos and think in dollars for once. Five hundred pesos was less than twenty bucks, a more palatable amount. Even if it had been more, I didn't have a choice. I thanked the woman and told her I would be back as soon as I could with the blood.

I didn't want to do this on my own. In fact, I didn't think I could. Fernando was company and he was savvy in some things, but I wanted a co-worker, someone who knew how these things were supposed to work. But who to call? Eli and Núria had left that afternoon for Santiago to visit a sister organization there. Ana lived so far in the northeastern suburbs she wouldn't be able to get out and make it to the city center easily, especially without a car. And even if she could, she would have to leave her kids alone. It was not yet ten o'clock. Héctor was my only viable choice. He lived nearer than the others. I dialed his number praying he would answer.

"Hello," his voice was laconic, but not sleepy.

"I've got a problem Héctor, an emergency." I started to explain.

Héctor tried hard to keep his work-life and home-life separate. "I don't know, Jon. It's not safe to get out of my neighborhood at this hour. I'd have no way to get down to the hospital. And Brenda's not been having a good time lately with the pregnancy."

"Héctor, I understand, but I don't know what I'm to do or where I'm supposed to go. Héctor, Eduardo looked bad, I mean really bad. They aren't going to operate on him if there's no blood." My voice wavered with the stress of the situation.

"Do you have money?"

"I'll have enough for the blood. I might have enough for at least one taxi ride."

He heard the anguish. Héctor was not an unkind man. "Listen, I'll call you back in five minutes. Let me go talk to a buddy of mine and see if I can't use his car. If I can get the car I'll be there, ok?"

"All right, Fernando," I put on the most authoritative, confident voice I could muster, "Are you with me on this one?"

He eagerly agreed. I knew it wasn't out of loyalty to Eduardo that he was interested in the outcome. We came out onto the street, slick and glossy from the earlier downpour. I paused, getting my bearings, remembering where the nearest ATM was that would allow access this late.

"Jon! Jon!" A voice called, coming from across the street. From against the doorway of the building in front of the hospital sprung up a figure of a man where he had been crouched. I didn't recognize him from where I stood. Because of the work we did, lots of people—kids as well as adults—knew who I was. I was pretty easily identified as the only shaved-headed gringo. I probably should have been more wary when my name was used, but I usually played along, even if I didn't recognize the person. Half the time they wanted money anyway. But tonight was not a night that I wanted to deal with listening to pleas for money or food. I had a situation on my hands.

Fernando recognized the figure coming toward us before I did. "Well, look who it is, Luisíto, the hero himself," he commented in a wry voice, somewhere between sarcasm and dry irony. I didn't understand the reference that Fernando made at that moment. I knew there was no amity between the two of them, but was unsure of the reason the bad blood existed. It went beyond territorial rivalry, though, and the usual animosity that Fernando elicited from most of the other kids. Luisíto had slowly moved into new realms of delinquency over the past few months, finding himself part of a thieving ring with two older men. My guess was that Fernando and Luisíto's bad relationship had something to do with Luisíto's new business relations.

Luisíto's transformation over the year since we had first met had been nearly total. A helpful, bright-eyed fifteen-year-old who took to the streets because of unspecified "neighborhood problems," Luisíto was now a sixteen-year-old deeply enmeshed in the world of robbery and drugs. It had been painful to watch as Luisíto kept drifting, moving from a peripheral position on the Malecón to being a central figure in the lives of the Plaza Güibia inhabitants. He had become moody and addicted to crack-laced marijuana cigarettes. He was violent, fighting his way to a dominant position within his cohort. When I had first met him, I thought the streets would devour him. Instead, Luisíto fed off the streets and thrived.

He wore an oversized Yankees baseball cap, black, cocked to one side and pulled over the ears. His jean shorts and long grey polo shirt were dotted with dark stains. The shorts, in particular, had a dark velvety patch that extended over the right pocket and worked its way up under the shirt.

I was surprised by his calm. He jerked his head in an upward motion in recognition of Fernando's presence. I extended my hand out to shake Luisíto's, which he took. The feel of his ice-cold hands told me that there was something not quite right.

"What's up, Luisíto?"

"Jon, did you see Shoeshine Boy? Did you see him?"

"Yeah, I saw him. Fernando told me what happened. He's not too good. They say it was a deep wound."

"I know. I saw it go in. The damn thing was shoved in to the hilt."

"You saw it?"

"Yeah. I saw it. I was sitting right next to Shoeshine Boy on that wall there in Plaza Güibia, smoking a joint. Joaquín came by, exchanged words with Shoeshine Boy. Nothing weird or angry. Then he comes back five minutes later, comes behind us and drives this long blade, homemade, you know? The kind you make with a steal or copper shank. Shoves it all the way in, pulled it out and walked away.

"Man, he was bleeding. Blood was everywhere, pooling around. I took a t-shirt and held it on the wound, but the blood kept coming. I carried him to where the taxis sit, picked him up and carried him all the way there and paid a taxi 500 pesos to bring him here. They didn't want to do it, but I said, 'I got 500 pesos, who will go?' and then one I know said he'd go, he'd do it. So I pulled Shoeshine Boy in the cab and got him here."

Five hundred pesos would have been five times what that cab ride should have cost. I couldn't help wonder where he'd gotten that kind of cash, what he did to earn it. Then I remembered that Eduardo had started selling drugs. It might have been what Eduardo had on him, or maybe it was Luisíto's cut?

"Like I said," Fernando capped off Luisíto's story, "Luisíto the hero." The way he said it was ambiguous. It could have been praise, but Fernando didn't praise anyone but himself, let alone Luisíto. It was as if he was intimating that Luisíto was somehow involved in the stabbing, somehow complicit.

My phone rang: Héctor, as promised. He had found his friend and had use of his car. He'd meet us at the end of the Conde.

"You guys sticking around here or are you coming with me to find some blood?"

They both elected to come with me. I had hoped that one of them would have dropped out, like Fernando. Having them both with me was going to get awkward. Luisíto started to lose his calm when I explained Eduardo's condition. In light of Fernando's comment, I kept seeing Luisíto's behavior as guilt. And Fernando was along for the ride more than ever now; within his smooth veneer he was watching Luisíto closely. He wanted to see what happened and how Luisíto would react. Yet, despite the complications, I didn't want to go this alone.

We waited outside Paco's Cafeteria, the only thing open besides the bars. The clients sat expectantly, some already dining with their young prospects. No one I knew by the looks—the regular crew of young hustlers, not any of our kids, thank God.

I kept looking at the clock on my cell phone. If it marked the seconds, I would have counted the ticks. What the hell was taking Héctor so long? Nearly forty minutes had passed since we left Eduardo on the stretcher outside the operating room. I saw his body as an hourglass and each minute was another minute of his life draining away. What if we didn't make it? What if I didn't return with the blood?

I tried to distract myself while we waited. "You did a brave thing, you know that Luisíto? You did right by getting Eduardo to the hospital."

"He's my best friend, my brother." Luisíto used the English word for brother, signifying not a blood relationship, but a street relationship. "I couldn't let him lie there after what Joaquín did to him." There it was again, this faint specter of guilt haunting his voice. It was the shadow of his words.

The minutes dragged a heavy weight. I paced the small section of sidewalk in front of Paco's. Fernando had struck up a conversation with one of the many taxi drivers that wait at the end of the Conde, obviously one that he knew well enough to joke with. Luisíto slunk back into the wall of the building, his body mixing with the concrete, trying to disappear. A half hour after calling, Héctor drove up in a beat up shit-brown 1970s Dodge Charger. He honked two times, a sharp long tone to announce his presence. Not exactly the cavalry, but close enough for me at that point.

I jumped in the front seat and the two teenage tag-alongs clambered into the back. "Thanks for coming, man," I greeted Héctor, offering my hand as I got in, "I don't think this is something I could do on my own, you know? It's not something I've done before."

"I understand. It's just Brenda, with the pregnancy, she gets kind of weird when I leave at night. She's getting close, and she keeps thinking it's going to end up like her first," the one born with birth defects. Héctor put the car in gear, "The Red Cross, right?" I nodded. "I know where it is. We had to give blood when my nephew had his appendix removed. You know how this is, don't you?"

"What do you mean?"

"You can't take blood out without putting blood in."

"You mean like donate blood?"

Luisíto spoke up from the back, "Like stick a needle in and take the blood out?"

"Just like that, yes."

"I'll do it," Fernando volunteered. "That sounds like fun."

"Yeah, man, me too. I'll give my blood if they need it." Luisíto was not going to be outdone by Fernando.

Héctor lowered his voice, "Jon, I can't give blood because of my kidney problem. If only you donate, we will be able to get only one pint of blood."

I felt a hollow in the pit of my stomach. It would have to be enough.

We arrived in less than ten minutes. The streets were quick, the traffic light, and Héctor sped through the side streets to get to a large chain-link fenced-in building. It was a part of the city I had never explored. At night it appeared vaguely industrial, with jutting, angular debris littering empty lots and darkened commercial sites sprouting like growths. Héctor pulled up to the guard, explained what we needed, and parked on the gravel surrounding the courtyard. Half the building was lit, the other half hiding against the blackened backdrop. There was one entrance illuminated and signifying on-duty personnel. We walked into the yellowish light and down the foyer to the first window. I hung back with the teens, allowing Héctor to explain what we needed.

It was much as Héctor had described. Because of the shortage of blood and the lack of tradition of donating blood, the blood bank required a deposit for any withdrawal to be made. The economic language of the transaction put in sharp relief the commodification of the human body. In a moment of difficulty and extreme need, all emotion is sifted out, leaving the frigid and bare economic terms of the dilemma. We had to donate to save the life of our friend. It couldn't possibly be seen as an altruistic act, either, because it was no one-to-one exchange. It wasn't blood for blood. It was blood for blood and cash.

The nurse came out through a set of double doors, into the waiting room. She held a brown pressed-wood clipboard against the stark white uniform. She was cheerful and wasn't going to let any of her own concerns shine through her public face.

She looked at Héctor and then me, making eye contact with each of us. "Now, who is going to donate?"

Before either of us could speak up, Luisíto replied, "I will. I'll do it." His voice, steady, resolved, surprised all of us in the room, including Luisíto.

"I'm sorry, my son," the nurse continued with that innocuous smile, "but both you and your friend are not eligible because of these." She motioned to her left earlobe with the right hand and touched the gold hoops with the pen she clasped between her fingers. Luisíto's hand went up in mirror of the nurses, touching his own faux-diamond studded ear. Both he and Fernando had their ears pierced; they had had it done on the streets, by one of their friends, with a found needle. But how could the nurse have known that? I suddenly felt self-conscious of the closed over holes in my own lobes. Could she see those dark pinpricks that looked like two well-placed moles?

"You're going to do it, right, Jon?" Héctor asked, reaffirming the decision that was all but stated in the car.

"Damn, man, what they do, drain you dry?" Fernando asked as I came out from the procedure room. "You look pale."

"Yeah, well, I almost fainted. I guess I'm not used to giving blood." I sat down next to Héctor, pulled my wallet from my back pocket and handed him some pesos. "Can you go get the blood?"

At that point the transaction was simple, like buying groceries. Héctor went to the unmarked window, paid the required amount, and waited. The woman came back with a brown paper bag folded neatly at the top, and a receipt stapled to the top left corner.

The ride back to the hospital was silent. No one, it seemed, not even Fernando and his boisterous mouth, had the desire to speak. We all knew what the end possibility could be. I checked my watch: nearly two hours had passed since I had seen Eduardo on the gurney. And how long before that had he been waiting there? When had Luisíto dragged Eduardo into the hospital? At what time had he been shanked? It could have been as many as four hours ago, maybe even five. The bigger question was, how long could Eduardo wait without surgery?

They hadn't been able to tell me where and how much Eduardo bled internally. That was the urgent need for blood. If they opened him up and it was discovered he'd bled like a stuck pig, that the wound had entered his stomach, for example, he could die bleeding to death on the operating table. They weren't going to take that chance.

Down the hall, around two corners and back to the blood bank, the paper bag with my deposit crackling all the way. A steady knock on the door and when the same large, smiling woman, white teeth gleaming with starch lab coat, opened the door I proudly held out the pint of myself for her. "Here's the blood," I couldn't help but smile proudly, like some dog with a retrieved ball for his owner, tail wagging.

"Oh, good, honey. Tell me the patient's name again?"

I gave her Eduardo's full name. In the space of her reply I offered a prayer. It was no bargain, no this-for-that transaction with God. Just a simple plea: Please, God, let me have arrived in time.

"Listen, dear," her face a blanket of concern, "this is great that you've come back with the blood. I knew you would, so I did a favor after you left. I sent up two pints of blood for another patient's surgery tomorrow. They only used one, and now with this pint, we are all settled and that other patient can have his surgery tomorrow, no problem. Your friend should be coming out of surgery soon. They are just sewing him up."

It took several breaths to let her words sink in. I stood blankly before her, still, and then dropped all pretence. I rushed at her, forgetting where I was, and put my arms around this stranger who, more than me, more than Héctor or even perhaps Luisíto, had saved Eduardo's life. "Oh, God. God bless you. God bless you." The stress of the past two hours broke through. I tried to explain through the tears that I thought we were going to arrive too late. At some point my Spanish failed me. I simply held on to this woman I did not know. If she were surprised she did not show it. With the insides of her wrists, careful not to touch me with the latexed hands, she patted my back and cried as well.

I regained my composure, released the nurse, and wiped the tears with the sleeves of my shirt. She smiled gently. "Go, check and see if he's out yet. Intensive care is on the other side of the courtyard. They should let you in and will be able to tell you more information, ok?" I thanked her one more time and turned out the door.

Eduardo looked as comfortable as possible for having been stabbed in the back. Propped up on one side with crumpled bedding, his off-kilter body was less pale than when I had seen him last. A long white pad of gauze and tape bisected his torso, wrapped tight like a sarong. His eyes were shut, and there was a faint odor of ether around his face. I stood looking down upon his long body, relieved beyond words to see his chest rise and fall in a steady, if shallow interval.

"He's just come from surgery, so he won't be awake for a while still."

I lifted my gaze to the light-blue scrub nurse at the far edge of the room. Eduardo was in good company. The seven other beds in the long, rectangular room were filled with patients in various states of critical condition. Here, there are no mechanical accompaniments like heart monitors or lung machines. All the patients had two plastic bags hooked to their recumbent bodies with tubes, one for the IV and one for the catheter.

"Can you explain to me, please, what they operated on him for?"

She appraised me, questioning visually my relationship with the patient. I quickly explained, falling back on my standard reply. That loosened her guard.

"They opened him up to see if the knife hit any of the internal organs. He was very lucky, you know? The wound entered at a very critical area, where lots of internal organs meet, the kidneys, the stomach, the appendix.

The knife missed all of those. He lost a lot of blood but he wasn't critically wounded."

So he's out of trouble?"

"He'll recover, assuming there's no infection. Will you be staying with him?"

The thought hadn't entered my mind. I looked down at Eduardo and my hands resting on the edge of the mattress. My hands! The phone number Eduardo gave me was slightly smudged from the cold sweat of my palms, but legible. "We'll see," I replied. "I'm going to try to contact his family first. It's more important that they be here when he wakes up in the morning."

She nodded and turned back to her desk and manila files of paperwork. Back out in the main waiting room, Héctor and Luisíto sat side by side, Héctor had nodded off and Luisíto sat with his chin in his hands and elbows on his knees. Fernando was nowhere to be found. Seeing me approach, Luisíto tapped Héctor, who jumped awake.

"They operated on him while we were gone," I explained without waiting to be asked. "He's out of surgery and they think he will recover."

I excused myself from the two of them and went out on the hospital's front steps. The night had calmed down considerably, with a sweet sea-smelling balmy breeze. No one was on the street; it was a quiet yet reassuring emptiness.

If I were a smoker I would have lit up. Instead of a pack of cigarettes, I pulled my cell phone from my bag. I had to make that call, as cold as it would be. The fact was, no one in the organization had ever made contact with Eduardo's family. We knew very little about most of the older kids' family situations if they hadn't been participating with us for long. Teenagers who recently came to the streets, like Eduardo, never seemed to attract the same kind of excitement as the ten- and eleven-year-olds, especially if they were as physically big and self-confident as he was. You got the sense they could take care of themselves and you didn't prod them as much; they would tell you what they wanted when the time came. Besides, regardless of the age, personal histories revealed themselves in bits and pieces, evolving over time as you built a relationship with a kid. What they told you at initial contact might be only the bare scaffolding around the truth. After months or even years, new elements would come to light.

What I did know about Eduardo's family life, then, was slim. He had been raised, with his younger sister, by his grandparents. This I knew because one day on a field trip, I sat next to Eduardo as the bus crept along the slow current of traffic up Gómez Street. Eduardo nudged me on the shoulder and pointed out the window, "That's where I live, you know? My grandma's house is in that second building there, on the fourth floor." It was always interesting to hear the kids describe their natal residence. Very few claimed to have the street—or their particular stretch of street—as their home. Most, like Eduardo, claimed to belong to some place, unwilling to make the clean break and declare the asphalt and brick their ultimate place of origin. They would claim allegiance to their street territory—Güibia's my zone, I sleep in the abandoned mansion, I work the Conde—but they didn't come from there. Home, or rather, having a home, still meant something and separated them from the truly "homeless" palomos.

During that same bus ride, I had asked as nonchalantly as possible after Eduardo's mother. "No, she lives in Los Cocos, with my stepfather. My grandpa sent me to live with them because I had a little problem at my grandma's house. My stepfather and I don't get along. He beats my mom and I don't like that. I had to leave her house. I left her house for the streets."

That was the closest I had heard from Eduardo about why he opted for the streets. Had we not been driving by the concrete blocks that made up the apartment complex where his grandparents lived, I might not have known even that little bit of information.

It was nearing two in the morning. Whenever a phone rings late at night, we assume an emergency. I could imagine that Eduardo's family would be no exception. Late-night phone calls rarely bring good news.

I entered the numbers and pushed send. The phone connected and there was a ring on the other line. Once. Twice. Three times. On the fifth ring a groggy feminine voice answered. "I apologize for calling so late," I began in as cordial a voice as possible, "But I must speak with Doña Amalia. I have news of her grandson, Eduardo."

As I explained the situation, Doña Amalia's fortitude convinced me she was tough as steel. She did not wail, nor did she raise her voice at me, although she did call out a man's name, asking him to come to where she was. I assumed it was her husband.

"I see. And Eduardo's in Padre Billini, you say? I'm not surprised. I told that boy he was headed for trouble, that he needed to be careful. I want you to know that we've tried everything we could think of to get that boy straightened out but we're at the end of our rope."

"I understand, Doña Amalia, but your grandson needs the presence of family right now. He was very close to dying. Maybe this could be the incident that will help Eduardo reevaluate his life."

"I don't know if we can make it to the hospital tonight. It is his mother that should go. He didn't give you her number, huh? Well, I'll have to contact her and get her out there. I've got work tomorrow morning. I can't spend all night in hospitals."

"Ma'am, with all due respect, myself and my colleague have been with your grandson and helped him all evening long. We care about Eduardo very much, but we are not family. His family should take responsibility for his care. We will continue to help, but we cannot and will not be the sole ones in charge. It would be a pity if something were to happen and Eduardo were to be alone." The intent of my message must have shown through the sweet words. There was a silence on the other end, only a muffled noise, like the phone had been pressed against the body and Doña Amalia was discussing the situation with someone. After a moment, her voice came back. "You are right. Someone will come tonight to be with him," she said with resignation. There was little, if any, conviction in her voice.

I thanked her again and gave her my number and the office number. "I will pass by in the morning to see how things are and see if Eduardo is awake." I clicked end on my phone, slipped it back into my bag and took a deep breath of the salt air. We could confidently leave, or, rather, I felt we accomplished all we could for the evening.

I rejoined Héctor and let him know I had contacted Eduardo's family. At the threshold Héctor turned to Luisíto, asking if he was heading back to the plaza.

"Yeah, I'm going back to Güibia."

"Come on, I'll drop you off."

Luisíto was quiet on the short drive up the Malecón. Héctor pulled in on a side street that paralleled the row of abandoned, ramshackle mansions where Luisíto slept. He made to get out of the back seat of the Charger.

"Listen, Luisíto," I said as he was halfway out of the car, "You did good. You know that, right? Eduardo would be dead if you hadn't brought him in"—regardless of whatever other role he might have had in the stabbing of his best friend. But I couldn't add that; it was only suggestive, a suspicion.

Luisíto didn't sound the proud hero, "Yeah, I know." And then, something I rarely heard from any of the kids we worked with: gratitude. "Thanks for being there. I didn't think anyone would come and help."

Luisíto got out of the car, slunk across the street to the chain-link fence that ringed the property and effortlessly lifted himself up and over into the overgrown weeds on the other side. I lost sight of him in the shadows before he entered the skeleton of the house where he slept.

## AFTERMATH

It was going to be another steamer of a day. Nine A.M. on the Conde and already the bricks radiated heat like it was mid-afternoon. I couldn't sleep in—something in my body had propelled me up at seven thirty, despite the late night. By the time I had climbed into bed in the wee hours the night before, the adrenaline of the evening had worn itself out and I collapsed onto the mattress, lights out. In the morning I felt rejuvenated and ready to go.

On my way to the hospital I called the office. Word had already reached them about Eduardo. Estívaliz, the director, thanked me for checking in on Eduardo. "But if his family is there make them take charge of his care. We aren't his family."

As I turned onto the Conde, I ran into Ferndando sitting on a bench outside of Paco's. "You disappeared last night. What, did it get boring for you?"

"Nah, man, I just had somethin' I had to do."

"At two in the morning?"

"You know how it goes."

"Thanks for telling me about Eduardo last night."

"Yeah, well, sometimes people get what they deserve. Sometimes it's a raw deal. He got screwed over."

"What've you heard?"

He gave a sarcastic chuckle. "You want me to give up my sources?"

"Well, if you aren't going to let anything go, I'll tell you what I think you know."

"Really? And what do you think I know?"

"That even if it was Joaquín's knife, he had help."

"Really? That's what you think I know?" A thin smile spread across his face.

"Yeah. And I'll even go further. You think it was Luisíto that gave the order."

"You think I know a lot." But the smile widened, flattening his lips to his teeth.

I took a further guess to see where it would take me. "And I know you don't start selling without permission. It can cause a lot of problems."

Fernando raised his hands to chest level, palms out, and shrugged his shoulders. "Now you know more than me 'cause I don't do that shit."

"Well, I'm just speculating." I had it nailed. "Listen, I'm off to see how Eduardo's doing. Should I send your best to the patient?"

"Don't bother. He won't believe anyone but his best friend." Meaning Luisíto.

To my surprise, Ana was in the cavernous hospital waiting room, talking on her cell phone, when I arrived. I gave her a hug in greeting.

"You didn't have to come here this morning. How did you know he was here?"

"I'd talked to Héctor this morning. Instead of going to the office I came straight here. I had to see him for myself."

"How's he look?"

"Like he's been stabbed in the back. He's weak and with some pain, but otherwise he looks ok. If he can stay clear of infection, the recovery should be quick."

"Did he tell you how it happened?"

"That it was Joaquín? Yes. I can't believe it. I've worked with Joaquín a long time, known him for many years. It's hard to accept. His mother is in there with him. She and his stepfather and grandfather got here early in the morning. It was good that when he came to this morning his mother was there."

Eduardo was still in the same post-surgery/intensive care room he had been taken to the night before. Out in the courtyard was a large, dark-skinned woman drinking a small carton of milk. She sat on the bench lining the wall, looking out onto the dilapidated greenery of the courtyard. Bags of medical waste sat in the open space among the verdant ivy and white chipped paint.

The large woman set down her drink as we approached, and greeted Ana. "Jon, this is Soreida, Eduardo's mother."

I did a mental double-take. How could this squat, frumpy woman be the mother of someone so tall and squarely built as Eduardo? Perhaps there was something in her cheekbones and slope of the forehead that vaguely resembled Eduardo, but that was as far as I could see the similarity. And she was young—maybe in her early thirties, to add a few years on her. Eduardo was sixteen.

I extended my hand in greeting. Something told me to keep my distance.

"Oh! You're the gringo that called. The one that saved my son. Oh, thank you!" She started to tear up.

"Really, ma'am, there were lots of people involved. My colleague Héctor, for example, plus the kid who brought Eduardo here to begin with." And the nurse at the blood bank, I thought, paying her private homage.

"But you gave your blood to my boy."

I changed the subject. "How's he doing?"

Her face turned somber again. "I got here at three-thirty, four o'clock this morning. I had such a time getting out of my neighborhood. No taxis will go in at that hour. I had to walk out to the main street—me and my husband—to wait for a taxi. When I got here and saw my son—my little boy"—she teared up—"he looked so bad. Pale, and sleeping so deeply his chest barely moved. I thought he was dead! I know, God save me from the thought, but I believed him to be dead!"

She didn't really answer my question, but I let it go. I gave Ana a sidelong glance and said, "I think I'll go in and see him now if that's all right." I didn't wait for a reply.

Eduardo didn't look that different from when I had left him eight hours before: still sleeping, his body awkwardly articulated on the bed. There was evidence of care, however, and of his family's presence. The blood-spotted sheets had been replaced and the area around the hospital bed was neat. Hanging off one of the corners of the bed was a child's pink backpack with Barbie's disembodied head pictured in the center, large parts of the decal peeling away.

I stood at the side of the bed and looked over the long, pale body. The gauze on the wound had not been changed and maintained that sickly brown color of dried blood. Even the white tape that framed the opaque window of the gauze had taken the crusted appearance of the blood. I caught the attention of the intern who was checking the IV of a patient three beds down and asked when the dressing would be changed.

"After the doctor makes his rounds at 10."

"Do you know if they've given him any medications in case of infection?"

"Again, the doctor will discuss that when he makes his rounds." The intern didn't look up from across the beds.

Eduardo squirmed, shifting his body, his arms and legs getting tangled in the plastic tubing of the IV drip and catheter. Male patients with catheters often catch painful infections, so that any short pull on the tube will elicit double the pain—one of having the tube in the slit of the penis and the other of the infected conjunction of the body's piping with that of the medical profession's. I looked down at where the tubing connected with the plastic bag, like an external bladder, full of dark yellow urine, pushed under the bed. That needed to be changed, too. It was for the auxiliary aspects of patient care that patients needed someone to watch over them besides the overstretched hospital staff.

Eduardo tried turning from his side to his back, the pain sharpening as he lay on the wound. That woke him up. He moaned out, "Son of a bitch." His eyes fluttered open. I stood there, smiling over him.

"And good morning to you, too."

It took him a couple of blinks to adjust to where he was. You could see it click, remembering that he was in the hospital. He lifted his head, looking at me sideways, dropped it to the pillow again and closed his eyes briefly. Then, the eyes opened with more certainty and clarity. "Ana said you'd come."

"And here I am. How're you feeling?"

"I got a pain in my back and a pain in my front." He indicated with his top hand the wound and the catheter.

"Yeah, well, that's a good sign. Means you are still alive. You scared us big time last night with your bleeding trick."

He tried to laugh and grimaced instead. "I remember seeing you last night. I thought it was a bad trip or something. I kept thinking, why can't I move? Why is Jon here? You called my mother?"

"You gave me your grandma's phone number. I called her."

"I didn't want to see me mother."

"You needed someone here with you. Your grandma called your mom."

He closed his eyes again. "I didn't want them to see me like this, you know?"

I didn't know how to take that. Did he mean wounded in the hospital, or did he mean coming in off the streets?

"Your mom know where you been living?"

"No. My grandma neither. I told them I was with my dad in San Cristóbal. That's where I was supposed to be."

"Well, they know now, more or less, everything."

Eduardo didn't reply at first, then said, "My grandma is going to lay in on me when she sees me. My mom can say whatever she wants, do whatever she wants, but it's my grandma that is going to hurt. She's the one who raised me."

"It can't hurt any more than getting stabbed in the back."

He raised his head and saw me grinning. "No. I don't suppose it will."

I didn't want to ask him the obvious question, at least not yet, about how it happened—or, more important, why. I figured the how was self-evident. It was the why that may never come out because the why may also be self-incriminating. Attacks on the street, especially attacks resulting in such violent retribution, never arise out of nowhere. I hated to agree with Fernando on this, but what he said rang true. Eduardo was no innocent bystander—he had done something to touch off this reprisal, broken some code or perceived code of the street—but he didn't deserve this. There were other forms of retribution, ways of hashing out a problem, and they almost all involved an ambush of some sort. Ganging up on a guy to beat the living daylights out of him. Gang raping both girls and guys. Setting someone's feet on fire while they slept. Sending the cops after someone so that the police did the double dirty work of pummeling the guy and giving him an arbitrary length of stay in the local holding cell. Stabbing someone in the back fit into the ambush, surprise nature of such reprisals. They wanted to send a clear, unambiguous message: you screw me/us over, we'll lay you out whenever, wherever, however. It was about the twin elements of surprise and fear.

"They tell me I've got your blood in me now," Eduardo said.

"That's right," I lied, "so you'd better take care of it."

"That means I can go get a visa now."

"How do you figure that, Eduardo?"

"Oh—I just go to the embassy and tell them that I have gringo blood now and that I'm partially you. They have to give it to me, since my blood would be legal." He was joking, of course, but the joke revealed his desire to escape.

"I don't think that'll work, Eduardo. Besides, you didn't lose all your blood, thank God. What was mine is now mixed with yours. You can't tell the difference. All blood is basically the same—Dominican or gringo."

"If all blood were the same, then why do they have embassies and laws that keep people out of some countries?"

He had me there.

"Speaking of blood," I segued, pushing the conversation to where my curiosity lay in wait, "Do you know how you got to the hospital?"

"Yeah. Luisíto paid a cab to bring me here. He dragged me to the curb and got me in the cab and brought me here."

"That was a smart and brave thing." I fished around, throwing comments like bait.

"And I would have done the same for him, you know. He's my brother."

The sentiment was reciprocal, then. Eduardo, too, used the English word, pronouncing it like two pieces of a broken dish—brot-her.

"So he was there when you got stabbed?"

"Listen up! This is how it happened." Eduardo became animated, lifting his arms and motioning with his hands as he talked. "Luisíto and I are sitting on the wall looking out to the sea, talking."

"Just talking?"

Eduardo equivocates. "You know how it is. Talking and having a smoke. So we're sittin' there doin' nothin' when Joaquín comes by, passes behind us and starts talkin' shit. He'd been talkin' shit to me all day. The police had come to the plaza earlier and Joaquín is telling me it's my fault that I didn't fight with the police when they came, which is bullshit. How am I gonna fight with some police? But later he apologized and shit, and I thought it was for real. So I was sittin' on the wall. And Joaquín goes down to the beach and asked Débora to lend him a knife. Luisíto and I don't hear him, he comes behind us and stabs me, just like that. I didn't feel it at first, just like a tingling. I didn't know I was stabbed until I fainted."

"He stabbed you like that, without motive?"

"What do you mean, without motive?"

"Like, without a reason as to why he would stab you."

"I don't know. I'm sure he had his reasons."

"You hadn't done anything to him?"

"No, man, Joaquín and I always got along fine. He can be a little shit sometimes, thinkin' he's all big and shit, but we never fought like this."

"Any business gone bad between you two?"

Eduardo tried to laugh again. "Business? You think you know what goes on?"

"No, I'm not too wise. I just know how this goes sometimes, why you guys fight like this, because I've seen it before. It's either because of a girl or money or drug. Or all three. Which one put you in trouble?"

Before he could answer—because he was going to, he thought about how he would say it, I could see the contemplation on his face—but before he could answer, Ana and his mother entered the room. He saw them come in, his face changing, and he clammed up. He wasn't going to talk about any of this in front of his mother.

My eyes followed his line of sight. "We'll talk more later on this."

"It's not important, Jon. He did this to me and now it's my turn to return the favor. That's all that is important."

He was already thinking revenge. Maybe Eduardo was right. Maybe the why didn't matter anymore, after the first act. In escalation, maybe the foundations of conflict were unimportant, the deep history obscured by the most recent events. Retaliation only went so far back as the time immediately before.

The underlying conflict, however, did seem important to me, if for no other reason than to satisfy my curiosity. Power struggles and interpersonal relations changed quickly on the street, especially in the Plaza, where it seemed that the drugs and money influenced who was with whom on a daily basis. Any insight into the conditions that bred such violent reprisals would have been welcomed. It would have made a logical pattern out of the apparent senselessness.

I was convinced that Eduardo would make a complete recovery. A couple more days in the hospital and he'd be out. Of course, the lingering question was, where to?

"It's going to take you a while to be back to your old self," I said. The three of us ringed Eduardo's bed, standing over him like sentinels. "You need to give some thought about what you are going to do and where you are going to go."

Ana was more direct. "You go back to the Plaza, back to the street, and you'll get an infection for sure. With a wound like what you have, you can't be moving around that much. You have to be calm."

"You understand they sewed you up from the inside? You've got stitches not just outside but inside, too."

Soreida released a big puff of air. "I don't know, Ana. He's my son, but if he were to come back to the house, he'd have to change. Things can't be the same. He's not a little kid. Look at him! He's a man. He needs to take responsibility for himself in my house." Eduardo's face turned sour. I remember what he had told me about his relationship with his stepfather. "He would do weird things," Soreida indicated Eduardo again. "He'd come back late at night. He wouldn't sleep on the couch or on a bed. Uh-huh. He'd climb under the bed to sleep like some sort of animal! He'd bring such habits from the street and be a bad influence on his younger brother. He'd fight with his stepfather. I can't have that kind of disruption in my house."

Throughout Soreida's condemnation, Eduardo stayed silent and took it. He didn't stage any interruptions or protest. He didn't try to justify his behavior. Even now that Soreida had finished, Eduardo remained placid in the face of his mother's rejection. It was a different Eduardo that answered his mother, a more rational and mature young man than I had ever seen. "A household cannot have two heads," he replied. The meaning was clear. Eduardo felt pushed out of his mother's house by his stepfather, his role as provider and protector of the family usurped by this other man.

"You will have to talk to your grandparents if you can't live under someone else's authority. In this world you don't always get to do what you want to do." Bitter resignation saturated Soreida's voice.

"The important thing is that we identify options now," Ana tried to mediate, "then we can work on resolving the problems getting along better. You need to understand, Soreida, that your son is in need and, at least temporarily, may need your assistance, including living with you until he recuperates if there is no other option. And you, Eduardo, must understand that you are vulnerable right now and must accommodate to the rules of others, be it ours, the doctor's, or your family's. You need to see what is in your best interest. Your mother is right about one thing. You are not a little kid. You are sixteen years old and can take responsibility for yourself and your actions."

Eduardo did not reply. It was rare to silence him so I didn't know what his reticence meant. Was he contemplating his options or was it defiance?

Five figures in sea foam–green scrubs and white coats entered through the door like a single living and breathing organism. The resident on duty stood up from the desk in the corner and announced in an authoritative voice, "The doctor is here to see the patients now. Please exit the room until he is finished."

The visitors of the other patients gathered their things and went out to the courtyard. We followed suit. Ana and I told Eduardo we'd stop by in the afternoon. As we took our leave, Ana took Eduardo's hand, patting it, and said, "We care for you very much, Eduardo. Think about what I said, ok?"

I wanted to ask Soreida what the problem was between Eduardo and his stepfather, from her perspective. What she had mentioned about Eduardo sleeping under furniture raised many red flags for me. She was wrong. Such behavior had little to do with Eduardo's cavorting in the streets. It usually indicated fear; victims of abuse would protect themselves any way they could. Hiding under furniture so their attacker could not find them or would have a more difficult time cornering their prey seemed like an effective survival tactic. It was hard for me to imagine a young man as brawny as Eduardo could be threatened to such a degree that he'd go cowering under beds, but that seemed to be the case. And it wasn't physical abuse of which such nocturnal behavior was symptomatic, but sexual violence. Eduardo, I thought, was too large a young man to be coerced into sex. But then I met his stepfather.

Outside in the courtyard on the same stone bench that Soreida had been sitting on earlier was a man as big as a door. His back leaned against the hospital wall and the long, thick legs extended out, feet crossed. Next to him was a small paper bag, which he grabbed off the bench when he saw Soreida. He stood up and marched toward us, this large man clutching the comically small paper bag as if it was a lady's pocketbook.

The man stood behind Soreida, a good two heads taller. He thrust the grease-stained bag into her hands, saying in a deep, rough voice like gravel, "Here are your empanadas, dear." He didn't have to make any verbal commands. His presence alone demanded that we introduce ourselves.

Soreida did the introductions, presenting her husband as Ernesto, but fawningly calling him Neto. She played to him, relied on him, and this dependency became obvious as I watched their interactions, in the way she subtly looked for his approval, searching his eyes for confirmation. Yes, I thought, I could see Eduardo pushed out of his mother's circle of care by this man. Her submission was total and left no room for Eduardo. Ernesto was the type that would demand such things from his family, and a kid as headstrong as Eduardo would not give them.

Ernesto placed both hands on his wife's shoulders, standing firm behind her. "We are going to find out who did this to Eduardo and make him pay. I've got friends of mine—police—who will help. That piece of trash will regret the day he ever messed with Eduardo." Ernesto went on to elaborate the plan, how he and his friends had already been to Güibia and asked around. Eduardo, to his credit, had not told his stepfather every detail of the evening. He had not divulged who had stabbed him, although our conversation had made it clear Eduardo knew full well who it was.

"Eduardo gave me a description. He said it was someone he didn't know. But I got information from those hooligans at the Plaza. We'll be waiting for this guy." Ernesto's voice was a violent tranquillity, exacting and passionless. I could only believe he'd go through with his threats, although why he cared so much I didn't know. Did he do it for Soreida's sake? Or out of some sense of wounded personal pride? Someone messed with a member of his family; even if it was his wife's no-good son, they weren't going to get away with the insult.

"You know who did this to Eduardo?" he asked Ana and me point blank.

I didn't hesitate. "You know, Güibia's one of those places that attract a lot of different people, people who come and go. We don't know everyone down there. Last night, the young man who told me Eduardo was here in the hospital, he told me it was a newcomer to the plaza." I couldn't believe I just looked straight in this man's eyes and told a blatant untrue version of events. I didn't know why Joaquín would stab Eduardo.

Ana addressed Ernesto's comments more fully, "With all due respect, sir, I think you should allow the justice system to work and find the person who did this to Eduardo. I don't think vigilantism is the answer."

Ernesto's face transformed into a threateningly banal look—detached, calculating. "We don't want justice. We want revenge."

Outside the hospital, into the brightness of the day, the full force of Eduardo's stepfather's expressed threats weighed upon Ana and myself. I didn't doubt he would follow through, and said so to Ana.

"No, you are right. We need to find Joaquín before Ernesto does, tell him to disappear. This is not a good situation. This is not the Joaquín I remember. He has changed so much, no longer the same kid who went to the Christians."

Three years earlier, Joaquín had been a roly-poly eleven-year-old with puffy cheeks and a baby-fat smile. I had seen pictures of events stored in the office's computers—trips to the zoo, activities in the park, baseball games—with Joaquín cheerfully playing along. A ministry that had come on weekends to preach to the homeless kids in one of Santo Domingo's parks along the Malecón picked out Joaquín and his friend Estarlín to go live in their residential center for troubled youth in a town two hours east of the capital. The two boys eagerly went, lured with hopes of a better future. Ana had not heard from them again until six months earlier, when both Estarlín and Joaquín appeared at their old haunts, back on the streets, eventually making their way to Güibia where all the action was to be had.

Joaquín came back from "the Christians" thirty pounds thinner, and Estarlín came back nearly a foot taller. Those had not been the only changes. Both had become cynical and wary. Joaquín expressed it in his sneering machinations, Estarlín in his calculated laziness. Neither had returned to their respective families. According to Estarlín, the center "decided to let all the older kids go. They didn't want us anymore, only the little kids. We worked really hard at the center. We helped build it. We cooked every day, cleaned it. We did church three times a day. And then one day the pastor says to us that we are ready to go out and preach the Word, that we have to leave. What shit is that? After you help build a home you have to leave it?"

They had received bus fare to return to their families in the capital—families they hadn't had much contact with in the intervening years. The two of them got off the bus and returned to the streets as if nothing had ever changed.

"So what do we do?" I asked. "Go to Güibia and see if Joaquín is around?"

"Or, if he's not, we can at least leave a message. He knows what he's done and should be smart enough to disappear."

We called the office, let them know what our plan was, and made arrangements with Epifanio to meet us there in the pick-up.

"You heard it was Luisíto that brought Eduardo to the hospital, didn't you?" I wasn't sure what Ana knew, although as per usual she seemed to be well informed.

"Oh, yes. That Luisíto, he did a good thing."

"Yeah, well, don't praise him too much yet," I replied. Ana looked quizzically at me. For once I had street knowledge she didn't. It was a hollow victory. I told her about my conversations with Fernando and my growing doubts about Luisíto's motivations for his heroism. Is heroism motivated by a guilty conscience still considered heroic?

"So I wouldn't praise Luisíto too much. He did the right thing, but telling him too many times is only going to make him feel worse."

"If he was involved." Ana didn't want to believe the worst.

"Yeah, if he was involved. Although, Ana," I pressed on, "Luisíto's got a good hold on the Güibia group. He's becoming one of the leaders. It would be inconceivable that he would allow that to happen if he hadn't known or gave the ok." I paused, letting Luisíto's possible actions settle in. "Or worse yet, he ordered it." Too much speculation would lead us in circles. There was no way to know unless Luisíto or Joaquín told us, and even then, it would not be truthful. The only truth we had was that Eduardo was stabbed and it was probably Joaquín who did it.

"Let's see if we can find Estarlín first. We know where he is likely to be."

Ana finished my thought, "And Estarlín will know about Joaquín."

Estarlín was one of three or four regulars who washed car windows at an intersection on Maximo Gómez. Window washing was an effective way to make enough petty cash to meet everyday expenses for street kids. Though it was not a get-rich-quick scheme, an industrious window-washer could net between 150 and 200 pesos in a day if the stoplight worked and there was enough traffic flowing through the intersection. That was enough money to buy a greasy fried meal, including rice, a hit of crack cocaine, and even enough for some post-crack marijuana to mellow out with. Of course priorities depended on the kid and what he was into that day. A couple of the kids washed windows to pay exclusively for their crack habit. They were the industrious ones, who were out there early and stayed late, because one hit of crack no longer had the desired effect. They needed two at least, sometimes three or four. What they couldn't make honestly window washing, they made up in other activities. Sex was the easiest form of exchange, but the window washers unanimously agreed it was better to make what you could at the intersection because sex for money wasn't steady and clients could be fickle.

Ana and I left the taxi two blocks north of the intersection where Estarlín and the other kids washed windows and walked down Maximo Gómez, heading toward the sea. They had chosen an ideal location for their business. Not only was it close to their home base on the Malecón, it was also the only main arterial flowing traffic to the east. It was a one-way street that, during rush hours would be backed up quite a long ways. They would wander through the stopped cars and target as many vehicles as possible.

It was nearing the middle of the day. Even on the tree-lined sidewalk the heat could be felt, insinuating itself with the double helix of humidity, winding under clothes and dripping the sweat down the back. A block before the intersection sits a large, Spanish-style mansion—creamy stucco walls and orange-tiled roof, set back from the avenue and surrounded by a low garden wall. The building may have been used as an embassy at one time, as farther up the street sit the representatives of Argentina, Ecuador, and the Vatican, but since I could remember, the building had been vacant with a large sign proclaiming its availability. Each passing month the house lost more of its vibrant grandeur as it succumbed to the lack of maintenance and vandals. Much of the ironwork had been taken piecemeal, and the teak double-entry doors boarded over so they would not be stolen. At the side entrance, against the low stucco wall, was a small, thin Haitian man with a large black cauldron of oil, frying pieces of plantain, yucca, sweet potato, and a nauseating array of unrecognizable meats—sausages, of course, but also long stringy sections called *bofe*, flattened and hanging from the wall behind the owner.

Sitting on the wall, next to the strung meat, sat the two Juan Carloses, holding in their hands pieces of brown coarse paper topped off with sausage and plantains. Their oversized t-shirts draped down their skinny bodies. The motion of their jaws as they chewed filled out their naturally gaunt cheeks. These two not only shared their first names, they shared a crack habit that cost between 500 to 700 pesos a day. Juancho and Juan Carlos had grown to look like each other over the months, despite Juancho's teased out afro and *café con leche* colored skin and Juan Carlos's shaved head and pitch-black coloring. Juancho had been on the streets for over five years, slowly descending into each new depth of vice and danger with aplomb and apparent glee. Juan Carlos had been living on the streets for little over a year. After meeting Juancho, the change in demeanor and physical appearance had been rapid. He went from marijuana to crack as his primary drug of choice. Juancho had started pimping Juan Carlos, with his exotic features and welcoming smile, and taught him the basics of pick-pocketing and breaking and entering. Between remunerated sex, petty thievery, and washing car windshields, they fed their habits and shared everything between them. They were both fifteen years old.

Ana greeted the two boys with the Spanish equivalent of *bon apetit*, a phrase not just used for the finest of foods, but for any meal, even the lowliest of street vendor food. They ate with gusto, chomping hard on the thick plantain chips. The proper response, so ingrained in Dominican culture, is to offer what you are eating to those around you. To not offer is to deny people the basic human dignity of sharing a space at the metaphorical table. Juancho did not disappoint, offering up to Ana and me the glistening bits of greasy food in his hand. Ana demurely declined. I sat next to Juancho on the wall and picked up a still-hot piece of plantain from his hand. Juancho cackled with glee, "This is what it is!" His broad smile held a piece of yellow stuck to the incisors.

"We heard Güibia had a lot of excitement last night," I said, ignoring Juancho's reaction to my eating from his hand. The plantain wasn't that bad. A bit dry, very salty, and hard to chew. Mostly it tasted of grease and a faint tinge of meatiness.

"You mean the thing with Eduardo?" Juan Carlos spoke for the first time.

"Yeah," Ana replied, "the thing with Eduardo."

"We don't know shit about that," Juancho answered back. "Last night we were working the Malecón, ain't that right, Juan Carlos? You know how it is, Jon, you gotta make the money for the rock." An illusion to crack, as a hit in Spanish is called *piedra* or a stone or rock of crack. Juan Carlos offered the curled up fist of his left hand to be bumped by Juancho's reciprocal fist, the nonverbal equivalent of saying "right on."

Juancho continued. He was going to give us every last detail of their night searching for cash. "We only had 200 pesos, which ain't enough to buy shit. We had to go on the search, you know? But we're lucky 'cause I think we can find a client. Down there by Montesino we see a guy who's looking for it. This dude wants it so bad he's drooling after Juan Carlos here. I send my boy out," Juancho acknowledges his companion with a bob of his head in Juan Carlos's direction, "and the two of them go behind the monument in the dark, out in the weeds. I give them a few minutes and then sneak around the other side of the monument. Ha! Juan Carlos is there on his fucking knees, chokin' down that faggot's sausage, man." Juancho mimicked the action, rounding his lips in a big 'O' and exaggeratingly rocked his head back and forth. Juan Carlos did not say a word, but looked down, concentrating on the grease-stained paper in his hands. "I mean, my buddy's givin' it to him like he means it! I gotta rock and just as the faggot's getting' ready to spew his cream I conk him on the head. The dude falls down cold." Juancho cackles again at the memory. "The faggot's loaded, too. He's got 500 pesos wadded up in his wallet. Juan Carlos and I get enough to smoke all night."

"Yeah, man. We went up to Benito Street and bought what we could right there. When we get back everyone's talkin' about how Joaquín knifed

Eduardo. We just went to our corner of the mansion and started smokin'. Everyone was all worried the police was gonna come and shit and we just sat back in our corner and smoked. The cops may come to the plaza but they never enter the mansion."

I told them about Eduardo's stepdad's threats, about how Güibia might be seeing a lot of cops or people saying they're cops. "They don't know who did it, but that means they could think it was any one of you guys. Just be alert and careful."

"Shit, man, he can come to me. I'll tell him where that fucker Joaquín is. I'll lead him right to the guy." Juancho had no trouble playing the turncoat, either. So much for solidarity. "You know what that fucker's been doin'? He walks around like he controls the goddamn plaza. Like we gotta buy from him."

"We ain't gotta buy from nobody. We go where we can buy for cheap," Juan Carlos interjected, indignation in his voice at the thought of having to pay more for crack.

"That's right, Juan Carlos. We may have our affliction," Juancho pronounced the word like it was a piece of cast-off clothing, "but that don't mean we gotta buy at too high a price. Joaquín starts acting like we can only buy from him. That's bullshit."

"So Eduardo started selling cheaper?" Undercutting prices, introducing competition, and taking away Joaquín's profits could have precipitated an attack.

Juancho turned his head to look me full in the eye, a knowing smile etched on his face. "Yeah, man. Eduardo found a source." Uncharacteristically, Juancho wasn't going to say any more on the topic. A brief silence fell upon us. The boys went back to chomping on their fried goodies, teeth grinding in short revolutions.

Ana caught my eye, signaling we should move on. "Is Joaquín still hanging around the plaza?"

"I saw him this morning, that was it. The fucker was still trying to sell." Juancho grumbled into his food. His mood had changed quickly, signaling it was time for us to go.

As we walked the next block down I tried to sort things out in my mind. I didn't doubt the root cause of the incident now—that Eduardo had been encroaching on the sales territory of Joaquín. I had a feeling Joaquín had a silent partner in his drug dealing, someone who may have provided him with the contact or even had set him up with the initial cash, but wasn't going to do the dirty work of selling. It had to be Luisíto. It didn't sound like it was common knowledge. In fact, I wondered if Eduardo had even known when he started selling that he was cutting into his best friend's earnings. He may have offered Luisíto a cut, or maybe not. It may have been Luisíto's idea to scare Eduardo off from selling or maybe it was Joaquín's, and Luisíto just went along with it. Luisíto was at least guilty by being complicit, that was one thing I was sure of by now.

We reached the near corner of the next block. The window washing crew, minus the two Juan Carloses who were still on their coffee break, wove in and out of traffic, throwing their sponges on windows in hope the driver would assent to the cleaning. Sometimes the driver would turn on their wipers to say no, other times they would curse and yell out the window or honk obnoxiously. The kids would flip these drivers off. Some of the more aggressive or high kids would grab their crotches obscenely, telling the cab drivers and pristine working girls alike to suck it. They got a great kick off of doing this, roiling with laughter at the cars' inhabitants' reaction. It only spurred them on.

Estarlín was out among the cars, easily recognizable because of his tall stature. His head and shoulders floated between the tops of the cars. He knew how to communicate with his body, signaling to anyone who would read the signs that he wasn't going to take shit. His long arms thumped his chest from time to time while he argued with cab drivers. He'd bounce about, chest first in a confident strut, his lanky body sometimes moving in two opposing planes at the same time. Estarlín knew how to use his height to his advantage.

The light changed and the traffic impatiently roared on. The boys skidded back into place along the sidewalk. Many offered us a warm greeting, but Estarlín hung apart, feigned not noticing us. Ana motioned that I stay put. She went to Estarlín alone. I kept myself busy playing thumb wars with two of the twelve-year-olds.

After a few minutes, Ana called me over. "Estarlín here thinks we're lying to him about Eduardo's stepfather, Jon."

"No, I don't think you are lying, Ana," Estarlín became defensive, lifting his head up and jostling his torso about with every word, "I just don't think it's that serious. They don't know it was him."

"You don't think they can find out?" I countered, "Come on, Estarlín, I know all these guys are your friends," I motioned to the far end of the corner where a group of six kids were play-fighting, waiting for the light to change, "But any one of them would sell his best friend if the money was right."

"They ain't my friends. It's just Joaquín and me. We've been through a lot."

"All the more reason to keep him out of harm's way, my dear one," Ana put on a placating, imploring voice. "This man's already been here asking questions. He's going to come back. It's just a matter of time."

"All we want you to do, Estarlín, is suggest to Joaquín that he either go home or find a different territory for a good three months. Either way he can't stay here."

"Why can't you talk to him, Ana?"

"First of all, because I'm very upset with him for what he did. I don't care about why he did it, you and I both know that's not how we resolve problems. Second, if we see him, we are obligated to bring him to the cops. He committed a crime and should go through the justice system. People would say that Niños del Camino harbors criminals if we didn't. Do you understand that? As much as we care for Joaquín, he did wrong. We don't want to see him get hurt by this man."

Estarlín considered this, wringing out the excess water in the piece of sponge he carried. A dark spot on the cement where the water dripped grew at his feet. "All right. I'll talk to him. I'll tell him he needs to disappear for awhile."

Ana was right—we definitely didn't want to see Joaquín, for our own liability. But Joaquín wasn't the only kid who performed acts of violence. To some degree or another, they all did. It was one of the defining features of street culture, inculcated in the very fibers of social relationships. We'd be fools to think we could change that when the culture was so much more intricately connected with elements we, as an organization, had no contact with or control over. How different was Juancho's attack and robbery of his client from what Joaquín did to Eduardo? Both involved premeditated, egregious violence for material gain. And yet I barely batted an eye when Juancho recounted his story, didn't even comment or admonish him. Maybe I thought the guy deserved what he got for picking up a minor for sexual services. My morals were getting out of whack, relativizing to the point of losing any absolutes. I could see the logic behind the actions. Not that it justified what had taken place, but it made it more difficult to rashly condemn. The more exposed I had become, the more desensitized to the elements of street life, the less willing I was to make blanket judgments. I was losing perspective as things became more normal and the kids' daily life shocked me less.

I remember early on, in my first months working, I had asked Ana about her relationships with the kids and how she reconciled what she knew about them with her work. She had replied simply, "I don't have to like every kid we work with. Some of them are tremendous. There have been a few that made me tremble on the inside. But I do have to offer all of them the same treatment and compassion."

## COMMENTARY

One of the consequences of structural exclusion, as outlined in Chapter 2, is that communities without access to the social, economic, and cultural resources of dominant society must rely on their own systems of support. As entrance to the formal economy, for instance, is hindered by a number of barriers (high unemployment, the need for specialized skills or education), forms of work in the informal and illegal economies are viable, even preferable, ways of making a living. Likewise, social norms on the street that are indigenous to those communities come to have greater value than the social norms guiding the lives of middle- and upper-class citizens, even while certain aspects of dominant society, such as access to high-end goods, are idealized and may motivate involvement in the illegal economy. Economic and social relationships on the street are intimately intertwined, to such a degree that it is difficult to examine one without viewing the influence it has in on the other. This is not so much a consequence of survival as it is the result of stark exclusion from participation in "respectable" society. While street groups draw on many of the same cultural forms and symbols as other social and economic classes, these forms and symbols are inflected in a different way.

We can see this in the influence that the drug economy has on shaping the values and interactions of street groups. As both addicts and business proprietors, street groups like the one centered loosely at Plaza Güibia weave a complex set of interpersonal relationships around access to and use of drugs, particularly crack. It is no surprise, then, that many of the interpersonal conflicts that arise involve drugs, particularly as drug use involves a hierarchy of desperation as one's addiction deepens. In other words, even while crack and marijuana are shared among close friends, tension arises when a peer takes advantage of other group members' addiction by selling them drugs. As long as members of the peer group purchase drugs from outside of the scene, a kind of détente, even mutual support exists, but once one member sets himself up as dealer to his friends, the situation turns more violent, even deadly.

This process is evident when we examine the close interpersonal relationships described in the above narrative. What first appeared to me as a more or less cohesive street group based on shared geographic boundaries within the city would slowly be revealed as much more dynamic and complex. Although groups of kids and youth did identify with areas of the city where they spent their time—as being associated with Plaza Güibia or Parque Hostos, for instance—this identification never expanded to include a sense of solidarity or group cohesion that melded geographic place with an investment in one's peer group. In other words, there was no larger group to which they pledged allegiance. Instead, individuals developed close relationships with some others in their environment, usually describing these relationships, as did Luisíto and Eduardo, in kinship terms—calling a particularly close friend or associate a broter, or brother, or other commonly used slang terms such as pana and pana full.

Marginal conditions forged tight bonds between pairs of youth, drawing them together because of the dangers they shared while trying to make it on the streets. Unlike the relationships with members from outside the street scene, as explored through the lives of Panchito and Nico in the previous chapter, relationships forged with one's peers on the street are less about comparative advantage and ways of gaining access to social and economic capital otherwise unavailable from the social networks springing from the street milieu, and more about reinforcing one's position vis-à-vis the resources available within the street environment. These relationships are no less exploitative, to be sure, but elements of cooperation, as well as conflict, characterize their tenor.

Juancho and Juan Carlos are a good case in point. Drug addiction and petty crime are woven throughout the history of their friendship. Their pursuit of covert activities only serves to strengthen this bond between them. They relish one another's company and the friendship that has developed as a result of their crack use. In the two years that I knew them, they worked toward a common goal each day—scrounging together enough money to meet their addiction needs. Despite this apparent harmony and friendship, their relationship was based on a deep asymmetry. Whether it was through personal charisma or force, Juancho clearly had the upper hand, with the ability to persuade Juan Carlos to take greater risks than he might have done had Juan Carlos been on his own. It was Juancho who initiated involvement in sex work and, more often than not, set Juan Carlos up as the bait for their con. Even though Juancho had his own history of sex work prior to meeting Juan Carlos (and he went back to intermittent sex work after Juan Carlos left the streets), he convinced Juan Carlos that he should be the one to interface more with clients, while Juancho stood in the wings and reaped the benefits. Juan Carlos freely accepted this arrangement, motivated by Juancho's encouragement and personality as well as his greater street savvy. Exploitation here is a mutual agreement. Indeed, it may not even be recognized as exploitative because it forms the very core of the friendship. Juan Carlos would stay closely tied to Juancho while he lived in Plaza Güibia, only having that relationship severed when Juancho was sent to prison. When Juancho eventually returned to the streets after being incarcerated for a year, it was with much more guile and a deeper dependency on crack. Juan Carlos, however, had moved on, replacing Juancho as his primary relationship on the street.

The immense contradiction between mutual trust and exploitation is clearly evident in the friendship of Luisíto and Eduardo. From nearly the first days that Eduardo began hanging around Plaza Güibia, there was immediate connection and rapport; the two teens were inseparable. Compared with the friendship of Juancho and Juan Carlos, Eduardo and Luisíto's relationship was, from the beginning, much more egalitarian. This may be because when Eduardo arrived in Plaza Güibia for the first time he was already considerably more streetwise than Juan Carlos had been. Eduardo had lived in an urban zone with a bad reputation and had been exposed to (and participated in) criminal activity prior to leaving his grandparents' home to live on the streets fulltime. Indeed, Eduardo would later tell me he left his grandparents' neighborhood because things had gotten "too hot" there—a bland euphemism for the fact that there were folks in his neighborhood who were out to get him because he had robbed the wrong business. He would transfer these skills to a broader geographic area when he began living on the Malecón. Eduardo's street savvy matched that of Luisíto, as Luisíto had learned much from his street peers in the initial six months of his living in the Plaza. Eventually, Luisíto would gain the respect and relative trust of several of the adults in the zone who, because he was under the legal age for prosecution, used Luisíto to transport drugs around the city. Perhaps the lack of daily drama and conflict between the two youth had much to do with the fact that the two "specialized" in different livelihood strategies and were not dependent upon one another. Although they drank together and shared marijuana cigarettes, neither was an addict in the same way that Juancho and Juan Carlos were.

All this changed, however, when they both became involved with selling drugs in Plaza Güibia and around the Malecón. Luisíto was beginning to be paid in product and not cash for his services transporting the crack and marijuana. His adult associates gave him permission to sell the excess product that he wouldn't use. Luisíto would smoke the marijuana—even share it with his peer group—but, because he wasn't interested in crack, he wanted to find a market for it without having to sell it on his own. Learning from his adult associates, Luisíto contracted the sales of the crack out to Joaquín, passing on the danger and hassle along with the drug. Meanwhile, Eduardo had gained access to a different drug source and also started selling crack in the same area as Joaquín, but undercutting Joaquín, who sold the crack at a higher price for the convenience of purchasing right at one's zone (and not having to travel across the city for a point of sale), and because he was sharing the profits with Luisíto. While neither teenager would lay it out for me in this way, both youths denied that Eduardo had an overt conflict with Joaquín, leaving unstated the competition for sales. I do not know if Eduardo understood that Joaquín sold Luisíto's drugs, nor can I speculate that if he had known it would have made a difference in his decision to undercut Joaquín. What is certain, however, is that Luisíto agreed to punish Eduardo for the competition or, at the very least, agreed to scare him or remove him temporarily from the picture while Joaquín could finish selling the product. It is possible that Joaquín's actions went further than Luisíto had anticipated.

Using premeditated sneak attacks to sanction the actions of another member of one's street cohort was a common occurrence when access to drugs was the primary concern. During my time working outreach, there were three such incidents of premeditated violent attacks. In one case, the victim died at the hands of his peers. In the other two cases, including that of Eduardo, the victim of the attack sustained enough injuries to be out of the picture for a long period of time. While the means of attack was different in all three cases—one had been doused with gasoline and immolated, another had been severely beaten by two members of his peer group as warning, and Eduardo was literally stabbed in the back—the roots of the conflict came back to either hoarding drugs or sales competition. While sharing of food, clothing, and other material goods was common in these street scenes, setting oneself up as seller, and thus having access to larger amounts of drugs than normal, violated a sense of common identity. Selling placed a youth in a position of power; in the eyes of his cohort, that would be the same as lording it over them.

It is through this lens that we should view Luisíto's deed of helping Eduardo to the hospital. His actions were not unusual. On a number of occasions, in emergency situations a sense of camaraderie and mutual support prevailed, with youths helping friends who were victims of violent attacks or accidents get to the hospital. What makes Luisíto's actions remarkable is precisely the fact that he had condoned the sneak attack. Fernando, in his way, was pointing out the contradictions in the professed closeness of Luisíto and Eduardo's friendship. Indeed, youth who choose to stay on the outskirts of the core street group, like Fernando, may do so because they recognize the double-edged sword of close affiliation. While such youth are neither able to lay claims to mutual support in times of crisis nor can they rely on pooling resources for purchasing drugs, they are able to rise above the fray, as it were, and not get drawn into the interpersonal conflicts that inevitably arise when the peer group consists of both drug consumers and drug sellers.

Social dynamics on the street are complex. Relationships of exploitation and mutual assistance exist among different subgroups within the same cohort, relationships that change over time as the individuals involved gain knowledge and experience. Factors such as relative age on the street (newbie versus veteran), reputation, access to material goods and drugs, livelihood strategies, relationships with non–street denizens, physical and psychological health, and intensity of one's drug addiction all play a role in patterning expectations and interactions among group members. These elements are in themselves changeable and affected by the internal workings of the street group as well as environmental influences. Thus, social dynamics are also highly susceptible to outside influence, bordering on volatility due to changes in the social environment. Increased presence of the police, an influx of drugs, the tourist economy, urban redevelopment, and social assistance programs (including NGOs like Niños), are just a few of the external factors that shape social relationships. The confluence of internal and external influences on street children and youth pose a challenge for developing effective outreach intervention strategies, especially as outreach will have an impact on the street group. The best that one can hope for is to be aware of the sources of conflict and astutely observe the potential changes in the environment that could have repercussions in outreach. Given these limits, I address the relative impact and importance of outreach in the conclusion.

# CONCLUSION

EVEN AS I WAS preparing to leave Santo Domingo in late fall 2006, things were beginning to change. In the last month of my Peace Corps service, the city government had begun a clean-up project of the Malecón, self-conscious of the fact that the public areas needed a facelift to match the recent investment of private developers in the area. They started with Plaza Güibia. From the beginning, the redevelopment of the plaza had moral overtones. It was not just about improving the crumbling infrastructure and providing a venue more aesthetically pleasing than the chipped concrete benches and cement tiles. Güibia was chosen specifically to clean up its image as a point of prostitution, drug consumption, and hangout for the homeless. Almost overnight, city workers and the police descended upon the plaza, driving out the denizens who made it home. Tall pieces of metal sheeting were erected all along the sidewalk, blocking out views of the demolition.

While the homeless adults abandoned the area around Güibia relatively quickly for more lucrative zones elsewhere, the street children and youth that made this part of the city their homes were less apt to change their zone. Indeed, for a time quite a few of them shifted their livelihood strategies to include ripping off the construction site, stealing the scrap metal, rebar, and copper wire that was being torn up from the rubble of the old plaza. This was good business, far outpacing what they would have earned from washing windshields. Even kids like Juancho and Juan Carlos turned their focus from sex work to scavenging for metal because the potential earnings were so great. As the youths had greater access to money, their crack addictions began to soar. By the time I left, the majority of the Güibia crew—those that stayed in the area, sleeping in the abandoned mansions across from where the plaza had once stood—had entered into a dangerous phase of spiraling drug consumption. When the cash cow of easy construction scavenging disappeared, as it surely would, they would be left with the need to find new sources of income, and would be willing to take greater risks in the crimes they would commit or their interactions with johns.

At the same time that the city was tearing down Plaza Güibia, the Tourist and National Police forces increased their surveillance of the Colonial Zone, chasing out undesirables such as beggars, itinerant merchants, and bootblacks. In order to peddle goods and services in the Colonial Zone, merchants needed special identification cards and permits from City Hall. Most shoeshine boys didn't have access to the funds needed to pay for the permits. Beggars were imprisoned for loitering. The street kids that had made the Conde part of their scene disappeared or played a game of hide-and-seek with the authorities. In my last few weeks, it became less and less common for me to run into any of the kids with whom I normally worked. It wasn't that there were no longer street children and youth in Santo Domingo, but that the population had shifted, moved to other parts of the city. On our weekly evening street visits, we begun encountering kids we knew far afield from the zones they had once called their own.

Niños del Camino was changing too. After years of postponement due to lack of funds, a reevaluation of priorities, and second thoughts about the utility of such an endeavor, the organization was finishing the construction of a multibuilding complex that would serve as a rehabilitation center for street children. Located in a rural zone north of the city, the center had been the latent dream of the organization from the early days. The idea of the project was nurtured by the original staff and director and then passed on to each succeeding generation of staff. Wouldn't it be great to have a place where kids could be removed from the poison of the city and their toxic relationships? A place where kids could learn the skills necessary to cope with their families and be reintegrated into their communities? The watchword was always that it was an integrated plan, taking into consideration the physiological, emotional, and social well-being of the child.

I had been skeptical from the start, having read accounts of the failures of such institutions elsewhere in Latin America. Even with the best of intentions and the best integrated plan, rehab centers had a low success rate and were only one kind of answer for some street children and youth. In part, this had to do with the high rate of children "escaping" such centers when their bodies started to go through withdrawal symptoms, the half-life cycle of the drugs stored in their body's fat and muscle tissue. Being submitted to regular schedules without the freedom to do as one pleases was also a jarring adjustment for children not accustomed to following rules laid out by others. Even some of the international funders expressed doubts about a residential rehabilitation model that didn't have a good track record elsewhere. Yet, plans had been in motion for over five years. A wealthy member of the organization's executive board had donated the land and was willing to bear some of the construction costs. He and other members of the board were dead set on seeing this project realized, with unrealistic expectations about the number of children to be served. International funding agencies, primarily from Spain, provided monies for the start-up costs, and plans were in the works as I was leaving the country to open the residential program with the first cohort of sixteen children.

I hoped for the best, but harbored my suspicions that the enterprise was doomed to fail. I worried that the organization was taking on too much. We continued with an outreach program, did house visits to families, and nine months earlier had opened a drop-in center for programming and attention that was just starting to operate smoothly. Although the infrastructure was paid for, the workload had increased without a concomitant increase in personnel, nor were operating funds for staff secure, relying on grants and international volunteers. The same staff that ran the drop-in center did outreach and assisted with family visits. They were doing an admirable job trying to balance the various demands and not burn out. The stress of opening the residential center and the desire to see it succeed (and the necessity of having it succeed, given the time and monetary investment) could shift resources and focus from what the organization had achieved. Mostly, however, I feared that the ideology of solidarity manifested in outreach that made Niños unique and had attracted me to the work to begin with was no longer a priority. Rehabilitation and social reinsertion are worthwhile goals but are often at odds with the idea of accompaniment. Accompaniment doesn't place an emphasis on outcome, but rather on process. Rehabilitation is a model with an already established definition of success. There were kids and youth who would never reach the destination implied by rehabilitation.

I returned to Santo Domingo in January 2010 for a month's stay, after having been gone for a little over three years. The changes that had started before I had left had gone through other shifts. Three years is a long time in the life of a nongovernmental organization. Three years is an eternity, given the volatility of street scenes. Three years is a good span of time in the social development of a child. I had expected some change, but I didn't know how much would be utterly different. Most of my old co-workers were no longer with the organization, for one thing. Eli was globetrotting with her Belgian boyfriend, working for the UN. Núria had returned to Spain to work with children of Moroccan immigrants. After years of working with street and working children, Héctor had left the social services altogether and had his own business painting houses. Lidu had gone to work for a Jesuit organization promoting workers' rights for Haitian migrants.

Ana and Epifanio were still with the organization, two of the last holdovers from when I had been there, but things were precarious. Money was tight, as always, but given the downturn in the global economy, especially in the European countries where much of the funding came from, there was even greater scrutiny and oversight about outcomes. I took no joy in being right about the rehabilitation center. The first cohort of kids had been a learning experience. Trying to work with sixteen drug-addicted youths at the same time managed to burn through educators, creating a revolving door of workers that didn't help maintain stability. This had the effect of drawing personnel off of other work to cover the gaps at the center. The organization assessed the failures of the first cohort as the result of not being selective enough in the profile of who was to be admitted. Although they had gone through a winnowing process months in advance to divine the sincerity of a kid's desire to be part of the program, the reality of life in the center couldn't compete in many cases with street life. Ana, who was eventually called in to work at the center, claimed they felt obligated to chose from the children and youth with whom they had been working for the past years but that, in reality, many of them were too old, too addicted, too street wise to adapt to the new environment.

As members of the first cohort were either kicked out of the program (for stealing the computer equipment, doing drugs, fighting) or left on their own accord, an effort was made to center on a narrower demographic, eleven to fifteen year olds with a less entrenched history on the streets. This second cohort stabilized at ten children, none of whom had been part of the street scenes with which I was familiar. Eight graduated through the two-year program and were back with their families. The center had the capacity for over forty kids in two buildings at a time. I had arrived at a period of re-evaluation and transition. It was uncertain if the international donors who had funded the first three years of the rehabilitation center would be willing to invest again, given the low numbers. Were there even enough kids that would fit the program's profile?

It was a huge investment in time and money to graduate eight children through the center. Was it worth it? Integrated plans were not cheap. Funding organizations were starting to ask what made these kids so special. Wasn't it better to invest money in organizations with greater potential reach? At its heart, international funders wanted to know if money couldn't be better spent helping "worthier" child and youth populations, ones who weren't drug addicted and lived in marginalized communities but with families. Niños was saddled with infrastructure that took money to keep up but which they could not afford to maintain without donor assistance. There was talk from the executive board that maybe it was time to reevaluate the purpose and target population of the NGO in order to make the center function with more children. The organization's available infrastructure was such an attractive commodity—few organizations had been as successful in such a short amount of time of being awarded the number and value of grants that Niños had been—surely it should be put to some use, even if it was not with the intended target population. After all, these same voices reasoned, maybe the lesson is that street children cannot be transformed into valued, productive citizens.

When I returned again in the summer of 2011 for a couple of weeks, the situation was even graver than the year and a half before. The last of the organization's grants was wrapping up, with none in the pipeline. Nothing had been decided about the rehabilitation center, although the organization was letting local groups from the rural community where it was located have access to the facility under the guidance of a Peace Corps volunteer. Without international funds, the drop-in center was going to have to close its door because there was no money to pay for materials, let alone salaries for workers. Everyone was laid off or put on notice that they needed to take a hiatus until things got figured out. In the midst of this, the organization's director, Estívaliz, was called back to Spain by her religious order. She was given two weeks' notice to close up her life in Santo Domingo after over thirty years in the city. The organization seemed to be finished. It remained to be seen if the executive board would find someone to take over as director or close up shop for good. All programming ended. After over fifteen years in existence, Niños del Camino was no more.

Both return visits to Santo Domingo were a time for me to reassess what, if any good, might have come from the years I had worked so feverishly with the boys and young men on the street. I hadn't worried about outcome in the midst of doing the work, but now I had this nagging concern: had it been worthwhile? As the organization roiled in its financial troubles and existential crisis, I wondered in what ways the work we did had a long-term impact. I set out to find some of the children and teenagers I had worked with closely in hopes of gauging, however piecemeal, their trajectories.

I began by going to the old haunts, the areas of the city where we used to work. The transformations along the Malecón were yet to be completed, even after three years of work. Plaza Güibia had been razed and mostly rebuilt. It was unrecognizable. The final design would include a recuperated beach, volleyball courts, swing sets, and twenty-four-hour security, including security cameras beaming directly into the National Police office. Renovation had not stopped with the plaza. Across busy George Washington Avenue, the lots facing the plaza were altered. The movie theater had received a much-needed facelift. I stood looking at the building, feeling that something was off. Then it hit me. The two abandoned mansions on the corner had been torn down and the rubble cleared. It was now one large empty lot, waiting for redevelopment. What had once been the center of drug consumption and the home for many of Santo Domingo's homeless was gone. I felt oddly nostalgic and saddened by the transformation, like I was missing my connection to the city, my sense of place. It wasn't just that the buildings were no longer there, but the Malecón felt lifeless to me without the characters I knew. I wandered north from the plaza, up Gómez to the intersection with Independencia to see if there was anyone I still knew washing windshields. The traffic light was broken, the cars rolling through the street on their way to the Colonial Zone. No one would be out working the intersection under these conditions. I stood on the southwest corner in the full midmorning sun looking into the shaded area. Standing near the curb in their blue aprons, holding the day's headlines slackly in their hands, were three newspaper saleswomen. I trotted across the street, dodging the flow of traffic.

They were the same women as had been there over three years before, the same weary faces and tired eyes. They recognized me immediately, commenting on how long it had been since they had seen me last and gently rebuking me for not coming around more often. I explained I no longer lived in the country, that I was back visiting, and amazed at the number of changes along the Malecón. Oh, it's incredible, they agreed, hardly the same place anymore. And the young men? I asked, referring generically to *los muchachos*, although it was abundantly clear that I meant the group of windshield washers. Many had left the area, but there was still a small group who worked the zone. One of the women pointed west down the street, saying I could find them at a small overgrown lot between the bank and the car rental. I thanked them and wandered that way.

Another large tree, with thick roots overflowing onto the sidewalk through the cement, shaded the area. Crowded around the space between the tree trunk and the cinderblock wall was a bunch of crouched figures, some on their heels, some bent over, all eyes intent on the rolling of dice against the wall. After each roll there was an exchange of money and a raucous lament by the loser of the round. I stood at the back edge of the group, watching, unnoticed. I recognized several of the young men, even if a few of their names escaped me. The figure holding court, however, the one directing the exchange of money after each roll, I knew quite well. Nico looked a mess. His ill-fitting jeans were smeared with grime. The short-sleeve Oxford shirt unbuttoned on his torso hung loose, revealing a less formidable musculature than I remembered. Something was eating away at him, some kind of addiction or disease. He distractedly registered my presence and asked gruffly what I wanted. I laughed, replying, "Oh, Nico, is that any way to greet an old friend?" The group turned their attention from the dice to me. There was a pause and then an effusive greeting. "Ay, Jon, *mi hermano!* Welcome back!"

I made for the wall, jumping up to sit on the rough cement. Nico came alongside me, leaning lazily, surveying the movement of the traffic. Juan Carlos sat against one of the roots of the tree, distractedly picking at his shoeless feet. He, too had visibly aged, now nearing twenty years old. The youthful vigor of his face was still apparent, despite its gauntness. I could only assume he was still on crack, although Juancho was nowhere to be seen. Several of the other youths I knew crowded around, excitedly explaining to the others who I was. We talked about the changes in the area. I told them I didn't recognize Güibia anymore and they laughed. "We're not welcome there," Juan Carlos informed me. The police, at the behest of the city government, periodically raided the sleeping areas on the Malecón, even after they torn down the mansions and everyone was kicked out of

Güibia. "There are no palomos on the Malecón," Juan Carlos summed it up. I couldn't help notice the slip of the tongue. Did Juan Carlos now consider himself a palomo? "They took a whole bunch of us to La Victoria for doin' nothing but sleeping in the abandoned lot," Nico continued, "Luisíto, Shoesine Boy, Juancho and me, and Juan Carlos. We were there for over six months for nothing. Juancho is still there."

With Juancho in prison, gone from the street for over a year, Juan Carlos had shifted his allegiance to Nico. When Juan Carlos asked Nico for a match to light his cigarette, he addressed him as *cuñado*, or brother-in-law. I'd never heard this form of address before on the street—much more familiar were other kinship terms like *hermano* (brother) or *primo* (cousin). I jokingly asked, "Nico's your cuñado now? What, did he marry your sister?" Turns out it wasn't much of a joke. When the two of them got out of La Victoria at the same time, Juan Carlos took Nico to his folks' place, where Nico met Juan Carlos's seventeen-year-old sister, Johaira. Nico earnestly chimed in, "Aye, this little woman has me crazy in love, Jon, I tell you the truth." Johaira, it seems, had a newborn of her own. Nico claimed Johaira was making him an honest man. He quickly slipped to the back of the empty lot, rummaging through his backpack. He returned with four small jars of baby food held high, proud of this proof of love, providing for a baby that wasn't his.

If Nico was now with Juan Carlos's sister, that meant he was no longer with Luisa. When I asked after her, Nico got a pained look on his face, replying that the two of them had been long since separated, since the last time Nico was in La Victoria. When Nico finally found her on the streets, he said, she was already in a really bad state. "She looks like an old lady of eighty now," he claimed. "The doctor told her to her face she has AIDS." Juan Carlos nodded in agreement. If it were true, it didn't bode well for Nico or Johaira. I would see Luisa twice before I would leave, both from a distance. The first time, I was sitting in an idled public taxi at the corner of Gómez and Bolívar; I did a double take of the figure sprawled out on a bench in the plaza, thinking at first glance it was an elderly woman. The second time was out front of the gates to the public university, the students giving wide berth on the broad sidewalk to a wild figure muttering to herself. Luisa had always been unpredictable, but appeared more so now. I had never had the same kind of relationship with her that Ana or Kennedy did. I was too much of a coward to go speak to her as she wandered erratically down the edge of the street.

When Juan Carlos told me that Juancho was still in La Victoria, I figured I would go. Having been before, I now thought I could manage a visit on my own, knowing more or less what to expect. Since I was staying with Ana and her family in the northern suburbs of the city, it took less time to get to the prison than it did to get downtown. So on a Wednesday morning I got in a public taxi outside of Ana's house and went for a jail visit. I had a mental list of who might be there and their possible location within the prison, thanks to my conversation with Nico and Juan Carlos.

The layout of La Victoria makes it difficult to navigate if you don't know where to find a particular inmate, and more so if you don't know the name of the place they are at—names like "la cuchara," "la plancha," and "el calentón," which act as much as descriptors as they do undiscovered continents. After greasing my way to the front of the line with a fifty-peso bribe (haggled down from one hundred), I was back in the same courtyard, milling around with the inmates and the family members that came to visit.

Juan Carlos had told me that Juancho was in the prison's Hogar Crea, the private cold turkey drug rehab center that had facilities all over the country. I told the man who I chose to be my guide where I wanted to go and we were off down the corridors and into another, smaller courtyard protected by a large overhang. When I handed over the five pesos to the guide, he told me to go talk to the director, also an inmate, Ramón. Ramón was a tall man with an ugly toothy mug that wouldn't quit smiling, but he was nice enough—or perhaps curious enough—to help me out. I gave him the full legal names of a couple of youth I had expected to find, including Juancho's. They all struck out. Most of the names he didn't recognize, and Juancho had left Hogar Crea to go back to the general prison population a month before.

As Ramón was giving me this information, someone tapped me on the back. I turned around and before I could see clearly who wanted my attention, a body came toward me, moving to give me a hug. In an automatic response, I returned the hug, hearing a voice tell me what a miracle it was to see me. When he released me, and stood back at a slight distance, it was Francisco, dressed in what passes for the Hogar Crea uniform for new recruits—shorts and a Hogar Crea polo shirt. I was surprised at the reception, because the Francisco I remembered had been too tough to display excitement or care for anyone. Yet here he was, eager and surprised at my presence.

Francisco had seen some rough times, but claimed he was on the better end of it. He had multiple scars on his arms—two sets of puffed up tiger stripes near the biceps of both arms, looking too symmetrical to be accidental—and a general wear and tear on the face that signaled hard living. The most alarming physical change was that the index finger on his right hand was missing. In its place stood a broad, thick stump. He pointed at where the finger would have been, telling me that Luisíto attacked him with a machete five months earlier, explaining vaguely, "You know, shit from the streets." I thought back to Eduardo's stabbing and Luisíto's role in the event. It was very possible that Luisíto had continued—perhaps even consolidated—his position as the drugs point man.

We sat on the stone picnic benches inside the Hogar Crea compound, facing each other. Every so often, as if to make sure I was not a hallucination, Francisco grabbed my hands, touched them, and then released them, as if a shock had passed through my hands to his. This was entirely out of character for the young man that I remembered as being full of bravado, and who would boldly state how he couldn't trust anyone but himself. He'd been in prison for four months. He corroborated the story told by Juan Carlos and Nico, that the local police, who were given orders by the city to clean up the Malecón, rounded him up in a general sweep of the sleeping areas. When he went before the judge, he was fingerprinted and sentenced to one year in jail. The judge told him in no uncertain terms that his time on the Malecón was through. Whether or not he and the other youth were truly not charged with any offense or if it was the enforcement of a general anti-vagrancy law, from their perspective their only crime was sleeping in a semi-public space.

Ironically, it was Juancho who convinced Francisco to join Hogar Crea. I don't doubt that for Juancho it was an instrumentalist argument. If I were in La Victoria, I would be scared enough to join the rehab program; if I didn't have an addiction I would feign one. The benefits are obvious. Even the strict schedule, the almost evangelical zeal mixed with Trotskyite self-criticism sessions, and limited freedom within the prison—these hindrances are nothing compared to the relative security members receive. Program participants have a guaranteed bed, decent bathroom facilities, a locker to guard personal items, access to purified water, and much better food than what would be received within the prison. Prison life in the Dominican Republic is expensive, if only because cash flow is limited. In this sense, Hogar Crea allows one to live well as long as one submits to the program. For Francisco, the benefits were augmented by the fact that his family did not know he was there. He had no way of contacting his mother in their rural home. He mentioned an aunt in the capital that he would periodically visit, but they had moved neighborhoods and he didn't know how to get a hold of her, either. It looked like he would be in La Victoria for a while.

Juancho had left the confines of Hogar Crea a few weeks before. When I asked after him, Francisco gave a cynical laugh, a trace of the teenager I remembered, and said, "He wasn't in it to change. He just wanted a rest from his addiction. Juancho is nothing but a *pipero*," a crack addict. After I had sat with Francisco for over an hour, he and another young man from the center (in the Hogar Crea program, participants are never allowed to travel away from the facility without being accompanied by another member) were given permission to walk me back to the front gates. Once we were out of view of the center, I asked Francisco if he knew where Juancho might be and if we would be able to speak to him. Francisco eyed his companion, saying that they didn't have permission to wander all over the prison. After several back-and-forth exchanges, the two agreed we could "pass by" the cafeteria where Juancho sometimes hung out. It was on the way. If he wasn't there, however, we weren't going to go searching all over La Victoria for him. Francisco's attention to the authority of others seemed further proof that he had changed.

As the day warmed, the number of inmates escaping the caldrons of their airless cells increased, pushing them into the public courtyards and open hallways looking for breeze and shade. We walked through one courtyard into the next and then through a darkened door. As we stepped in from the bright day, I could barely make out the dark outlines of the cavernous room we were now in but distinctly made out the smell of old cooking oil. As my eyes adjusted to the dank and dim surroundings, I saw thirty or so cement tables and benches, firmly secured to the floor. This was the cafeteria. We were gruffly greeted just inside the door by a man who informed us the next service wasn't for another half hour. Instead of chafing at the brusque encounter, Francisco politely asked if Juancho was in the back, telling the man that he had a visitor. Had Hogar Crea really changed Francisco's demeanor in such a short time that he wouldn't have replied with his characteristic bluster? The man nodded, walked halfway across the room and then yelled Juancho's name into the kitchen area. A minute or two passed. Then, dishrag in hand, a wiry figure emerged from behind the cement petition. Juancho swaggered over to us. When he recognized me, he threw up his hands and gesticulated in wide arcs, exclaiming, "Oh! What the hell! It's Jon! What the fuck are you doing here?"

We shook hands and did a half hug, patting each other on the back. Juancho climbed up to sit on the tabletop facing us. He wore a baggy pair of cargo shorts and a tank top, both too big for his slim frame. If he had been off crack for any amount of time, I couldn't tell. His bicep muscles hung loosely from the bone, the crack having stripped away the fat that helps hold the body together. He was all muscle and tendon.

I told him Juan Carlos had said he would be here. "That faggot?" Juancho replied, "He left me stranded. Just because Nico starts fucking his sister he up and leaves his buddy." The venom in Juancho's voice took me by surprise. There was some deeper issue between the three of them. "And this one," he pointed at Francisco, "wants to stay in Crea like an idiot. You know you miss the taste of the pipe," meaning the crack pipe. Francisco gathered his proselytizing zeal as a prophylactic against Juancho's temptation. "You were the one who brought me to Crea. You said to me, 'We should change our lives, find refuge in Crea.' Now I am on the path but you have lost your way. You drown yourself in crack and make yourself ill."

"That's bullshit," was Juancho's reply. "I told you to join Crea to take a break and get adjusted to La Victoria, not to stay. You're missing out." Juancho looked at me with a broad, mischievous grin on his face. "I like my crack. It makes me feel alive. It's my daily bread." The reference was not just to the Lord's Prayer, but also to the morning affirmation that Hogar Crea participants say daily, their "one day at a time" credo.

Juancho was being belligerent and intentionally confrontational. Seeing Francisco smug in his Crea uniform and being reminded of Juan Carlos's supposed abandonment had set him in a foul mood. I had seen enough. "You'd better get back to work," I told him, "besides, I've gotta get going."

We left Juancho to the kitchen. I couldn't help but think how hard he worked, how single-minded his focus was. When he and Juan Carlos had been living on the street, at least he had someone to share his addiction with, someone with whom to enjoy the struggle. He had hoped to make Francisco into that person—that was clear from the tense interaction between them. Instead, he was alone with his addiction. It seemed as if, for the time being, the good times were done.

While I had been working with Niños, I had done countless house visits to children and youth who wanted contact with their families or who were back in the home after a period of time on the street. I had even made cold contacts in cases of emergency. I had never done these alone, however, always with Ana, Epifanio, or others who knew their way through the maze of alleyways and side streets to arrive at the house in question. They also knew what to look out for in some of the more dangerous neighborhoods in order to keep themselves safe. There had been a time in the history of the organization, before there were funds to buy a pick-up truck and hire a driver, when Ana did all the house visits herself, traveling on public transit and using motorcycle taxis to get from the neighborhood entrances into the inner sanctums.

Some of the house visits were one-off experiences for me, never to go back. A few I visited with such regularity that I can still recall the turns and twists to get into the neighborhood, which staircase to go down to emerge at the right door. There were a few kids who I had worked with who were rumored to be back home, having gone back on their own accord. As the transformations were taking place in the Colonial Zone and along the Malecón, some of the kids aged out of street life and, surprisingly to me, reintegrated into their households with little or no support from the organization. Things had changed; the kid had grown up into an adolescent or young man who took greater responsibility for himself or, through some kind of activity (possibly illegal) provided much-needed income to the family. Such was the case of Hilário and his older brother, Andrés, whom I visited in January 2010.

When Andrés left for the streets at age thirteen, his eleven-year-old brother, Hilário, quickly followed. After four years in and out of programs and on and off the streets, Andrés and Hilário both went home to their grandmother's house. When I spoke to the two of them, sitting out on the corner across from where the alleyway to their house intersected with the main street, Andrés told me the decision was relatively easy. He knew his grandmother would gladly take them back in, having always offered them a place to stay in the past. The deciding factor, however, was that their youngest brother was following in their footsteps and wanted to spend time with them on the streets. "That was it," Andrés earnestly told me. "The streets are no fun. They are full of struggle. I didn't want Junior to go through what Hilário and I did." He didn't have to name it. I remembered their crack use to deaden the pain of having lost both their parents to HIV/AIDS. I also remembered Andrés's violent and ragged outbursts, so different from the self-contained eighteen-year-old dressed in nice jeans and a knit shirt I was now talking to. Hilário agreed, saying "We did things on the street that Junior shouldn't have to do."

What I wanted to know was what were they doing now that they were back home. Things hadn't changed that much—their grandmother still lived hand to mouth. Andrés shrugged, "I can find things to do here in the neighborhood for a guy who has connections. I need to go get my national ID card, too, though, so maybe I could find legitimate work." In other words, Andrés did jobs for some kind of criminal—it was unclear if he was a fencer or a drug dealer. Andrés wasn't going to say more out in the open like that. He had found an alternative to being on the streets. It wasn't necessarily one free of danger, nor was it the narrow path to the legal economy, but it was, by far, the better option. I wondered if Hilário would follow in his brother's footsteps again.

Andrés and Hilário were not unique. Ana told me about other kids we had worked with who had transitioned away from living on the street on their own accord. The key was that they no longer slept on the street, but that didn't mean they were no longer street-oriented. She told me how she encountered more than one on public transit collecting passengers' fares. Willy found legitimate work at a fast food restaurant and lived with his wife and daughter. Máximo was gaining notoriety as a drug dealer in the neighborhood of Capotillo. The biggest surprise came when Ana told me in 2011 that Luisíto had become an Evangelical Christian and was seen traveling the city with Bible in hand, preaching on buses. He was training to become an associate pastor in the congregation he attended. That was a far cry from selling crack on the Malecón.

No one I talked to, however, knew what had become of José Alberto. Ana said his case was dropped not long after I left due to constraints of time and money. It got too expensive to drive out to San Cristóbal to do visits regularly. Plus, with the emphasis shifting toward the rehabilitation center, many of the family visits were suspended without warning. Besides, Ana reasoned, José Alberto had a lot going for him that would have indicated a more positive outcome—most important, parents who genuinely cared about him and had welcomed him back home with little consternation.

I had visited Don José's house enough times that I felt confident I could find it on my own. Plus, San Cristóbal was on my way to visiting the juvenile detention center in Najayo, where I had hoped to go and talk to the new director about continued implementation of the legal reforms associated with the 2003 child protection code. I figured it wouldn't do any harm to see if I could track José Alberto down. I hopped off the bus in the downtown plaza and walked fifteen minutes down the main avenue to the turnoff into José Alberto's neighborhood. As if on autopilot, I navigated the streets until I saw the basketball court and the mechanic's shop ahead of me.

I didn't recognize the middle-aged woman in the doorway of the apartment that I associated with José Alberto's family. If it was Segunda, she would have aged far beyond what would have been expected in the four years since I had seen her. I greeted her and she eyed me wearily. When I asked if Don José was at home she replied she didn't know who I was talking about. She'd lived in there for forty years, she said, and didn't know any Don José. A younger woman exited the adjacent door as I continued to explain who I was looking for and why. The younger woman became more animated, telling her neighbor, "No, you remember, the musician." Then she knew who he was. Don José had moved to the surrounding countryside not long ago. When I pressed them for details about Pepe, their remembrances were mostly negative.

"Oh, I know which one—the eldest child, the skinny one, the one that caused his father so much trouble, always on the streets," said the young neighbor. She leaned against the doorframe in her hot pink halter top that she would adjust every couple of minutes. The older woman in Don José's former house nodded in agreement.

"Is Pepe still living with his father?"

"I don't know," answered the older woman, "I heard he was in prison in Najayo. He would steal and bring trouble to his father's house. The boy was no good." Later that afternoon when I visited the juvenile detention center at Najayo, I asked after José Alberto, in case he might be there. If he had been remanded to jail, it would have been the juvenile facility and not La Victoria, because he was still under eighteen years of age. I was told that he had been released less than a week before. They weren't going to tell me why he had been in the center.

I tried to track Don José down in hopes of communicating with Pepe. I left messages with the young neighbor, anticipating that he might leave a phone number where I could reach him. I hired a motorcycle taxi to take me to the surrounding hills where Don José was said to live, asking at the entrance of every dirt track if the musician lived down the road. Maybe it was best that I didn't find him and didn't have to hear about how José Alberto had not lived up to expectations. I could imagine I might not be welcomed anyway, associated as I was with the organization that was supposed to have helped him but only abandoned the family. After roaming around the countryside for a couple of hours, I called it quits. I realized I much preferred to remember José Alberto as the sullen, hard-working adolescent I knew on the streets.

It was impossible for me to predict the life trajectories of the youths I had worked with on the streets. Although I was not surprised that Juancho was still entrenched in his addiction to crack, I hadn't expected to see Francisco in prison. If four years earlier I had had to guess who would still be living in their homes, Andrés or José Alberto, I would have said José Alberto. Andrés had eventually returned home by himself. I wondered if we had helped keep open the lines of communication, however tenuous, with their grandmother in the years we worked with him and his brothers. In reviewing the kids I knew and where they have ended up in the intervening years, I have come to the conclusion that, ultimately, we may have had little impact. Kids return home because they perceive it to be a better alternative to life on the street. Adolescents may test the streets for a period of time, go home for a period of time, and continue on that pattern until they eventually age out of the street. In other words, we worked with hundreds of different children and youth over the two years I was with Niños, but only a small fraction of these were actually dedicated to full-time, long-term life on the streets. Most of the kids would have returned to their homes without the presence of outreach educators in their lives.

I want to clarify that this does not mean that I am against social service programs directed at helping street children and youth. While the impact of outreach services on the long-term trajectory of a street child may be unknowable, the short-term benefits are paramount to the health and well-being of that child. Outreach is, in many ways, a form of social triage. Educators respond to the crisis environment of the street, including immediate medical and legal needs. Likewise, educators offer the psychological benefits of having someone with whom to talk and provide needed information about social service options and opportunities. This is the crucial work of outreach.

Although the possibility exists for outreach to sustain and aid children and youths' existence on the street, this is a small concern in comparison to its day-to-day benefits. The key is that the spirit and tenor of the work must be one of solidarity, and not clientelism. We are not offering assistance because of some greater benefit down the road, some potential payback. Solidarity is an act of standing with others, bridging the divides of class, race, gender, and age as much as possible. Empathy can only spring from mutual engagement and interaction. In fact, this may be the strongest case for continued humanitarian and human rights work with street populations. If we want to live in societies that value self-determination and dignity of all peoples, sustained mutual engagement with those on the margins matters.

# NOTES

## INTRODUCTION

1. Research was conducted between 2004 and 2006. I became a Peace Corps volunteer after having completed my doctorate in anthropology with a focus on youth violence in Latin America. I approached my service in the Peace Corps with the intent of using my academic knowledge and experience toward human services. I also aimed to use my time as a volunteer to gather data and research for a future project, the result of which is this book. See the December 2011 issue of the *Anthropology News* (www.aaanet.org) for more on the long-standing relationship between anthropologists and the Peace Corps.

2. Agency is the ability to react, plan, and carry out plans of action on a moment-to-moment basis. It is a fundamental quality of human existence, much akin to will, determination, or desire. However, one's agency is shaped by the choices a given situation presents, the opportunities one can finesse, and the material and social resources one can marshal. Limitations such as personal identity (one's age, race, class, and gender) and material conditions can limit the type of agency one can exercise.

3. This distinction is, in many ways, an oversimplification, as many authors utilize a combination of the two approaches in their analyses of the lives of children. However, it does offer a broad characterization of research perspectives and the methodological and ethical considerations they entail.

4. See, for instance, Farmer 2004.

5. Huggins and Mesquita (2000) link scapegoating street youth for crime with moral exclusion and civic invisibility in Brazil.

6. See, for instance, Vigil 1988a, 1988b, 2002, 2003, and 2007.

7. Sharon Stephens's groundbreaking 1995 volume, *The Cultural Politics of Childhood*, and Nancy Scheper-Hughes and Carolyn Sargent's 1998 *Small Wars* both set the agenda for subsequent research about children at the interface of cultural and political debates. The chapters in both collections explore issues as diverse as state policies concerning demographic population shifts, pronatalist ideologies, cultural fears about uncontrolled children, and the macrolevel forces of economic and political policies that cause pain and suffering in the lives of children. As Liisa Malkki and Emily Martin (2003) point out, Stephens's contribution was in aligning ethnographic research with the investigation of the political lives of children. Despite their calls for child-centered research, both collections focused more on ideologies of childhood than the perspective of children. See also Wolseth and Babb 2008.

8. See, for example, Michel Foucault's 1980 discussion of the creation of the "schoolboy" in Western European education systems in volume 1 of the *History of Sexuality.*

9. In Latin America this is most clearly seen in studies of family structure and productive labor. Lewis Aptekar (1988) highlights the cultural kinship patterns of Colombian

working poor households, demonstrating that children working and living on the streets are part of an adaptive strategy for household survival. More recent work by Mary Kenny (2007) and Thomas Offit (2010) provide a stark picture of the necessity of child labor for household survival. Kenny's work illustrates that attitudes of children and parents vary, with some parents forcing kids to work and appropriating their earnings for their own consumption, and some children seeking out the opportunity to earn in order to be productive members of the household.

10. See the International Programme on the Elimination of Child Labour's (IPEC) campaign to end forms of child labor, a part of the International Labour Organization's (ILO) Decent Work Agenda. Find out more by accessing www.ilo.org/ipec/lang--en/index.htm.

11. See, for example, Hecht 1998, Huggins and Mesquita 2000, Inciardi and Surrat 1998, Kovats-Bernat 2006, Marquez 1999, and Salazar 2008, and Scheper-Hughes and Hoffman 1998, among others.

12. As was the case of the massacre of a group of street children sleeping on the steps of the Candelaria Cathedral of Rio de Janeiro in 1993. For the testimony of one of the survivors of the massacre, Wagner dos Santos, see the preface to Jones and Rodgers (2009).

13. This distinction has much resonance in the work on street children in Brazil (see Hecht 1998 and Scheper-Hughes and Hoffman 1998). J. Christopher Kovats-Bernat (2006), however, skillfully demonstrates that in Port-au-Prince, at least, such stark distinctions between home and street do not apply.

14. This is most evident in historic and contemporary circulation of children in Latin America within kin and fictive kin networks and to orphanages and other state-run and private child social service organizations (see Blum 2009, Fonseca 1986 and 2004, Leinaweaver 2008, and Wolseth 2011).

15. This was the response that Cuba has taken. See Lutjens 2000a and 2000b.

16. See the articles in Gareth A. Jones and Dennis Rodger's 2009 edited collection, *Youth Violence in Latin America*, for regional and country trends on the prioritizing of policing over social programs and its consequences, especially the overview chapters by Rodgers and Jones, and Ungar, and the chapter by Rocha Gómez on Nicaragua.

17. Although there is a history of child socialization studies, I trace the development of a child-centered approach to psychiatrist Robert Coles and his Children in Crisis series. Coles's work is characterized by an intense listening to the narratives children tell, connecting children's everyday experience to their moral development. Coles's insistence on the voices of children, to the point where explicit theorizing is eliminated, provides one model for presenting children as active moral agents in their own lives. Other social science researchers have built upon Coles's methodological insistence to develop related approaches. See, for example, his 1990 book, *The Spiritual Life of Children*.

18. For a concise history of ethnographies of childhood, see Robert A. LeVine's 2007 article, "Ethnographic Studies of Childhood: A Historical Overview." For an introduction to the anthropology of childhood's major theoretical debates, see Myra Bluebond-Langner and Jill E. Korbin's 2007 article, "Challenges and Opportunities in the Anthropology of Childhoods." For anthropology's troubled relationship with children, see Lawrence A. Hirschfeld's 2002 article, "Why Don't Anthropologists Like Children?" For a broader

history of anthropology's engagement with children, see the review by Robert Munroe and Mary Gauvin (2010) in *The Anthropology of Learning in Childhood.*

19. The inclusion of children as agentive, culture-bearing, individuals is likely to have as great an impact on ethnographic method and theory as the feminist turn has had since the late 1970s. Scuttlebutt within the discipline has it that studying children is "the new gender."

20. See, for example, Donna Lanclos's 2003 study of children's playground culture in Northern Ireland for a review of the folklore studies. Marjorie Harness Goodwin's 1990 work, *He-Said-She-Said,* looks at the connection between the communication and negotiation of conflict among African American children's play and their social development. See also Ashley E. Maynard and Katrin E. Tovote's 2010 review of child peer learning, "Learning from Other Children."

21. See, for example, Chin 1999.

22. Lawrence A. Hirschfield (2002) describes how children's understanding of social difference is not always the same as that of adults.

23. David Rosen (2007) has captured the tension between the phenomenon of child soldiers and the rise of a global definition of childhood based on middle-class Western norms. The work of Susan Shepler (2005) and Rosalind Shaw (2007, 2009) in Sierra Leone, Margaret Trawick (2007) in Sri Lanka, Harry West (2000) in Mozambique, Anna Peterson and Kay Reed (2002) in Central America, and Julia Dickson-Gómez in El Salvador (2003) all points to the wide-ranging social-psychological effects of a child or youth's exposure to gun battle. Trawick and West, for example, demonstrate that young women soldiers in Sri Lanka and Mozambique, respectively, experienced their training and battle experiences as liberating from more traditional gender dynamics both in the household and society at large. Peterson and Reed and Dickson-Gómez are less sanguine in their appraisal of the psychological damage done to children who are forced to fight against their own families and villages.

24. Studies of juvenile delinquency have long played a role in traditional sociological and criminological approaches, starting from the early work of the Chicago School. Concern had been primarily with how the children of immigrant families adjusted (or failed to adjust) to life in marginal urban communities and the role of delinquent behavior in that adjustment process. An exemplar of this ethnographic work is William Foote Whyte's *Street Corner Society* (1943), in which he detailed the lives and fortunes of residents in Boston's North End. The result is a richly textured portrait of social organization in an impoverished community. A central theme continues to be the relationship between the youth peer group and delinquent behavior, which carries over into research on juvenile gangs, especially in the foundational work of James Diego Vigil in Los Angeles (see Vigil 1988a, 1988b, 2002, 2007).

25. The scholarly literature on street children shares many of the concerns of the literature on child soldiers, child prostitutes, and juvenile delinquency and gangs because of the lifestyle and cultural characteristics of various street child populations.

26. For Colombia, see Goode 1987 and Aptekar 1988; for Russia, see Stephenson 2001.

27. Both Butler's 2007 work in Rio de Janeiro and Beazley's 2003 work in Indonesia recognize that prolonged exposure to uncertainty, violence, and a distinct moral universe

separate from middle-class concerns contributes to a unique sense of self-experience of emotion on the streets. For a discussion of resiliency and street children, see Panter-Brick 2002. For a cautionary response to the assumption that children are too resilient, see Boyden 2003.

**28.** For a review on peer socialization and street children, see Wolseth 2010. Laine Berman (2000) demonstrates how street children in Indonesia manage their relationships with one another and their own sense of self through the strategic use of narratives.

**29.** See the work of Campos et al. 1994 and Lockhart 2002, 2008 for more on the use of sexual violence to regulate the peer group in Brazil and Tanzania, respectively.

**30.** See Wolseth 2009 for more on street peer groups sharing resources and knowledge.

**31.** Researchers have investigated solidarity and drug use in many homeless environments, including solvent use in Brazil (Lucchini 1996), heroin use in San Francisco (Bourgois and Schonberg 2009), and crack cocaine use in Santo Domingo (Wolseth 2009).

**32.** Samuel Martínez (2007) charts this economic shift in Dominican *bateyes*, or sugar cane plantations, in his excellent longitudinal ethnography, *Decency and Excess*. Stephen Gregory (2007) discusses the impacts of globalization and its discontents in *The Devil behind the Mirror*. Lauren Derby (2009) provides ample historical evidence for the rise of the middle class and new consumptive desires in Santo Domingo.

**33.** See, for example, Safa 1995 and 1999. For an assessment of Safa's work in the Caribbean, see Bolles and Yelvington 2010.

**34.** Brennan 2004.

**35.** Padilla 2007.

**36.** For methodological innovation and ethical quandaries surrounding child-centered research, see Allison James 2007, "Giving Voice to Children's Voices: Practices and Problems, Pitfalls and Potentials," and M. Elizabeth Graue and Joaquín J. Walsh's 1998 research manual, *Studying Children in Context: Theories, Methods, and Ethics*.

## CHAPTER 1: OUTREACH WORK

**1.** Although many of the kids we worked with on the streets came from humble origins, Francisco's situation was by far one of the most economically desperate. As a general rule, economic necessity is but one of a number of factors (and rarely the overriding one) leading kids to live on the street. In Francisco's case, it was clear he left home to stop having the burden of being the sole male provider for all of his younger siblings.

**2.** For a literary account of the tyranny of Trujillo and the lives of the Mirabel sisters, see Julia Alvarez's *In the Time of the Butterflies* (1994). For social historical accounts of the Trujillo dictatorship, see Richard Turits's well-regarded 2004 *Foundations of Despotism: Peasants, the Trujillo Regime, and Modernity in Dominican History*; Eric Roorda's 1998 *The Dictator Next Door: The Good Neighbor Policy and the Trujillo Regime in the Dominican Republic, 1930–1945*; and Lauren Derby's 2009 provocative work on Trujillo, masculinity, and spectatorship, *The Dictator's Seduction: Politics and the Popular Imagination in the Era of Trujillo*.

3. During my tenure with Niños del Camino, the organization was shifting from primarily street programming to developing in-service care, with the hope of eventually having a residential rehabilitation center to help children transition back into their homes. This programming was closely modeled after North American and European programs for homeless youth and stood in stark contrast to traditional approaches of orphanage facilities, with a more or less open-door policy.

4. Phillipe Bourgois and Jeff Schonberg (2009) demonstrate the pull between exploitation and intimacy among homeless heroin addicts in the San Francisco area. Their descriptions of both heterosexual romantic partnerships (48–77) and male homosocial bonding (210–239) centered on a shared addiction resonates with the mixture of deep friendship and sexual exploitation present among the teenage boys and male youths who made the Malecón their home.

5. Hecht intimates that, at least in northeast Brazil, children who spend time in the streets may be doing so to provide for, or nurture, the home. In other words, "home" is not so much a physical space as a set of relationships and obligations, primarily with and to one's biological mother (1998: 107–110). This includes financial obligations. Thus, kids become unwilling to return home if they fear they have nothing to show for their time away.

## CHAPTER 2: STRUCTURAL CONDITIONS

1. Berman (2000) indicates that the narratives of street children are often tied to learning how to survive on the street and the spatial parameters of existence. Her insights relate to recorded narratives as told to her by children, however. Street gossip, on the other hand, is a narrative form that may help set those spatial parameters. See also Beazley's comments on the importance of peer group communication on the streets of Yogyakarta (2002: 1667).

2. Linda Whiteford's assessments (1990, 1992, 1998) of the Dominican health care and public health systems as they existed during the acute economic crises of the late 1980s and early 1990s describes the detrimental effects of underfunding. Although many things have changed—such as improved access to working technology and the use of generators that provide electricity during frequent blackouts—other aspects of public hospitals, such as reliance on family members to provide for patient care, remain constant.

3. Racial classification in the Dominican Republic is detailed and complicated by the dissimulation of African heritage in which many Dominicans participate. This is compounded by the nationalist distinction Dominicans make between themselves and Haitians, even while the two populations share a common history, origin, and certain other cultural features. For more about Dominican and Haitian relationships, see Michele Wucker's *Why the Cocks Fight: Dominicans, Haitians, and the Struggle for Hispaniola* (2000). For more on Dominican racial categories and the identity formation, see Ginetta Candelario's *Black behind the Ears: Dominican Racial Identity from Museums to Beauty Shops* (2007).

4. Caring for members of one's primary street group is a common feature of coping strategies for homeless populations, as highlighted in Conticini's work in Dhaka (2007).

However, this care in self-designated street families is often gendered and assumed to be an extension of women's work, as evidenced from Hansson's work with street girls in South Africa (2003) and Stephenson's work with street youth in Moscow (2001).

5. Bourgois and Schonberg (2009: 97–115) describe how medical professionals mistreated the homeless heroin addicts who sought medical attention, intimating that the hospital staff viewed the homeless as less than human because of the deteriorated state of their bodies. In María's case, her callous treatment by the doctor may have had as much to do with class differences as it did with acceptable medical procedure. I witnessed some medical professionals in the Dominican Republic treat María and other homeless with empathy and care.

6. *La Cárcel de La Victoria: El Cuarto Hombre* (2004), directed by José Enrique Pintor.

7. It is possible that Nico may have worked as a *bugarrón*, a local classification designated for Dominican young men who, generally, assume the active role in sexual activities with other (more often than not foreign) male clients. Padilla (2007) argues that male sexual subjectivities (like the bugarrón) in the Dominican Republic are being reshaped by globalization, in particular the tourist industry. Nico's unproblematic (for him) long-term relationship with the Puerto Rican while simultaneously being in a longer-term relationship with Luisa is illustrative of much of Padilla's argument.

8. *Boricua* is local slang for someone from Puerto Rico.

9. Ramoncito used *casado*, literally meaning married, but he did not mean legally married. Popular notions of marriage in the Dominican Republic do not require a legal or religious ceremony to claim this status. Instead, moving in with a partner indicates marriage.

10. Luisa used the term *maricón*, a local pejorative term for men who, when having anal sex with another man, take the passive role.

11. Also written as *panaful*. *Pana*, according to Deive's *Diccionario de Dominicanismos* (2002) derives from the English word "partner." In everyday Dominican Spanish, a pana is one's social intimate.

12. See Staples 2007.

13. See http://hdrstats.undp.org/en/countries/profiles/DOM.html.

# REFERENCES

Alvarez, Julia. 1994. *In the Time of the Butterflies*. Chapel Hill, NC: Algonquin Books.

Anthropology News. 2011. "In Focus: The Peace Corps." *Anthropology News* 52 (9), http:// www.anthropology-news.org/index.php/toc/an-table-of-contents-december-2011 -volume-529/.

Aptekar, Lewis. 1988. *Street Children of Cali*. Durham, NC: Duke University Press.

Beazley, Harriet. 2002. "'Vagrants Wearing Make-up': Negotiating Spaces on the Streets of Yogyakarta, Indonesia." *Urban Studies* 39 (9):1665–1683.

———. 2003. "The Construction and Protection of Individual and Collective Identities by Street Children and Youth in Indonesia." *Children, Youth, and Environments* 13 (1) (Spring), http://colorado.edu/journals/cye.

Berman, Laine. 2000. "Surviving on the Streets of Java: Homeless Children's Narratives of Violence." *Discourse and Society* 11 (2):149–174.

Bluebond-Langner, Myra, and Jill Korbin. 2007. "Challenges and Opportunities in the Anthropology of Childhoods: An Introduction to 'Children, Childhoods, and Childhood Studies.'" *American Anthropologist* 109 (2):241–246.

Blum, Ann Shelby. 2009. *Domestic Economies: Family, Work, and Welfare in Mexico City 1884–1943*. Lincoln: University of Nebraska Press.

Bolles, A. Lynn, and Kelvin A. Yelvington. 2010. "Introduction: Dignity and Economic Survival: Women in Latin America and the Caribbean and the Work of Helen I. Safa." *Caribbean Studies* 38 (2):vii–xxxvi.

Bourgois, Philipe, and Jeff Schonberg. 2009. *Righteous Dopefiend*. Berkeley: University of California Press.

Boyden, Jo. 2003. "Children under Fire: Challenging Assumptions about Children's Resilience." *Children, Youth, and Environments* 13 (1):1–35, http://colorado.edu/journals/cye.

Brennan, Denise. 2004. *What's Love Got to Do with It?: Transnational Desire and Sex Tourism in the Dominican Republic*. Durham, NC: Duke University Press.

Butler, Udi. 2007. "Embodying Oppression: Revolta amongst Young People Living on the Streets of Rio de Janeiro." In *Livelihoods at the Margins: Surviving the City*, edited by James Staples, 53–74. Walnut Creek, CA: Left Coast.

Campos, Regina, Carlos Mauricio, Marcela Raffaelli, Neal Halsey, Walter Ude, Marilia Greco, Dirceu Greco, Andrea Ruff, and Jon Rolf. 1994. "Social Networks and Daily Activities of Street Youth in Belo Horizonte, Brazil." *Child Development* 65(2):319–330.

Candelario, Ginetta E. B. 2007. *Black behind the Ears: Dominican Racial Identity from Museums to Beauty Shops*. Durham, NC: Duke University Press.

Chin, Elizabeth. 1999. "Ethnically Correct Dolls: Toying with the Race Industry." *American Anthropologist* 101 (2):305–321.

Coles, Robert. 1990. *The Spiritual Life of Children*. Boston: Houghton Mifflin.

Conticini, Alessandro. 2007. "Children on the Streets of Dhaka and Their Coping Strategies." In *Livelihoods at the Margins: Surviving the City*, edited by James Staples, 75–100. Walnut Creek, CA: Left Coast Press.

Deive, Carlos Esteban. 2002. *Diccionario de Dominicanismos*. Santo Domingo, DR: Editora Manatí.

Derby, Lauren. 2009. *The Dictator's Seduction: Politics and the Popular Imagination in the Era of Trujillo*. Durham, NC: Duke University Press.

Dickson-Gómez, Julia. 2003. "Growing Up in Guerilla Camps: The Long-Term Impact of Being a Child Soldier in El Salvador's Civil War." *Ethos* 30 (4):327–356.

Farmer, Paul. 2004. "An Anthropology of Structural Violence." *Current Anthropology* 45 (3):305–325.

Fonseca, Claudia. 1986. "Orphanages, Foundlings, and Foster Mothers: The System of Child Circulation in a Brazilian Squatter Settlement." *Anthropological Quarterly* 59 (1):15–27.

———. 2004. "The Circulation of Children in a Brazilian Working-Class Neighborhood: A Local Practice in a Globalized World." In *Cross-Cultural Approaches to Adoption*, edited by Fiona Bowie, 165–181. London: Routledge.

Foucault, Michel. 1980. *The History of Sexuality*, vol. 1: *An Introduction*. New York: Vintage.

Goode, Judith. 1987. *Gaminismo: The Changing Nature of the Street Child Phenomenon in Colombia*. UFSI (Universities Field Staff International) Reports 28, Latin America. Hanover, NH: UFSI.

Goodwin, Marjorie Harness. 1990. *He-Said-She-Said: Talk as Social Organization among Black Children*. Bloomington: Indiana University Press.

Graue, M. Elizabeth, and Daniel J. Walsh. 1998. *Studying Children in Context: Theories, Methods, and Ethics*. Thousand Oaks, CA: Sage Publications.

Gregory, Stephen. 2007. *The Devil behind the Mirror: Globalization and Politics in the Dominican Republic*. Berkeley: University of California Press.

Hagan, John, and Bill McCarthy. 1998. *Mean Streets: Youth Crime and Homelessness*. Cambridge: Cambridge University Press.

Hansson, Desirre. 2003. "'Strolling' as a Gendered Experience: A Feminist Analysis of Young Females in Cape Town." *Children, Youth, and Environments* 13 (1):1–19, http://colorado.edu/journals/cye.

Hecht, Tobias. 1998. *At Home in the Street: Street Children of Northeast Brazil*. Cambridge: Cambridge University Press.

Hirschfeld, Lawrence. 2002. "Why Don't Anthropologists Like Children?" *American Anthropologist* 104 (2):611–627.

Huggins, Martha K., and Myriam Mesquita. 2000. "Civic Invisibility, Marginality, and Moral Exclusion: The Murders of Street Youth in Brazil." In *Children on the Streets of the Americas: Globalization, Homelessness, and Education in the United States, Brazil, and Cuba*, edited by Roslyn Arlin Mickelson, 257–268. London: Routledge.

Inciardi, James A., and Hillary L. Surrat. 1998. "Children in the Streets of Brazil: Drug Use, Crime, Violence and HIV Risks." *Substance Use and Misuse* 33(7):1461–1480.

James, Alison. 2007. "Giving Voice to Children's Voices: Practices and Problems, Pitfalls and Potentials." *American Anthropologist* 109 (2):261–272.

Jones, Gareth A., and Dennis Rodgers, eds. 2009. *Youth Violence in Latin America: Gangs and Juvenile Justice in Perspective.* New York: Palgrave MacMillan.

Kenny, Mary Lorena. 2007. *Hidden Heads of Households: Child Labor in Urban Northeast Brazil.* Buffalo, NY: Broadview Press.

Kovats-Bernat, J. Christopher. 2006. *Sleeping Rough in Port-au-Prince: An Ethnography of Street Children and Violence in Haiti.* Gainesville: University of Florida Press.

Lanclos, Donna. 2003. *At Play in Belfast: Children's Folklore and Identities in Northern Ireland.* New Brunswick, NJ: Rutgers University Press.

Leinaweaver, Jessaca. 2008. *The Circulation of Children: Kinship, Adoption, and Morality in Andean Peru.* Durham, NC: Duke University Press.

LeVine, Robert A. 2007. "Ethnographic Studies of Childhood: A Historical Overview." *American Anthropologist* 109 (2):247–60.

Lockhart, Chris. 2002. "Kunyenga, 'Real Sex,' and Survival: Assessing the Risk of HIV Infection among Urban Street Boys in Tanzania." *Medical Anthropology Quarterly* 16(3): 294–311.

———. 2008 "The Life and Death of a Street Boy in East Africa: Everyday Violence in the Time of AIDS." *Medical Anthropology Quarterly* 22(1) (March 2008): 94–115.

Lucchini, Ricardo. 1996. *Niños de la Calle: Identidad, Sociabilidad, Droga.* Barcelona: Los Libros de la Frontera.

Lutjens, Sheryl. 2000a. "Restructuring Childhood in Cuba: The State as Family." In *Children on the Streets of the Americas: Globalization, Homelessness, and Education in the United States, Brazil, and Cuba,* edited by Roslyn Arlin Mickelson, 149159. London: Routledge.

———. 2000b. "Schooling and 'Clean Streets' in Socialist Cuba: Children and the Special Period." In *Children on the Streets of the Americas: Globalization, Homelessness, and Education in the United States, Brazil, and Cuba,* edited by Roslyn Arlin Mickelson, 55–65. London: Routledge.

Malkki, Liisa, and Emily Martin. 2003. "Children and the Gendered Politics of Globalization: In Remembrance of Sharon Stephens." *American Ethnologist* 30 (2): 216–224.

Marquez, Patricia. 1999. *The Street Is My Home: Youth and Violence in Caracas.* Stanford, CA: Stanford University Press.

Martínez, Samuel. 2007. *Decency and Excess: Global Aspirations and Material Deprivation on a Caribbean Sugar Plantation.* Boulder, CO: Paradigm Publishing.

Maynard, Ashley E., and Katrin Tovote. 2010. "Learning from Other Children." In *The Anthropology of Learning in Childhood,* edited by David F. Lancy, John Bock, and Suzanne Gaskins, 181–205. Lanham, MD: AltaMira Press.

Munroe, Robert L., and Mary Gauvin. 2010. "The Cross-Cultural Study of Children's Learning and Socialization: A Short History." In *The Anthropology of Learning in Childhood,* edited by David F. Lancy, John Bock, and Suzanne Gaskins, 35–63. Lanham, MD: AltaMira Press.

Offit, Thomas A. 2010. *Conquistadores de la Calle: Child Street Labor in Guatemala City.* Austin: University of Texas Press.

Padilla, Mark. 2007. *Caribbean Pleasure Industry: Tourism, Sexuality, and AIDS in the Dominican Republic.* Chicago: University of Chicago Press.

Panter-Brick, Catherine. 2002. "Street Children, Human Rights, and Public Health." *Annual Review of Anthropology* 31:147–171.

Peterson, Anna L., and Kay Almere Reed. 2002. "Victims, Heroes, Enemies: Children in Central American Wars." In *Minor Omissions: Children in Latin American History and Society,* edted by Tobias Hecht, 215–231. Madison: University of Wisconsin Press.

Rocha Gómez, José Luis. 2009. "Understanding the Logic of Nicaraguan Juvenile Justice." In *Youth Violence in Latin America: Gangs and Juvenile Justice in Perspective,* edited by Gareth A. Jones and Dennis Rodgers, 149–165. New York: Palgrave Macmillan.

Roorda, Eric. 1998. *The Dictator Next Door: The Good Neighbor Policy and the Trujillo Regime in the Dominican Republic, 1930–1945.* Durham, NC: Duke University Press.

Rosen, David. 2007. "Child Soldiers, International Humanitarian Law, and the Globalization of Childhood." *American Anthropologist* 109 (2):296–306.

Safa, Helen I. 1995. *The Myth of the Male Breadwinner: Women and Industrialization in the Caribbean.* Boulder, CO: Westview Press.

———. 1999. "Free Markets and the Marriage Market: Structural Adjustment, Gender Relations, and Working Conditions among Dominican Women Workers." *Environment and Planning A* 31 (2) 291–304.

Salazar, Guadalupe. 2008. "Second-Class Citizens in the Making: The Rights of Street Children in Chile." *Latin American Perspectives* 35 (4):30–44.

Scheper-Hughes, Nancy, and Daniel Hoffman. 1998. "Brazilian Apartheid: Street Kids and the Struggle for Urban Space." In *Small Wars: The Cultural Politics of Childhood,* edited by Nancy Scheper-Hughes and Carolyn Sargent, 352–388. Berkeley: University of California Press.

Scheper-Hughes, Nancy, and Carolyn Sargent, eds. 1998. *Small Wars: The Cultural Politics of Childhood.* Berkeley: University of California Press.

Shaw, Rosalind. 2007. "Memory Frictions: Localizing the Truth and Reconciliation Commission in Sierra Leone." *International Journal of Transitional Justice* 1 (2):183–207.

———. 2009. "Afterword: Violence and the Generation of Memory." In *Remembering Violence: Anthropological Perspectives on Intergenerational Transmission,* edited by Nicolas Argenti and Katharina Schramm, 243–253. New York: Berghahn Books.

Shepler, Susan. 2005. "The Rites of the Child: Global Discourse of Youth and Reintegrating Child Soldiers in Sierra Leone." *Journal of Human Rights* 4 (2):197–211.

Staples, James, ed. 2007. *Livelihoods at the Margins: Surviving the City.* Walnut Creek, CA: Left Coast Press.

Stephens, Sharon, ed. 1995. *Children and the Politics of Culture.* Princeton, NJ: Princeton University Press.

Stephenson, Svetlana. 2001. "Street Children in Moscow: Using and Creating Social Capital." *Sociological Review* 49 (4):530–547.

Trawick, Margaret. 2007. *Enemy Lines: Childhood, Warfare, and Play in Batticaloa*. Berkeley: University of California Press.

Turits, Richard Lee. 2004. *Foundations of Despotism: Peasants, the Trujillo Regime, and Modernity in Dominican History*. Palo Alto, CA: Stanford University Press.

Ungar, Mark. 2009. "Policing Youth in Latin America." In *Youth Violence in Latin America: Gangs and Juvenile Justice in Perspective*, edited by Gareth A. Jones and Dennis Rodgers, 203–224. New York: Palgrave Macmillan.

Vigil, James Diego. 1988a. "Group Processes and Street Identity: Adolescent Chicano Gang Members." *Ethos* 16 (4):421–445.

———. 1988b. *Barrio Gangs: Street Life and Identity in Southern California*. Austin: University of Texas Press.

———. 2002. *A Rainbow of Gangs: Street Cultures in the Mega-City*. Austin: University of Texas Press.

———. 2003. "Urban Violence and Street Gangs." *Annual Review of Anthropology* 32:225–242.

———. 2007. *The Projects: Gang and Non-Gang Families in East Los Angeles*. Austin: University of Texas Press.

West, Harry. 2000. "Girls with Guns: Narrating the Experience of War of Frelimo's 'Female Detachment.'" *Anthropological Quarterly* 73 (4):180–194.

Whiteford, Linda. 1990. "A Question of Adequacy: Primary Health Care in the Dominican Republic." *Social Science and Medicine* 30 (2):221–226.

———. 1992. "Contemporary Health Care and the Colonial and Neo-Colonial Experience: The Case of the Dominican Republic." *Social Science and Medicine* 35 (10):1215–1223.

———. 1998. "Children's Health as Accumulated Capital: Structural Adjustment in the Dominican Republic and Cuba." In *Small Wars: The Cultural Politics of Childhood*, edited by Nancy Scheper-Hughes and Carolyn Sargent, 186–201. Berkeley: University of California Press.

Whyte, William Foote. 1943. *Street Corner Society: The Social Structure of an Italian Slum*. Chicago: University of Chicago Press.

Wolseth, Jon. 2009. "Good Times and Bad Blood: Violence, Solidarity, and Social Organization on Dominican Streets." In *Youth Violence in Latin America: Gangs and Juvenile Justice in Perspective*, edited by Dennis Rodgers and Gareth Jones, 63–82. New York: Palgrave Macmillan.

———. 2010. "Learning on the Streets: Child Peer Socialization in Adverse Environments." In *The Anthropology of Learning in Childhood*, edited by David F. Lancy, John Bock, and Suzanne Gaskins, 421–442. Lanham, MD: AltaMira Press.

———. 2011. "Circulating through the System: Juvenile Justice and the Mobile Lives of Street Children in the Dominican Republic." *Children, Youth, and Environments* 21 (2):34–56.

Wolseth, Jon, and Florence E. Babb. 2008. "Introduction: The Cultural Politics of Youth in Latin America." *Latin American Perspectives* 35 (4):3–14.

Wucker, Michele. 2000. *Why the Cocks Fight: Dominicans, Haitians, and the Struggle for Hispaniola*. New York: Hill and Wang.

# INDEX

# ABOUT THE AUTHOR

JON WOLSETH holds a PhD in anthropology from the University of Iowa. He has published widely on the intersection of violence, marginality, and adolescence in Latin America, including the monograph *Jesus and the Gang: Youth Violence and Christianity in Urban Honduras*. He is currently pursuing a degree in urban and regional planning.

CPSIA information can be obtained at www.ICGtesting.com
Printed in the USA
BVOW08s1922080913

330511BV00002B/3/P